The Archaeology & Architecture of Afghanistan

The Archaeology & Architecture *of* Afghanistan

Edgar Knobloch

First published in 2002
Reprinted 2011, 2022

The History Press
97 St George's Place,
Cheltenham, Gloucestershire GL50 3QB
www.thehistorypress.co.uk

Copyright © Edgar Knobloch, 2011

The right of Edgar Knobloch to be identified as the Author of this work has been asserted by him in accordance with the Copyrights, Designs and Patents Act 1988.

All rights reserved. No part of this book may be reprinted or reproduced or utilised in any form or by any electronic, mechanical or other means, now known or hereafter invented, including photocopying and recording, or in any information storage or retrieval system, without the permission in writing from the Publishers.

British Library Cataloguing in Publication Data.
A catalogue record for this book is available from the British Library.

ISBN 978 0 7524 2519 1

Printed by TJ Books Limited, Padstow, Cornwall

Contents

List of illustrations • 7

Preface • 10

Introduction: Afghanistan's cultural heritage • 11

1 The country and the people • 13

2 History • 25

3 Notes on architecture • 47
    Early Iranian architecture
    Early Buddhist architecture
    The art of Gandhara
    The Parthian and Sasanian architecture
    The Kushan and late Buddhist architecture
    Early Islamic architecture
        Architectural decoration
        Islamic calligraphy
        The Samanid, Ghaznavid and Ghorid architecture
        The Seljuk architecture
    Timurid and Late Islamic architecture
        General
        Architectural form
        Architectural decoration
        Calligraphy and carpets
        Late Islamic period

SITES AND MONUMENTS

4 Pre-Islamic • 73
    Mundigak and Deh Morasi Ghundai
    Ay Khanum
    Surkh Kotal
    Samangan-Aibak
    Old Kandahar

The Hoard of Kunduz and the Ashoka fragments
Begram-Kapisa
Shotorak and Paitava
Sites and monuments in the Kabul Area
Hadda
Bamiyan and Kakrak
Fundukistan and Foladi
Balkh
Tepe Rustam and Takht-i Rustam
Tepe Sardar
Tilla-Tepe, Delbardjin, Dokhtar-i Nushirwan

5 Early Islamic — 103
Medieval Kabul
Medieval Balkh
Dawlatabad, Sar-i Pol, Baba Hatim
Ghazni
Lashkar-i Bazar
Medieval Herat – The citadel, the Friday Mosque
Monuments in the Herat area
The Minaret of Jam
Shahr-i Zohak and Shahr-i Gholghola

6 Timurid and late Islamic — 131
Timurid Herat
   The citadel
   The Musalla
   Gazurgah
Other monuments in and around Herat
Timurid Balkh – The Mosque Abu Nasr Parsa
Mazar-i Sharif - The Shrine of Hazret Ali
Ghazni
Kandahar
Kabul
Takht-i Pol
The Tashkurghan and Kunduz Area

Notes and references — 163

Glossary — 169

Bibliography — 174

Index — 186

List of illustrations

Text figures

1. Geographic zones of Afghanistan
2. Geographic zones 2: mountain systems
3. The Kabul Gorge
4. Rivers of Afghanistan
5. Mountains in central Afghanistan
6. The Band-i Amir Lakes
7. Ethnic groups of Afghanistan
8. Nomads on the move
9. Afghan business
10. Achaemenian satrapies
11. Movements of Alexander the Great
12. The Mauryan Empire
13. The Sasanian and Gupta Empires
14. Eurasia
15. The Ghaznavid and Ghorid Empires
16. The Moghul and Safavid Empires
17. The Empire of Ahmad Shah
18. Russian advances in Central Asia
19. British retreat route
20. Archaeological sites
21. Ancient Balkh, the citadel
22. The tower of Masud III, Ghazni. Detail
23. The tower of Bahramshah, Ghazni. Detail
24. The mosque Noh Gumbad. Detail of ornament
25. Alabaster carved panel from the palace of Afrasiab, Samarkand. Tenth to eleventh century
26. Ghaznavid calligraphy
27. The façade at Hadda
28. Ornament at Balkh, Noh Gumbad
29. The site of Surkh Kotal
30. The monastery at Aibak
31. The *stupa* at Aibak
32. Interior of the monastery at Aibak
33. The Guldara *stupa*

List of illustrations

34	The Guldara *stupa*
35	Hadda, Tapa-i Kafariha
36	Capitals at Hadda
37	Bamiyan, the valley and the cliff
38	The large Buddha at Bamiyan
39	The small Buddha at Bamiyan
40	The large Buddha at Bamiyan: niche and frescoes
41	Aerial view of the site of Balkh
42	The site of Tepe Sardar
43	Mosque Noh Gumbad. Detail
44	The tower of Masud III, Ghazni
45	The tower of Bahramshah, Ghazni
46	The tower of Bahramshah, Ghazni
47	The tower of Bahramshah, Ghazni. Detail
48	The tower of Masud III, Ghazni. Detail
49	The citadel, Herat
50	The Friday Mosque, Herat. Eastern *iwan*
51	The Friday Mosque, Herat. Detail
52	The Friday Mosque, Herat. Detail of inscription on the southern side
53	The Friday Mosque, Herat. Inscription on the northern side
54	The cauldron at the Friday Mosque, Herat
55	The Pol-i Malan Bridge, Herat
56	Shahr-i Zohak
57	Shahr-i Zohak
58	Shahr-i Gholghola. View from the citadel
59	Kala-i Dokhtaran
60	The Musalla, Herat
61	Mausoleum Gawhar Shad, Herat. Detail
62	Mausoleum Gawhar Shad, Herat. Detail of the interior
63	Mausoleum Gawhar Shad, Herat. Detail
64	The shrine at Gazurgah
65	Gazurgah, Herat. The eastern *iwan*
66	Gazurgah, Herat. Detail of the southern wall
67	Gazurgah, Herat. Detail of the eastern *iwan*
68	Gazurgah, Herat. Detail of the western *iwan*
69	Gazurgah, Herat. Detail of the western *iwan*
70	Gazurgah, Herat. Detail of the courtyard
71	The shrine of Abu Nasr Parsa, Balkh
72	The shrine of Abu Nasr Parsa, Balkh. Detail
73	The shrine of Abu Nasr Parsa, Balkh. Detail
74	The shrine of Abu Nasr Parsa, Balkh. Detail of *iwan*
75	The shrine of Abu Nasr Parsa, Balkh. Detail of the interior
76	The mosque Takht-i Pol
77	The mosque Takht-i Pol. Interior

78　The mosque Takht-i Pol
79　Aerial view of Mazar-i Sharif
80　Mausoleum Hazret Ali, Mazar-i Sharif
81　Mausoleum Hazret Ali, Mazar-i Sharif. Detail
82　Mausoleum Abdul Razzaq, Ghazni
83　Mausoleum Abdul Razzaq, Ghazni

Colour plates

1　The Bamiyan Valley
2　The Band-i Amir Lakes
3　Women at Shahr-i Gholghola
4　A Hazara girl
5　The Pol-i Malan Bridge
6　The Babur Gardens, Kabul
7　The village of Tashkurgan
8　An Afghan family
9　Detail of the mosque Abu Nasr Parsa in Balkh
10　Detail of the mausoleum Gawhar Shad in Herat
11　The site of Surkh Kotal
12　Detail of the Friday Mosque in Herat
13　Detail of the mosque Noh Gumbad, Balkh
14　The Kuh-i Baba range and the valley of Shahr-i Gholghola
15　The citadel, Shahr-i Gholghola
16　The mausoleum Hazret Ali, Mazar-i Sharif
17　The citadel, Tashkurgan
18　The tower of Masud III, Ghazni
19　The tower of Bahramshah, Ghazni
20　Gazurgah, Herat. Detail
21　Entrance of Gazurgah, Herat
22　A landscape in the Hindukush
23　Timurid walls, Balkh
24　One of the minarets of the Musalla, Herat
25　The Friday Mosque, Herat

Preface

There are very few studies devoted to Afghanistan and, as far as I know, there is none dealing exclusively with its archaeology, art and architecture. Instead, information is scattered throughout a number of articles in a variety of languages (French, Russian and Italian as well as English), which were often published in fairly obscure journals and magazines. Many of these no longer exist, and copies are difficult to find. The main purpose of this book has been, therefore, to concentrate as many references as possible within a single publication, and so make them available as a collection to those who are interested in the subject. This task, however, presented a number of difficulties.

One was the transcription of Oriental names, whether Arabic, Turkish, Persian or other. There are indeed as many ways of doing this as there are Orientalists, and I had to make my own choice. Another problem was the arrangement of the sites described in chapters 4-6. Two possibilities presented themselves: by area and region, which would have advantages for the traveller, or by historical and cultural affinity. I opted for the latter, principally because travelling in the country is not going to be easy for some time, and also because this book is, after all, intended for students of history and art, who would prefer to find monuments of the same period and style grouped under the same heading. The drawback of this approach is that, inevitably, places such as Balkh and Herat which contain monuments belonging to different periods figure in more than one chapter.

I accept in advance any blame for inaccuracy, incompleteness or superficiality in my descriptions. Although I have tried to keep my bibliography as complete as possible, there is a fair chance that some references, including important ones, have escaped me.

I am indebted to Professor Robert Hillenbrand for his critical comment and useful suggestions, and to Professor Tom Gouttierre for his encouragement and appreciation of my work. I am also grateful to the School of Oriental and African Studies, the British Museum, the Royal Geographical Society and the Náprstek Museum in Prague for showing exhibitions of my photographs of Islamic Architecture and Middle Eastern Archaeology.

Edgar Knobloch
London-Quillan, December 2001

Introduction: Afghanistan's cultural heritage

The character of Afghanistan, its ethnic composition and its long and chequered history pose a number of problems to anyone who tries to categorise the country under a single heading. What is Afghanistan? Who are the Afghans? What were the cultural trends and influences that shaped their history? The answer to each question would differ according to the specialisation of the scholar asked, and more often than not there would be different approaches even within the same discipline, be it pre-history, graecology, indology, the history of Iran or that of Islam. In each of these cases, the main subject of the study would lie elsewhere, and Afghanistan's role and contribution would be treated merely as a kind of fringe element, its importance regarded as more or less secondary.

The matter is further complicated by two major deficiencies. One is study into the role of the steppe nomad: the great unknown in historical and social contexts, cast aside by most observers as uncivilised, barbarian and, on the whole, merely destructive. And yet their role, their repeated invasions of the lands of settled agrarian civilisations, left deep marks in the history of the country, brought about profound changes in its political orientation and contributed significantly to its cultural pattern. We know next to nothing of the nomads' administration, their legal and fiscal systems, their social organisation – nor of their art. Having no fixed abode, they had no tradition of monumental art – that is of architecture, painting or sculpture. Their artistic genius instead expressed itself in accordance with their environment and their way of life; in music and dancing, in flat ornamentation used in embroidery and carpets, or sometimes in small metal objects (used for decorating dresses, or as harnesses, buckles, brooches, buttons and so on). But inspiration from this source can be detected in the art, notably in the ornament, of their settled neighbours or subjects.

The second main drawback is the undeniable fact that research has been carried out almost exclusively by Western scholars, who quite naturally treated Oriental studies from the point of view of their own values, criteria and standards. These combined to make it often difficult to grasp the real significance of certain events, trends or even entire periods in the country's development.

A number of other, lesser, drawbacks could be added. Western scholars operating on the basis of archaeological evidence and literary analyses tended to prefer, or accentuate, such periods and aspects of history for which this kind of evidence was available. Settled civilisations were therefore the focus while the nomads, who left no such evidence, were largely ignored. On the other hand the period of Islam's dominance in Afghanistan, for which ample evidence was available, was treated as no more than an appendix of wider Islamic studies and, within this framework, especially of Iranian history, while its own complexity and specific features were hardly ever analysed in depth.

Geography and the ethnic composition of the population complicates the situation even more. Lying between two great civilisations, the Iranian and the Indian, the country was open to political, military and cultural influences from both – and the repeated incursions of the nomads from Central Asia have made no little contribution. A mosaic of warring tribes of different linguistic, ethnic and religious affiliation, as well as the character of the country itself, with its high mountains, steppes and deserts, produced no kind of cohesion; a deficiency which is, at the time of writing (2001-2), becoming yet again tragically evident. And yet every period, every influence, whether Iranian-Zoroastrian, Indian-Buddhist, Islamic or nomadic, left its mark in the country's cultural make-up, despite the undeniable tendency of every new power to denigrate, neglect or even destroy the heritage of its predecessors.

Turning to the present, the destruction of the Bamiyan Buddhas, the looting of the Kabul Museum, the pillage of Ay Khanum and other sites as well as the general neglect of standing monuments, and the deliberate destruction by the Taliban of even Islamic treasures like the burning of the Nasser Khosrow library with its priceless manuscripts, provoked a reaction from scholars, universities and other interested parties in the West. So UNESCO sent experts to assess the state of some monuments; the Musée Guimet in Paris took care of some of the objects salvaged from the Kabul Museum; SPACH (Society for the Preservation of Afghanistan's Cultural Heritage) tried to recover some lost pieces from the antique markets in Pakistan and to catalogue those that remained in Kabul; the Afghanistan Museum in Exile was founded by private initiative in Switzerland as a temporary shelter for Afghan art; and other organisations such as AFRANE (Amitié Franco-Afghane) or ISCHA (International Committee for the Salvation of the Cultural Heritage of Afghanistan) were set up to retrieve, restore and protect the dispersed artefacts. These efforts, however, have had only a modest effect so far – partly due to the dispersal of qualified Afghan personnel all over the world.

In the general context of rebuilding the devastated country, the salvation and preservation of its cultural heritage is only one of the many tasks with which the international community is faced. Food, shelter and security will have to be provided first; and here, unfortunately, the old tribal rivalries do not help. Some areas are still affected by banditry, bombing or revenge killings; skirmishes between hostile families or clans flare up here and there; deliveries of food and resources are often looted; and foreign troops whose task it is to provide security are not always welcome.

Nevertheless, so far there has not been an open challenge to the interim government. If this situation continues, Afghanistan appears to have at least a fighting chance to break out of the vicious circle of poverty, displacement and violence that have plagued it for so many years, and to become again a member of the community of civilised states as opposed to being what so many today view as being nothing more than 'a bunch of fanatics and terrorists sitting on a pile of rubble'.

1 The country and the people

Afghanistan is a huge country by European standards; covering 683,000km² it is one-sixth larger than France, and about the same size as Great Britain, West Germany, the Benelux countries and Austria together. However, its population of 24 million is only a little more than that of Austria and Belgium (April 2002 estimate: this total includes some four million refugees in Iran and Pakistan, substantial numbers of whom are returning or expected to return). Before the Russian invasion in 1979, only Kabul had over 500,000 inhabitants; the other two large cities, Kandahar and Herat, had populations of about 200,000 and under 100,000 respectively.

As a political entity Afghanistan is a fairly recent creation. A loose conglomerate of tribal territories until the eighteenth century, it developed into a state only in the nineteenth; its borders with Russia and India were fixed in the second half of that century and part of its frontier with Iran was not demarcated until the 1930s. Its political development and economic structure were largely the outcome of its ethnic composition, which in turn reflected the geographical and climatic conditions of the country. Due to the complexity of its topography, it is not easy to divide the country into geographic and climatic zones. The Danish geographer Humlum, writing in 1959, found as many as ten,[1] while, a decade later, Dupree established eleven zones on the basis of entirely different criteria.[2]

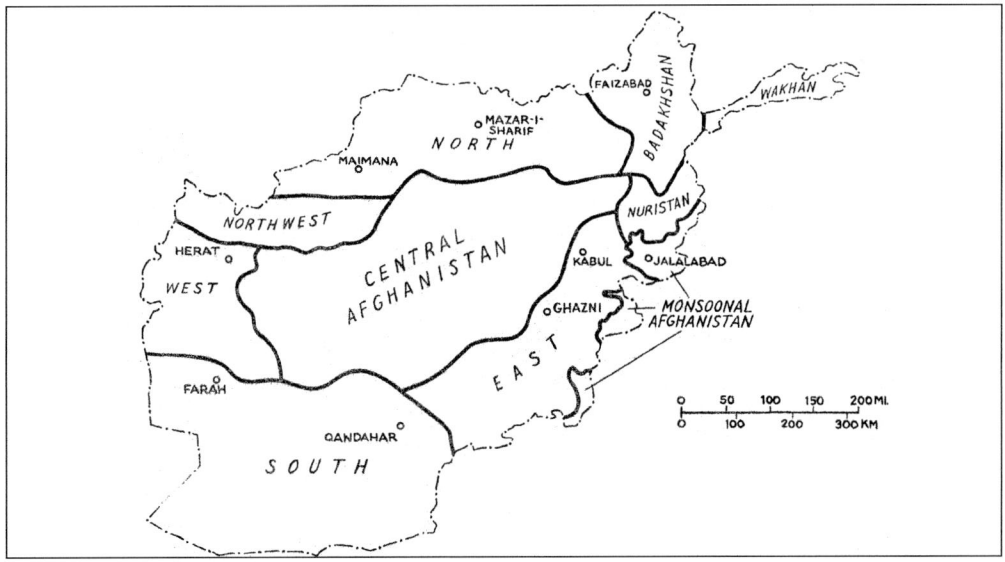

1 *Geographic zones of Afghanistan.* Dupree/Humlum (1959)

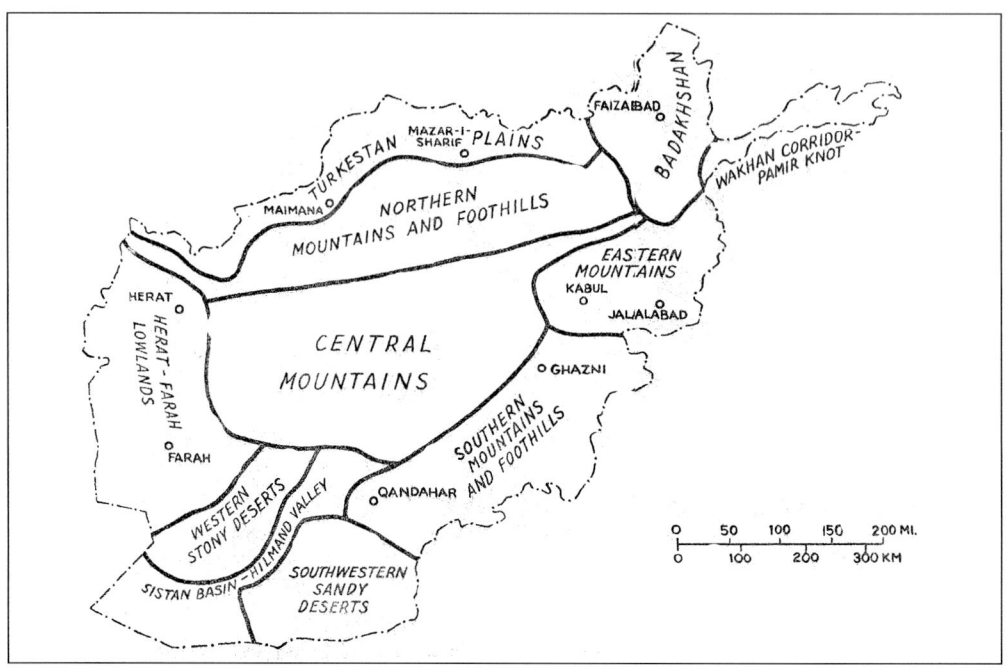

2 Geographic zones 2: mountain systems

A glance at the map shows that a huge mountain chain, composed of several ranges and running from the north-east to the south-west, divides the country into two unequal halves, steppe in the north and the north-west and desert in the south and the south-east. Closer inspection however reveals that this impression is somewhat deceptive. First of all, there are mountains elsewhere, all along the border between Afghanistan and Pakistan, rising over 4000m high in the northern part and coming down to 2000m in the south. Between these and the Hindukush – the central part of which rises to over 5000m – is an enormous wedge, widening to the south-west and consisting, at its tip, of the rocky and occasionally wooded valleys of Nuristan with the fertile Kabul area to the east, and the subtropical plain of Jalalabad to the south. The elevated uplands of Ghazni form a sort of transverse barrier, from which the south-western slope continues on, past Kandahar, to merge with the sandy vastness of the Registan desert.

Mountains are also found in the north. A chain called the Khwaja Muhammad Range separates the alpine pastures of the Badakhshan from the Turkestan plain to the west of it, which stretches between the Amu Darya and the Hindukush. Consisting mainly of steppe, it slopes gently westwards until it becomes the Kara Kum desert.

The central chain itself is composed of several sections, of which the highest is the Kuh-i Baba, culminating in Shah Foladi, 5143m, and bordered by the high plateau of Hazarajat in the south, and the fertile, sheltered valleys of Bamiyan, Kakrak and Foladi in the north. To the west, on the north bank of the Hari Rud, the

3 The Kabul Gorge

Paropamisus (Safid Kuh) Range stretches as far as the Iranian border; the desolate, inhospitable region of Ghor lies in its eastern section and the fertile, populous oasis of Herat in the west. South of the Hari Rud more mountains slope until they disappear in the flat, stony desert, the Dasht-i Margo, 'The Plain of Death'. The highest section of all is the extreme north-east: the Wakhan Corridor which leads into the Pamir and provides one of the very few crossings into Chinese Turkestan. According to Humlum, 83 per cent of the Wakhan-Pamir area lies above 3000m and the rest between 1800 and 3000m. There is permanent snow above 5000m.

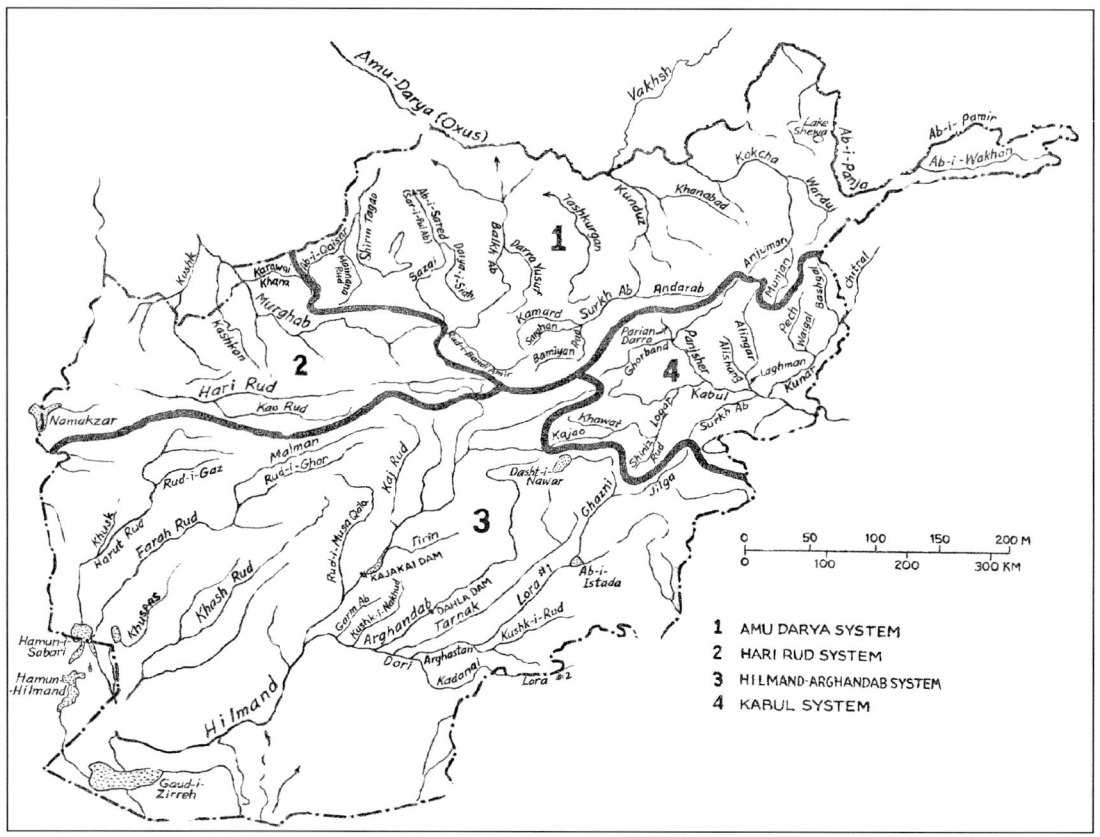

4 *Rivers of Afghanistan*. Dupree

Then there are the rivers, or river systems, crucial in the shaping of the country's profile, in the vital division between the deserts and the oases, the areas where man can live and find his food, and where he cannot. Afghanistan contains four such systems.

In the north and fed by the glaciers of the Pamir is the Amu Darya (the Oxus of the ancient Greeks and the Jayhun of the medieval Arabs), which forms the frontier with Uzbekistan and Sajikistan for over 1000km. It is called Panj or Ab-i Panj in its upper reaches, and Ab-i Wakhan at its headwater in the Pamir. Only two tributaries, the Kokcha and the Kunduz Ab, flow into it from its Afghan side. The latter, which is almost 500km long, bears the name of Bamiyan Rud near its source and irrigates, among others, the Bamiyan Valley. Several other rivers drain the northern slopes of the central mountains; all belong, technically, to the Amu Darya system, but all die before reaching the confluence, used up, for the most part, in irrigation networks.

In the east the Kabul River forms part of the Indus river system. The great watershed between the Aral Sea into which the Amu Darya discharges itself, and the Indian Ocean which the Indus flows into, is the Shibar Pass, (3285m). From here a tributary of the Bamiyan Rud flows to the north and the Ghorband, a tributary of

5   Mountains in central Afghanistan

the Panjshir, to the south. The Kabul River irrigates the Kabul valley and eventually, after passing through a spectacular series of gorges, the plain of Jalalabad; then it turns north and east into the Peshawar valley in Pakistan but does not flow through the Khyber Pass. Several tributaries flow into it from both its right and left bank, of which the Panjshir, the Kunar and the Logar are the most important.

In the west the Hari Rud flows first through a steep, narrow valley between the two ranges of the central Hindukush, then enters the plain and supplies water to the large oasis of Herat. Turning north, it forms the border between Iran and Afghanistan for 160km, before entering Turkmenistan under the name of Tedzhen, and finally disappearing in the Kara Kum desert. The Murghab, once perhaps its confluent, rises in the western Hindukush, flows north into Turkmenistan and meets the same end in the sands of the desert.

The southern system, probably the most extensive of all, is that of the Helmand and the Arghandab. The Helmand, 1300km long, rises in the Kuh-i Baba to the west of Kabul and flows south-west to the Iranian border where it makes a large bend to the north and empties into the Hamun-i Helmand, an area of lakes and marshes of which the larger part lies in Iran. Sistan, the large and fertile oasis around the Hamun, which is now divided between Afghanistan and Iran, used to depend for its prosperity on the water from the Helmand, of which the Arghandab, 560km long, is the biggest tributary. It irrigates the plain of Kandahar and joins the Helmand at Bost where the Ghaznavid sultans built their winter residence at nearby Lashkar-i Bazar in the eleventh century. Several rivers flow into the Arghandab from the east

The country and the people

6   The Band-i Amir Lakes

and the south-east, from the mountain ranges on the Pakistan border and from the monsoon forests of Paktia. In the far west of the country two rivers, the Farah Rud and the Harut Rud empty into the lake in northern Sistan.

Underground irrigation canals called *kanat* or *karez* exist in eastern, southern and south-western Afghanistan. These often run 10–15m below ground (sometimes even deeper), and from the air look 'like neat lines of anthills leading from the foothills across the desert zones to the greenery of the villages and towns'.[3] From the exits of the canals the water flows in open ditches into the cultivated land.

It can be seen from this overview that most of Afghanistan is desert or semi-desert, and that a large part of the cultivated land is restricted to irrigated areas. These can best be described as oases, large or small, although in some cases they are situated in the plains or on the fringes of the deserts; elsewhere they can be found at the foothills of the mountains or in isolated mountain valleys. Dry farming exists in some areas. The rest of the country, uncultivated as it is, can be divided into three different categories: the deserts, sandy or stony, mainly in the south, the south-west and the west; the barren stretches of mountainous country covering a large part of the centre and some of the north-east and south-east; and in the north the steppe, a grassy plain which can provide fodder for large herds of animals including camels, horses, cattle, sheep and goats. The steppe extends into the mountains in the form of the grassy uplands which can be found almost everywhere at altitudes of up to 3000m, and which the nomads use as their summer pastures. Forests are only found in Nuristan, north-east of Kabul, and in Paktia, which lies south of the city on the Pakistan border.

The climate is continental in its extremes of hot and cold. The south of the country is open and almost barren, swept by hot winds in summer, with the heat often rising to 45°C in the shade, and cold winds in winter, when temperatures drop to -10 or even -20°C. In the west and south-west, a samum, or hot wind from the desert, blows constantly from June to September, often bringing sandstorms. This wind is called the '*bad-i-sad-o-bist ruz*' or 'the wind of 120 days'. In the deserts water can sometimes freeze at night in summer despite the daytime heat. Needless to say that buildings suffer considerably in this climate, both from frost and surface erosion by wind and sand.

Rain falls mostly in spring, between March and early May, but also in winter in low-lying areas like Herat, Kandahar and Jalalabad. The effects of the Indian monsoons are occasionally felt in the eastern part of the country; Paktia is usually considered the monsoon area of Afghanistan, but summer rains are pushed as far as the Kabul Valley. The climate in the Jalalabad plain, sometimes described as subtropical with its virtually rain-free summers and infrequent frost, is the mildest in the whole country, and it is in this region that the richest vegetation can be found: flowering plants and shrubs, subtropical scrub and even some palm trees.

Elsewhere in the valleys and on the river banks there are plane trees, poplars, willows and mulberry trees, replaced at higher altitudes by oak, walnut, ash and juniper. Some deciduous trees (willows and poplars) can be found in the forests of Paktia and Nuristan; but conifers, pine, cedar, larch, fir and yew are most plentiful. Pistachio trees grow in the valleys, especially in the north-west of the country. Reed jungle stretches along the banks of the Amu Darya and dense tamarisk scrub along the Helmand. In the deserts, the steppes and at high altitudes the vegetation is limited to scrub, grasses and some seasonal plants.

The Afghan nation, as it began to emerge from the end of the nineteenth century, is still a vague and at times almost a fictitious concept. Ethnic unity is non-existent in Afghanistan and tribal loyalties still largely outweigh national ones in the conglomeration of tribes and tribal families which form the population of the country. These tribes belong to several ethnic groups which, although all Muslim, differ widely in language, customs, dress and, most important, in their way of life.

The main ethnic groups are the Pushtuns (about 7.5 million) who live in the east, the south and the south-west; the Tajiks (about 4 million) in the north and the north-east; the Uzbeks (over 1 million) in the north; the Hazaras (about 1 million) in the centre; the Aimaks (900,000) in the west and the north-west; the Persians (about 700,000) mainly in the Herat area; and some smaller groups, like the Turkomans in the north-west, the Kirghiz in the Pamir and the Baluch in the south. Small scattered communities of Mongols, Hindus, Sikhs and Arabs are also to be found. Two interesting groups are the Brahui of whom some 200,000 live in south-western Afghanistan, and the Nuristanis in the north-east. There used to be Jewish communities, too, but all have left.

The country and the people

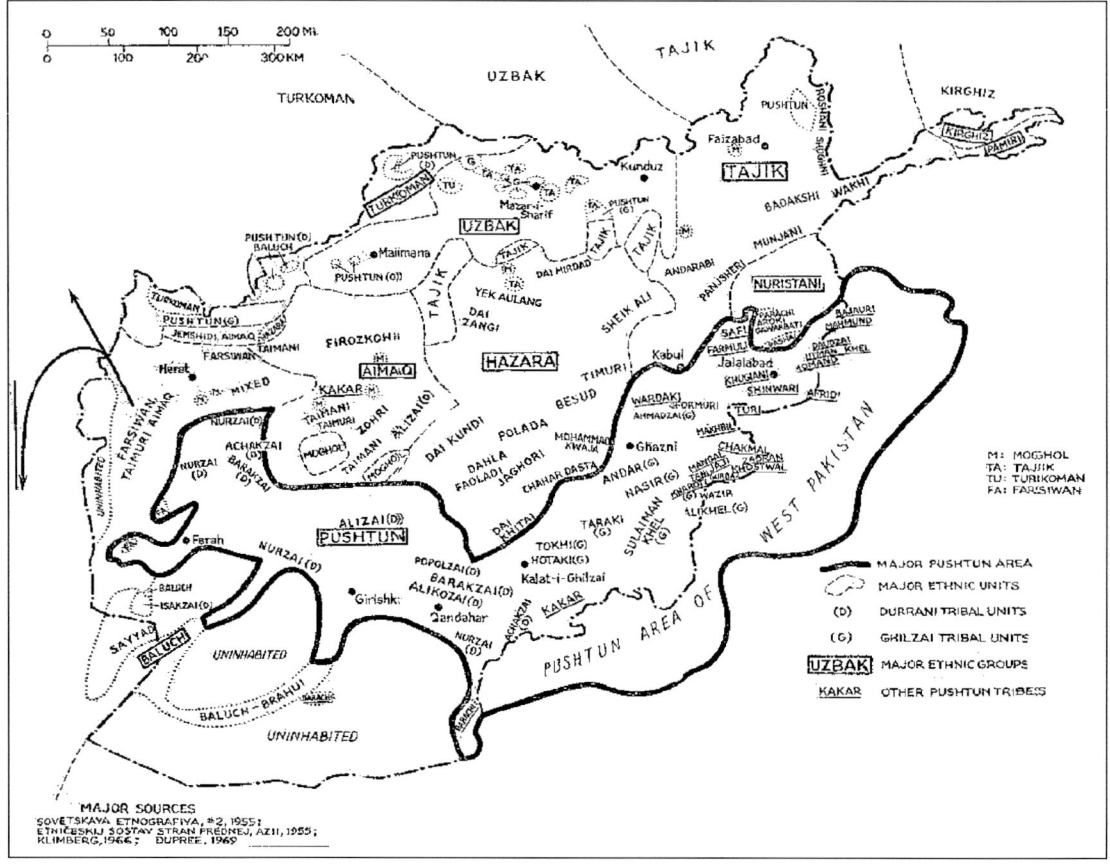

7 *Ethnic groups of Afghanistan*. Dupree

The Pushtuns, the Tajiks, the Persians and the Baluch are of Caucasian stock, whereas most of the others are Mongoloid. The Hazaras have typically Mongolian faces and are generally considered to be the descendants of the Mongols of Chingiz-Khan. They probably migrated into Afghanistan between the thirteenth and the fifteenth century, but their connection with the Mongols is only hypothetical. The Brahui alone are of Australoid (Indian-Dravidian) stock. The Nuristanis are conspicuous by their Mediterranean features and recurrent blond hair.

The Pushtuns are divided into two main tribal units: the Durrani in the west of the Pushtun area, and the Ghilzai in the east. An equal number of Pushtuns live across the border in the North-West Frontier Province of Pakistan. These divisions, however, are largely theoretical. Few areas in Afghanistan are ethnically homogeneous and the visitor soon learns to recognize the various types, and their varying costumes which make the bazaar in every town so colourful.

The two principal languages of Afghanistan, Dari and Pashto, belong to the Iranian family. Dari, which is close to Persian (Farsi), was until recently the official, or court

8 *Nomads on the move*

language, with its dialects spoken by the Tajiks, the Hazaras and the Aimaks. Iranian Farsi is spoken in Herat. The language of the Pushtuns is Pashto, which is spoken in a variety of dialects, while the Brahui use Dravidian. The second most important language family is the Turkic, which includes those used by the Uzbek, Kirghiz and Turkoman. All these languages use Arabic script with some additional characters and modifications, like in Persian. Literacy is increasing, but at the time of writing it was probably not more than 10 per cent; in 1961 it was less than 3.5 per cent.

As for religion, the entire population of Afghanistan is Muslim, mainly of the Hanafi Sunnite rite; the Parsiwan (Persians) of the Herat area and most of the Hazaras, Kizilbashi and Ismaili are Shi'ites. The Kafirs of Nuristan were shamanists until their conversion in the last decade of the nineteenth century. Shamanism is still practised across the border, in Chitral. The Hindu and Sikh communities, needless to say, practise their own religion.

The population of the country has consisted since the earliest times of two diametrically opposed formations, the sedentary agriculturists and the pastoral nomads. A whole range of sites containing evidence of nomadic peoples was found alongside the locations of agricultural settlements. This proves that the two types of society and economy co-existed in the country in the past, just as they do at present.

Ethnically, the nomads belonged variously to the Indo-Iranian, Turkish and Mongol families; descendants of each of these can still be found among the mosaic of the contemporary peoples in Afghanistan. It should be emphasized however that the mobility of the nomads poses serious problems to archaeologists. Traces of the nomads' way of life are confined almost exclusively to their tombs, or *kurgans*, as they are sometimes known. These are usually situated in isolated spots with hardly any connection between them and without any superimposed layers, thus making identification and dating extremely difficult.

The nomads needed high mountain valleys as summer pastures for their herds; and these were provided by the uplands along the upper Oxus, in the Hindukush and the Paropamisus. Several nomadic empires therefore centred on these regions, from where incursions could be made into the rich and fertile oases of Persia or into the Indian plain. The nomads were warlike peoples and they were often called on by the local rulers to intervene in their disputes, or were directly employed by them as mercenary soldiers.

In the field of art, the contribution of the nomads can be traced mainly in decorative arts and ornaments. They had neither architecture, nor painting or sculpture. The principal outlets for their creative talent were therefore the implements of their daily life, their clothes, arms, harness and carpets, and a few luxury objects, such as goblets, caskets and jewellery.

About three million Afghans, or one-sixth of the present population are still nomads or semi-nomads. Most are Pushtun, Baluch and Kirghiz. The semi-nomads are herdsmen who also practise some agriculture; only part of the tribe moves with the herds or flocks. Some scholars believe that all Afghan ethnic groups had a nomadic past. However, as agriculture has been practised in the oases since prehistoric times, it must be assumed both that the sedentary ancestry of some parts of the population is of a very long standing, and that the warlike nomads have been the ruling élite of the country for most of the time. This can still be felt in the higher social status enjoyed by some groups, predominantly nomadic, such as the Pushtuns, as compared with others who have been predominantly sedentary, such as the Tajiks or the Hazaras.

The nomads live either in tents or in portable huts called *yurts*. Black goats-hair tents are the typical abode of the Pushtuns, the Baluch and some Aimaks. There are several types of *yurts*, used mainly by the Turkic peoples in the north, the Uzbeks, the Tajiks and the Kirghiz, as well as some Hazaras. Until 1979 some 200,000 Pushtun nomads crossed regularly into Pakistan for winter grazing.

The agriculture in the oases was and still is based on artificial irrigation. Canals, some substantial in size, were drawn from rivers with permanent water branching off at a convenient place, where a dam was erected. The largest irrigation networks were on the rivers Helmand and Hari Rud. The dependence on irrigation had important repercussions in the social structure of the population.

Before the arrival of the Russians, four-fifths of the arable surface was taken by irrigated farmland, with the remainder being used for dry-farming. Three out of ten of the farming population were 'big' landowners, four were smallholders and three were landless peasants. Their work was based on a verbal agreement, and their reward was usually one-sixth of the harvest, occasionally increasing to up to one-half if the worker provided his own tools and seeds.

Irrigation was based on canals built and maintained by the village, and the distribution of water, governed by a complex system of laws and by-laws, was administered

9 *Afghan business*

by the *mirab* or 'lord of the water', appointed by the village council. From a military point of view, the key places of the irrigation network were also the most important strategically. More often than not the destruction of a dam rendered the entire oasis defenceless or even uninhabitable.

Trade routes crossed the country in various directions from the earliest times, linking China and India with Persia and, farther west, with the Levantine ports of the Mediterranean. Important settlements grew along these routes, such as Ay Khanum at the crossing of the Oxus, or Bamiyan near the difficult Shibar Pass across the Kuh-i Baba Range. These routes were used by pilgrims and traders as well as armies. As Buddhism penetrated north, the entire road between the Indus and the Oxus was lined with monasteries and *stupas*, but as the Hephthalites or the Mongols penetrated south they transformed that same road into a path of destruction.

Present-day roads follow to a large extent these ancient trade routes, but surface transport is a problem which still has not been solved satisfactorily. For centuries the north was connected with the south only by tenuous caravan tracks which were impassable for several months in winter. The first motor road across the Shibar Pass was built by King Nadir Shah in the early 1930s but it was not macadamized and it, too, was blocked in winter. The opening of the Salang tunnel in 1964 provided the first all-year road connection between Kabul and Mazar-i Sharif.

Other important roads are Kabul to Peshawar, Kabul-Kandahar-Herat, Herat-Islam Kala and Iran, and Herat-Kushka and the ex-Soviet Central Asian republics. There are no railways in Afghanistan, but in 1982 the Russians built a bridge across the Amu Darya at Termez, and a railhead on the Afghan side. As Afghanistan is a landlocked country, its very few river ports are all on the only navigable river, the Amu Darya. The major one is Sher Khan Bandar, formerly called Kizil Kala.

Under the last king, Zahir Shah, the economy of the country made substantial progress. During the Cold War it benefited from the superpower rivalry in various ways. The Russians supplied cheap raw materials and built factories and bridges in the north, while the Americans financed development projects and built airports and dams in the south. North-south roads were financed by the Russians, east-west ones by the Americans. During the Russian occupation the country suffered greatly from the guerilla war and afterwards even more from the factional strife that followed. Under the Taliban regime, since 1996, the country was, in the words of one observer, run 'like a grocery shop'. There was no financial policy, no budget, no systematic tax collection and no banking system either. The government's main revenue came from taxes on imported goods. Rubies and emeralds mined in Badakhshan province were an important source of income for the opposition which was based there. But the principal field of economic activity became the cultivation of poppy and the export of drugs, while the rest of the country's agriculture fell into steep decline due to several years of severe drought and, to no lesser degree, because the millions of refugees who fled the country left behind vast tracts of uncultivated land which rapidly turned into desert.

In education and healthcare the situation became even more catastrophic. The education of women was banned altogether, while the only educational establishment for boys became the *madrasas* (coranic schools). The Western NGOs which provided most of the medical and nutritional aid were constantly harassed, so that even before the beginning of the American bombardment, the last of them left the country.

Children's mortality, according to recent statistics, was 16.3 per cent, the highest in the world, while the life expectancy, at 41 years, was the lowest.

2 History

The earliest urban settlement so far excavated on the territory of Afghanistan is the site of Mundigak, north-west of Kandahar. It developed into a town in its Period IV (seven periods have been identified) which corresponds roughly to the years 2750-2250 BC. Certain similarities of construction and lay-out permit the belief that the town had contacts with the Indus valley civilisation of Mohenjo Daro and Harappa. However, after Period V (end of the third millennium BC) the site was abandoned for ten or twelve centuries and its last period (VII) corresponds approximately to the eighth to seventh century BC.

Afghanistan first entered history as a series of eastern satrapies of Achaemenian Persia between the sixth and the fourth century BC. Aria or Ariana was the name for the area around Herat, Bactriana was the northern part of the country, between the Oxus and the Hindukush, while Gandhara extended south of the mountains and east as far as the Punjab. Sattagydia lay between Ghazni and the Indus, Arachosia roughly between Kandahar and Quetta, and Drangiana was what later became known as Sistan.

When Alexander defeated the last Achaemenian king in 331 BC, the eastern satrapies tried to organize resistance against the invader. Iskander, as Alexander is still known in legend, invaded Ariana and founded his first city of Alexandria on or near

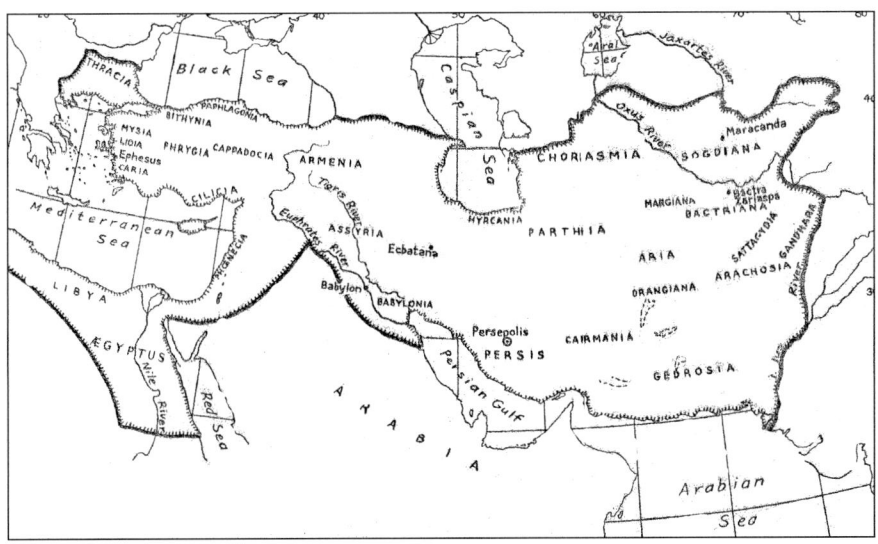

10 Achaemenian satrapies. Dupree/Wheeler (1968)

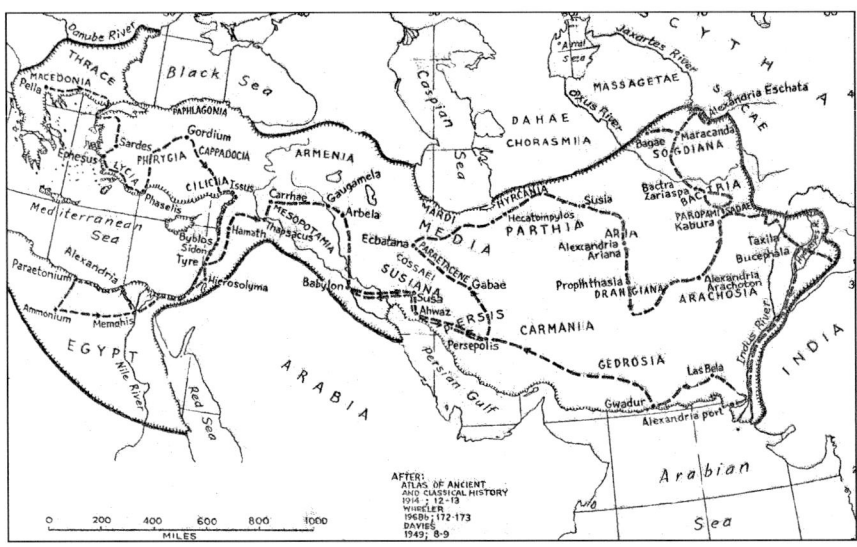

11 Movements of Alexander the Great. Dupree/Davies (1949)

the site of Herat. He then moved into Drangiana; Arachosia together with other satrapies of southern Iran subsequently submitted to him. Moving east along the Helmand river, he stopped at Kandahar and founded the second Alexandria. From here he pushed into the Kabul area and fortified another strategic site near the confluence of the Ghorband and Panjshir rivers, probably close to the point where the city of Kapisa was later built. In pursuit of his opponents who had retreated north of the Hindukush, he did not take the usual road through the Bamiyan passes but, to surprise them, chose the much more difficult passage farther east, through the Khawak Pass, and mounted his attack on the satraps' army in Bactria from Kunduz in the east, when they were expecting him to come from the south. Alexander followed the retreating satraps over the Oxus and penetrated as far as the Jaxartes, the present Syr Darya, where he founded his furthermost Alexandria, Alexandria Eschate, near modern Khojend. He waged campaigns in Transoxania, or Soghdiana as it was then known, for more than two years and when he eventually returned to Afghanistan, he travelled via Bamiyan, the Shibar Pass and the Ghorband Valley. He split his army into two near Jalalabad: one half followed the Kabul River into India, while Alexander himself moved north-east with the elite of his army into Bajaur and Swat, via the Kunar Valley. In 326 BC he was in the Punjab where having defeated the Indian army of King Porus on the river Jhelum he began his homeward journey down the Indus. He died in Babylon in 323 BC.

The eastern part of his empire, Persia, Bactria and India, was then governed by his one-time general, Seleucus, whose descendants failed, however, to keep their holdings intact, with the result that two Greek kingdoms split off in the east: Bactria north of the Hindukush, and, later, the Indo-Greek kingdom south of it. At the same

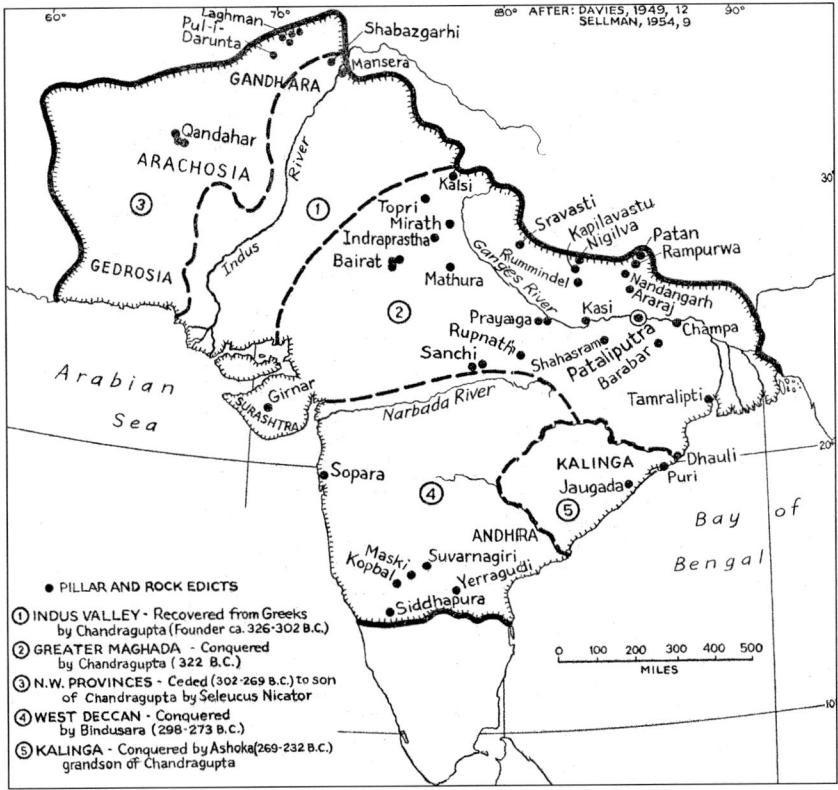

12 The Mauryan Empire. Dupree/Davies (1949)/Sellman (1954)

time, the Indian dynasty of the Mauryans began to push into Afghanistan from the east. Chandragupta, the founder of the dynasty, occupied the Indus Valley at the end of the fourth century BC; at the beginning of the third, his son concluded a peaceful transaction with the descendant of Seleucus, Seleucus Nicator who, realizing that he was unable to defend the provinces of Gandhara, Arachosia and Gedrosia, agreed to cede them to him for 500 elephants. The Mauryan empire reached its peak under Emperor Ashoka (269-32 BC), and declined following his demise, while the Bactrian and Indo-Greek kingdoms enjoyed a period of prosperity and expansion lasting approximately a century.

However, between 140-30 BC, Bactria was invaded by nomads from Transoxania. Heliocles, the last Greek king, was defeated and thus Greek domination of the country came to an end. The dominant tribe of this invasion would seem to be the Scythians or Saka who belonged, both ethnically and linguistically, to the Iranian family. Shortly afterwards another invasion from the north pushed the Saka across the Hindukush and into Drangiana and Arachosia. This is still reflected in the name given to Drangiana: 'the land of the Saka' or Sakastan, now Sistan. The new invaders were a group of tribes known as the Yue-che (Yüe-czï) who were most probably also of

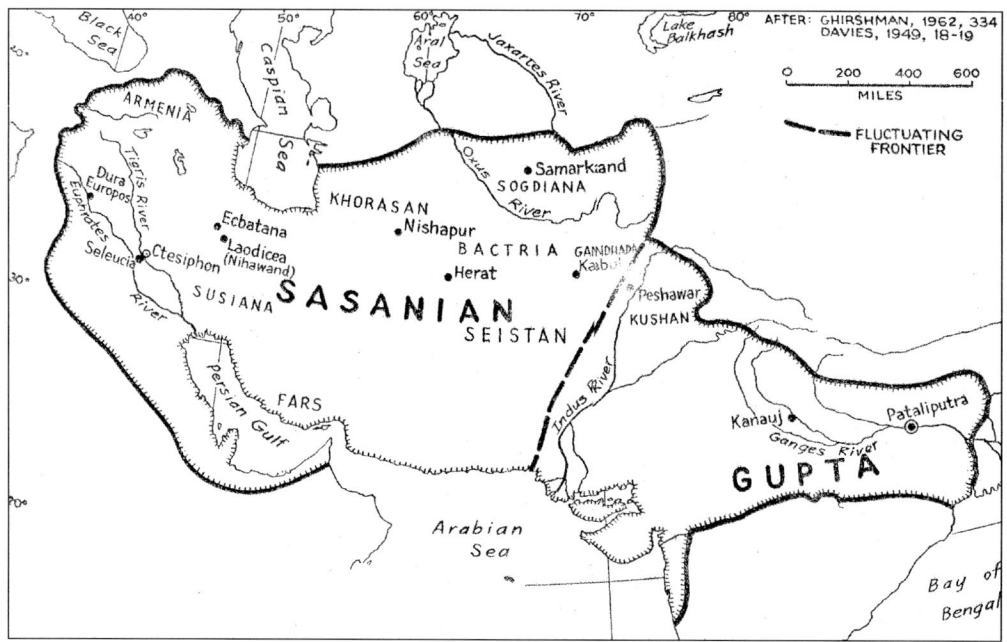

13 The Sasanian and Gupta Empires. Dupree/Ghirsham (1962)/Davies (1949)

Indo-European origin. One such tribe was the Tokhars who gave their name to Bactria – Tokharistan. The Saka penetrated into the Kabul area and into the Punjab, and when the Yue-che caught up with them, moved further east into India where, in Malwa and in Gujerat, their principalities continued to exist until the fourth century AD.

Gradually, most of the Greek states south of the Hindukush fell under Scythian suzerainty.[1] Bactria was split between five Yue-che clans, one of whom, the Kushans, founded a powerful dynasty around the beginning of our era. The golden age of the Kushan empire came with the reign of King Kanishka, who ruled over Transoxania, Afghanistan, and a considerable part of the Punjab. The date of his accession is subject to dispute and varies between AD 78 and as late as 278, with the year 128 being generally considered the most probable.[2] Irrespective of when he lived or died, Kanishka left an indelible mark on the Indian, Afghan, Iranian and even Chinese cultural landscape, for it was during his reign that Buddhism rose to its apogee in Central Asia and subsequently spread to the Far East and parts of South-east Asia. He made his capital Pushkalavati, the site of Charsada near Peshawar; his summer residence was Kapisa (Begram) north of Kabul. The decline of the Kushan empire came about in the third century AD when Bactria again became a province of Persia which was now under the Sasanian dynasty, who had replaced the Parthians at the beginning of the century.

The Sasanians had ruled for a century and a half when another steppe horde descended upon the eastern provinces: the Hephthalites, or White Huns, who were of Turco-Mongolian origin. They lived in the region of the Altai mountains and from there moved into the steppes of western Turkestan. Towards the middle of the fifth century they occupied the area between the rivers Ili and Talas in the east and the Aral Sea in the west. They then began to move south, across the Syr Darya, into Transoxania and Bactria, conquering the entire eastern part of the Sasanian empire, including the rich and important province of Khorasan. One of the shahs, Peroz (Firuz), was killed in battle; but overall Persia managed to withstand the onslaught.

Within 50 years the Hephthalites had become a formidable power. They continued to move southwards and, after replacing the last of the Kushans in Kabul, crossed the passes and invaded India which was then ruled by the Gupta dynasty. At the beginning of the sixth century they established their capital at Sialkot in East Punjab and from there raided and terrorized India for 50 years. The Hephthalites persecuted the Buddhist religious communities in the highly civilised provinces of Kapisa and Gandhara, massacred the population, destroyed monasteries and works of art and eventually wrecked the 500-year-old Greco-Buddhist civilisation. Their domination was broken in the second half of the sixth century, mainly due to another invasion from the steppes, this time by the Turks.

In the mid-sixth century the Turkish homelands in Mongolia and eastern Siberia were divided between the eastern and the western khanates. The western Turks invaded the Hephthalites' territory in the Talas region. A simultaneous attack from the Sasanians crushed the Hephthalites, and marked the end of their power. The Persians and the Turks divided the Hephthalites' possessions. The Turkish khan took Soghd and the shah (Khosroes Anushirwan) took Bactria. The arrangement was short-lived, for the Turks invaded Bactria almost immediately, penetrating as far as Herat. The diplomacy of this period shows some interesting political manoeuvring between the Turks and the Byzantine Empire against Persia.

While the Turks were holding Transoxania, the Hephthalite princelings continued to rule Bactria, south of the Oxus and north of the Hindukush, as vassals of the Persian kings. South of the mountains their principalities remained independent. In the south-east, the entire region between Kabul, Ghazni and Kandahar, which was known as Zabulistan, came under the domination of an Indianized dynasty of Turkish descent, the Turk-Shahis.

After the Arabs had defeated the Sasanians and made themselves heirs to their empire, they quickly dispersed the Hephthalites in northern Afghanistan. They conquered the entire province of Khorasan with the cities of Balkh, Merv and Herat, and the oasis of Sistan in the middle of the seventh century. From these holdings the Arabs conducted raids on the neighbouring countries, Transoxania in the north and Zabulistan in the east. Some 30 years elapsed before they were able to camp on the other side of the Oxus in winter for the first time, and they were not to conquer Transoxania finally until the beginning of the eighth century.

Meanwhile, the son of the last Sasanian shah, Peroz, sought help from China against the Arabs. He even promised to accept Chinese suzerainty in return for military assistance. The result was a historical curiosity – for a while, Persia became a Chinese province with the capital at Zaranj, in Sistan.[3]

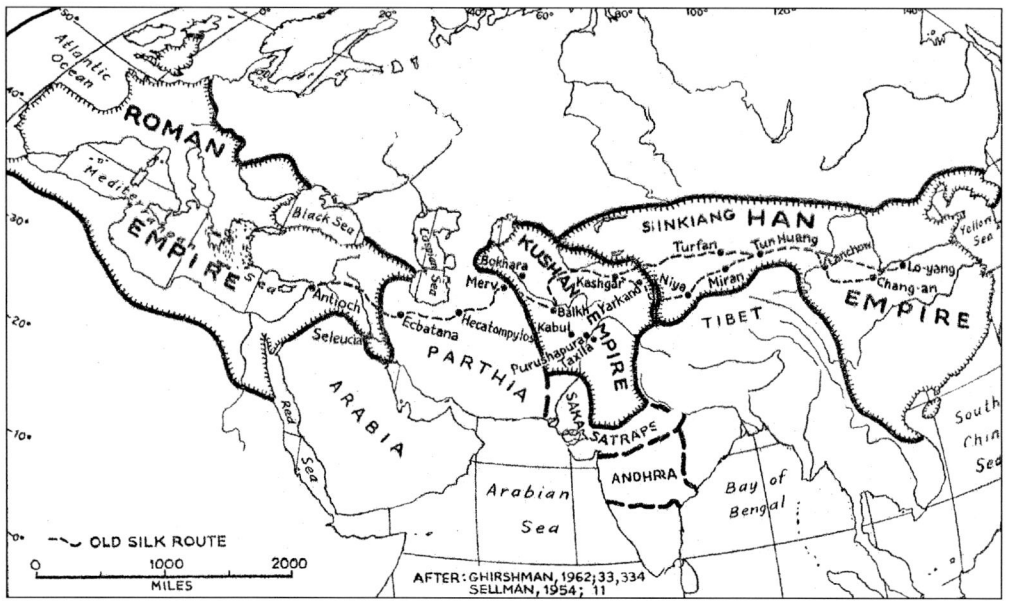

14 Eurasia, second century AD. Dupree/Sellman (1954)/Ghirsham (1962)

The raids into Zabulistan resumed as soon as the Arabs had re-established their grip over Sistan, but the Turk-Shahis generally managed to withstand the attacks. Some time around 850, the Turk-Shahis were replaced by another wholly Indian dynasty, the Hindushahi rajas who were most probably Brahmins. Since the seventh century, Buddhism had been in rapid decline, mainly due to rising militant Hinduism as well as the proselytizing force of Islam; but some of its centres, like Bamiyan (see below p.88), survived for another two centuries.

In the second half of the ninth century a dynamic local dynasty, the Saffarids, came to power in Sistan. For a time they extended their domination over much of Zabulistan and they even conquered Kabul, but could not hold it permanently. In the year 900 the Saffarids were defeated by the rulers of Transoxania, the Samanid amirs of Bukhara; but after a short spell a branch of the family managed to return to power and, for several centuries, survived successive waves of invaders – the Ghaznavids, the Seljuks, the Mongols – until the Safavid empire was established in Persia in the sixteenth century.

The Samanid empire, which for about a century included also Khorasan, Sistan and eastern Afghanistan, became a huge and loosely knit conglomerate of provinces stretching from Khorasan to the Ferghana Valley, and from the Aral Sea to the borders of India. In practice only the central provinces, Khorasan and Transoxania, were ruled directly by the amir, because the outlying regions (like eastern Afghanistan) were too remote to be controlled from Bukhara. They either tended to revert to their original, local rulers who may have received some sort of investiture from the amir and paid

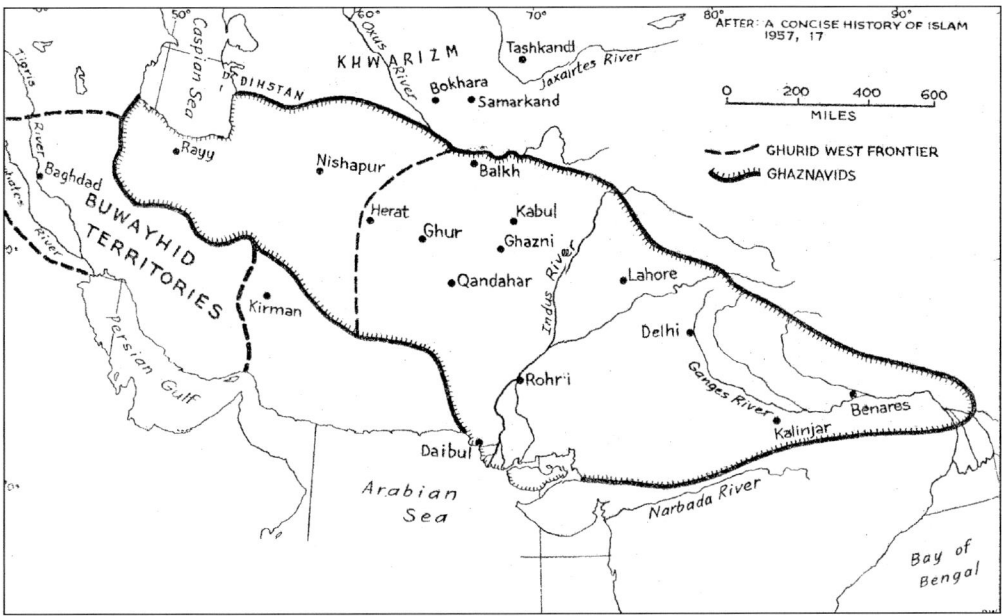

15 The Ghaznavid and Ghorid Empires. Dupree/A Concise History of Islam

tribute to him, or they were administered by military governors, for the most part Turkish slave officers, who were given – or appropriated for themselves – a considerable degree of independence. So for instance Alptigin, a former commander of the amir's forces in Khorasan, defeated the Hindushahi king of Kabul, conquered Ghazna and established himself there as governor in the name of the amir, not without repeated protests from the latter. A successor of Alptigin, Sabuktagin (Sebüktigin) exploited the decline in the Samanids' power to extend this holding over virtually all the territories south of the Oxus. In 1005, Samanid rule finally collapsed and Sabuktagin's son, Mahmud, became sultan in his own name. He quickly increased his father's territories by all the Samanid lands on the left bank of the Oxus, including Khorezm and Khorasan, and extended his empire on the other side deep into India, annexing the Punjab, Multan and Sind. Despite Mahmud's indisputable qualities as military commander and statesman, however, his successes were rather short-lived. His son, Masud I, lost an important battle against the Seljuks in 1040 and had to relinquish Sistan, Khorasan and Khorezm. The Ghaznavid empire, reduced to Afghanistan and northern India, began to gravitate more and more towards the east. Ghazna remained the capital for another century, but as it was now rather exposed, the sultans preferred to reside elsewhere, usually in Lahore. The Ghaznavids abandoned Ghazna altogether when it was sacked and burnt by the sultan of Ghor in 1149.

Setting out from their desolate and mountainous homeland in central Afghanistan, the sultans of Ghor expanded first west to Herat and south to Bost and Ghazna, and then eastwards, into the remaining Ghaznavid territories in India. By the end of the twelfth century, all Ghaznavid possessions were in their hands and the dynasty of Sabuktagin and Mahmud had ceased to exist.

In the west, the Seljuks continued their conquest of Armenia and Asia Minor. In 1071 they defeated and took prisoner the Byzantine emperor, Romanus Diogenes, and subsequently established the Turkish sultanate of Rum in present-day Turkey which, two centuries later, became the foundation of the Ottoman empire. Their sultan Sanjar, the last of the Great Seljuks and originally governor of Khorasan, intervened successfully in the Ghaznavid territories in Afghanistan and Khorezm, as well as in Transoxania. Sanjar died in 1157, and his once powerful empire disintegrated completely.

Thus, on the eve of the Mongol invasion, the entire eastern caliphate was ruled by Turkish dynasties. The Seljuks controlled central and western Iran and eastern Anatolia, the Khorezmshahs ruled in Khorezm and Transoxania, and the Ghorids were masters of all the lands between Herat and Delhi. Only the Saffarids in Sistan were probably of local – that is non-Turkish – origin. The first two decades of the thirteenth century saw a rapid and short-lived expansion of the ephemeral empire of the Khorezmshahs who penetrated into Afghanistan, occupied Khorasan and threatened Iran. But before they had time to consolidate their possessions, the Mongols struck.

The nomadic tribes who lived in the vast steppe area north and north-east of the Gobi desert were a mixture of Turks, Mongols and Tungus. The twelfth century saw the beginning of a slow consolidation process and, somewhat later, the Mongols emerged as a dominant force under their leader, Temuchin, who later became known as Chingiz-Khan. Native of a clan whose pastures lay between the rivers Onon and Kerulen, Chingiz-Khan gradually succeeded in subduing other Mongol clans and neighbouring tribes and in 1206 was able to convene a Grand Assembly, or kuriltay, of all Turco-Mongols, at which he was proclaimed emperor or Great Khan (Kha-Khan). In 1218 Chingiz-Khan sent Jebe Noyon, one of his best generals, to the west. In an extremely efficient and disciplined campaign, Jebe took Semirechiye and Eastern Turkestan; thus Chingiz-Khan became an immediate neighbour of the Khorezmshah. Chingiz-Khan first tried to establish commercial and political contacts with the Khorezmians, but subsequently prepared for war when a caravan carrying a Mongol envoy was massacred on the Syr Darya. The Mongol army that assembled on the upper Irtysh in the summer of 1219 contained between 150-200,000 men – far fewer than the Khorezmian forces, but with superior discipline and more coherent and efficient leadership.

The Khorezmshah adopted a defensive strategy based on his many fortified towns, but by doing so, he divided his forces and enabled Chingiz-Khan to capture the big cities one by one. Bukhara, Samarkand, Otrar and Gurganj fell in rapid succession. The Khorezmshah fled westward pursued by a Mongol detachment through Khorasan, Iran and Azerbaidjan until he died of exhaustion on an island in the Caspian in December 1220. In the spring of 1221 Chingiz-Khan crossed the Amu Darya and began the conquest of Khorasan and Afghanistan. The cities of Balkh, Merv and Nishapur were completely destroyed and depopulated in this campaign. The mausoleum of Caliph Harun ar-Rashid at Tus and the tomb of Sultan Sanjar

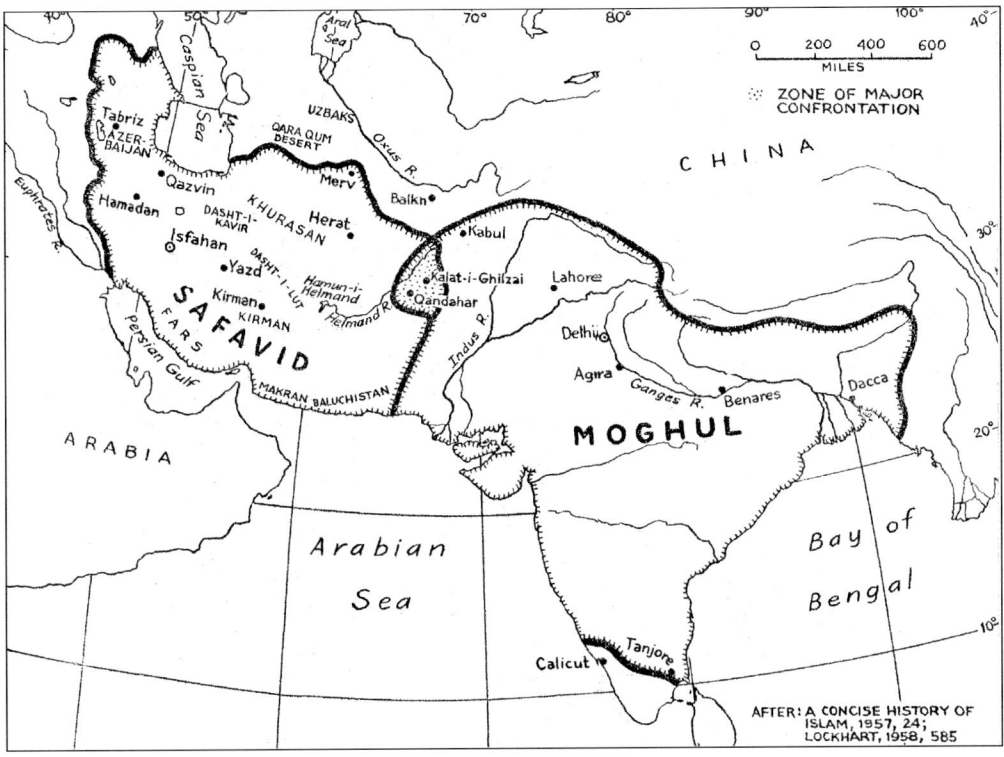

16 The Moghul and Safavid Empires. Dupree/*A Concise History of Islam*/Lockhart (1958)

at Merv were ruined, together with other monuments of Islamic civilisation. Herat, too, was sacked and destroyed, but Sistan with its capital, Zaranj, seems to have escaped the Mongol fury. Despite this, the damage inflicted on irrigation systems and cultivated land was so great that for a generation or so there was probably very little organised life at all.

Under Chingiz-Khan's successors Transoxania became part of the ulus, or apanage, of Chaghatay, Chingiz-Khan's second son. In Iran, after a period of rule by military governors, Hulagu, the grandson of Chingiz-Khan, became the founder of the dynasty of the Il-Khans of Persia. After the collapse of this rule, Herat was ruled by a local dynasty, the Karts, who acquired *de facto* independence at the beginning of the fourteenth century, but they were annihilated in 1381 by Tamerlane. The rest of the territory of Afghanistan was ruled by petty princelings of whom little is known. In the third quarter of the fourteenth century, one such prince was the amir of Balkh, Husayin, who was related by marriage to a little tribal chief from the region south of Samarkand. The name of this chief was Timur, who was later to become known as Timur the Lame, or Tamerlane. By then the original Chaghatay ulus was in a state of utter decay and Timur and Husayin together had to defend Transoxania against nomadic incursions from the east. Their association came to an end when

Timur besieged Husayin in Balkh and defeated him, thus becoming the sole master of Transoxania. In the thirty years of continuous campaigning that followed, Timur succeeded in eliminating virtually every rival, real or potential. Moghulistan (the country beyond the Syr Darya) and Khorezm were the first targets, followed by Khorasan and Persia, with all the lands once ruled by Hulagu. The Volga state of the Golden Horde governed by Timur's arch-enemy Tokhtamish was defeated in two campaigns and became so weak that it never recovered. Timur's army came within a stone's throw of Moscow, his victories over Tokhtamish enabling the Russian principalities to reassert themselves and later to unite and throw off the Mongol yoke.

A campaign to India which extended his territories to the Ganges carried Timur's grand design one step further, but again, such a vast empire without a proper organisational and economic structure was doomed to be short-lived. It collapsed and disintegrated almost immediately after Timur's death in 1405. Warring factions formed around Timur's sons and relatives who fought one another for power, while governors of distant provinces were quick to proclaim themselves independent. Within a few years the empire had shrunk to its very core, i.e. Khorasan and Afghanistan, which were ruled from Herat by Timur's youngest son Shahrukh. In Transoxania, Shahrukh's son Ulughbeg, who resided in Samarkand, ruled as his viceroy, with other members of the family holding some other fiefs. The long reign of Shahrukh and Ulughbeg, 1407-47 and 1410-49 respectively, was a period of prosperity and stability. However, with the assassination of Ulughbeg by his own son in 1449, the process of disintegration was given a further impulse. In the second half of the century the western territories gradually fell into the hands of the Turkoman tribes, the White Sheep and Black Sheep Tartars, while in the east the nomad Uzbek khans were able to arbitrate between the Timurid princelings.

In the late 1450s, Timur's great-grandson Abu Said attempted to restore the empire once more; but after some initial success he was defeated by the Turkomans, captured and executed in 1469. After his death the only significant Timurid principality was Khorasan which enjoyed a period of unrivalled prosperity and cultural progress (1469-1506) under the sultan Husayin Baykara, who resided in Herat.

Towards the end of the century Transoxania came under increasing pressure from the Uzbeks, a Turkish tribe now firmly entrenched on the Syr Darya line from the Aral Sea to Ferghana. In Ferghana, they forced out the Timurid ruler, a young prince called Babur, who had to abandon his fief and seek refuge in Kabul. In 1500 the situation in Transoxania was ripe for the Uzbeks' intervention. Their khan, Muhammad Sheybani, a Chingizkhanid from the House of Jochi, crossed the Syr Darya, occupied Bukhara and Samarkand, and proclaimed himself ruler of Transoxania. He established his capital in Bukhara and, as soon as he consolidated his power, pushed further south. In 1507 he entered Herat, which was defended by a young son of Husayin Baykara, and extinguished the line of Timurid sultans who had ruled Transoxania and Khorasan for over a century.

Meanwhile Babur, the last surviving Timurid, replaced his uncle in governing the tiny kingdom of Kabul and tried to make use of the rising power of Persia to recover his family's lost possessions. When the Safavid shah Ismail defeated the Uzbeks in

1510, Babur did indeed manage to restore Timurid power in Transoxania for a short time; but the Uzbeks returned two years later and reoccupied the country as far as the Amu Darya. Babur was then forced to return to Kabul and when he realized that any further attempt to regain his native Ferghana would be in vain, he turned his attention and all his frustrated energy towards India. In 1525 he left Kabul and marched against the sultan of Delhi whom he defeated in 1526, at the battle of Panipat. He subsequently replaced him, thus becoming the founder of the famous Moghul dynasty which ruled India until it was deposed by the British.

In the sixteenth and seventeenth century the territory of Afghanistan was disputed between the Moghuls, the Safavids and the Uzbeks. Kabul remained firmly in Moghul possession, but Kandahar and Balkh changed hands several times. The Uzbeks returned to Herat for a time, but were driven out by the Persians, who continued to hold the city until the early eighteenth century. The year 1648 marked the great retreat of the Moghuls, who were forced to abandon both northern Afghanistan and Kandahar. As the Moghul empire weakened, more and more Afghan tribes in the north and the east of the country became independent. As had happened so many times in the past, local chieftains commanding the loyalty of powerful tribes came to power in the big cities of Kandahar and Herat, first under the suzerainty of the Persians, then as independent rulers and eventually as founders of native dynasties.

With the two great powers in a state of decadence and with no threat of a nomad invasion from the steppes, the stage was set for an inter-tribal struggle and a quest for the domination of the country by an indigenous force. At the forefront of this struggle were the two main Pushtun tribes, the Ghilzai and the Abdali. The chieftain of the Ghilzai, Mir Wais, who spent some time at the Safavid court in Isfahan, became aware of the weakness of the Persians and in 1709 started a revolt against them. Although the Persians were helped by the rival tribe, the Abdali, the Ghilzai managed to hold Kandahar and forced them into retreat. Mir Wais died in 1715 and was buried outside Kandahar. After the Persian retreat, the Abdali revolted in Herat, defeated several punitive expeditions and proclaimed Herat an independent state. In the clash between the two dominant tribes which followed the Ghilzai again prevailed.

The power of the Ghilzai was now such that they felt strong enough to challenge the Safavids on their own territory. The 18-year-old son of Mir Wais, Mir Mahmud, twice captured Kirman in southern Persia and after these initial successes marched straight for the capital, Isfahan. He defeated the Persian army outside the city and laid siege to it for six months. The population was reduced to a diet of dogs, cats, old shoes and horse dung,[4] and some 80,000 people died of starvation and disease. In April 1722, the shah finally capitulated. The population of Isfahan probably numbered 650,000 in the early eighteenth century; after the defeat the city never regained its former importance though now its population is close to two million.

Mahmud proclaimed himself shah and pursued his occupation of Persia, but his atrocities provoked revolts among the Persians and eventually among his own followers. He was killed in 1725 and his cousin, Ashraf, was proclaimed shah.

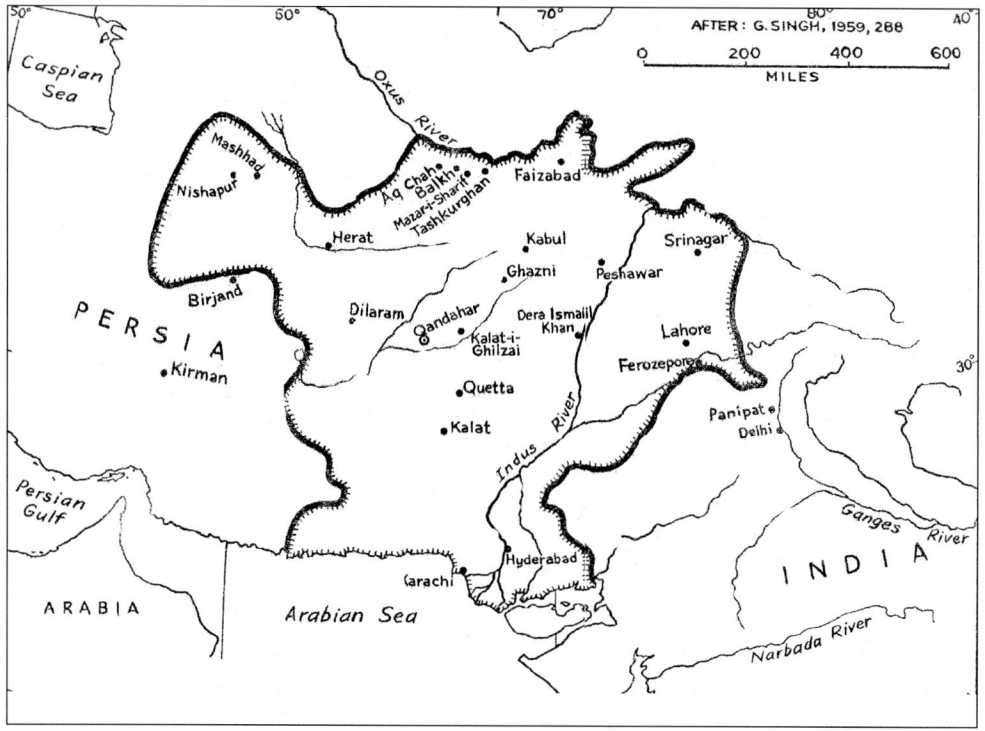

17 The Empire of Ahmad Shah. Dupree/Singh (1959)

Meanwhile, the last Safavid claimant, Tahmasp II, in flight from the Afghans, found himself in the hands of a Turkish adventurer, Nadir Khan, who rose from a cameleer to outlaw king with a large personal army. Nadir first attacked the Abdali forces in Herat, defeated them and then turned towards Isfahan. He defeated Ashraf in several battles and became himself an effective ruler of Persia. The Ghilzai and the Abdali now joined forces against him, but to no avail. They were defeated, Kandahar fell to Nadir and a switch of population followed. The Ghilzai were exiled to Khorasan and the Abdali were resettled in Kandahar.

Nadir Shah then followed the path of previous conquerors and invaded India in 1739. The Moghul court in Delhi which faced Nadir, pleasure-loving and laden with 'carpet-knights',[5] resembled the Safavid court in Isfahan which had faced Mahmud. The victorious Nadir Shah left Delhi after two months with an enormous booty which included the Peacock Throne and the famous Koh-i Nur diamond. He then moved past Herat into Transoxania, where he took Samarkand, Bukhara and Khiva. In 1741 he eventually returned to Mashad, which he made his capital.

After the death of Nadir Shah – who was beheaded by his own officers – the Abdali tribe rose to power in Afghanistan. In 1747 a young chieftain, Ahmad Khan, with a distinguished record of military command under Nadir Shah, was elected supreme chieftain. He changed his name to Ahmad Shah Durrani, and since then the Abdali have also been called Durrani. Kandahar quickly fell to him and Ahmad Shah, combining incredible luck with consummate skill, was on his way to creating the last great Afghan empire. While the Ghilzai, once masters of this part of the world, never again attained their former power or importance, the Durrani played the leading role in the country until the left-wing coup in 1978.

Ahmad Shah's road to glory was a fast one. In quick succession he took Ghazni, the last Ghilzai stronghold, and Kabul, still ruled by the Moghuls. Peshawar and Lahore followed. In 1748 the Moghul emperor ceded to him all his territories west of the Indus. Herat, still in Persian hands, fell after a siege lasting nine months. Mashad and Nishapur were also taken. The nomadic tribes north of the Hindukush, between the mountains and the Amu Darya, accepted the suzerainty of the Durrani shah. After another campaign to India, Kashmir too was annexed to the empire. In the fourth Indian campaign, in 1757, the Afghan army entered Delhi and penetrated as far as Agra. A fifth campaign, in 1759-61, was provoked by a revolt of the Sikhs and the Mahrattas. The defeat of the Mahrattas made it easier for the British to become the paramount power in India. By destroying the Mahratta force the Afghans inadvertently aided the British advance toward the north-west and, more immediately, the rise of Sikh power in the Punjab. The Afghans waged five more campaigns against the indomitable Sikhs, but the Sikhs remained masters of the Punjab in the end until the British demolished their power in 1849.

The Durrani empire soon began to crumble in a dispute over some northern regions; the Durrani shah and the amir of Bukhara agreed to accept the Amu Darya as a boundary dividing their interests. The amir presented Ahmad Shah with a kherka – a cloak supposedly worn by the Prophet – for which the Durrani shah constructed a special mosque in Kandahar. Ahmad Shah died in 1772 and under his son and successor Timur Shah (1772-93) the decline gathered momentum. The amir moved his capital from Kandahar to Kabul to escape the hostility of the local Pushtun tribes. Revolts occurred in Sind, Balkh, Sistan, Khorasan and Kashmir and, in the first ten years of Timur Shah's reign, all these regions were lost. Before the end of the century the empire was reduced to little more than the areas of Kabul, Kandahar, Herat and Peshawar, and parts of the northern steppe.

It was also in the last decade of the eighteenth century that the rivalry of the great European powers made itself felt in this part of the Asian continent. After his initial success in Egypt, Napoleon sent a mission to the Qajar shah of Persia – the Qajar dynasty rose to power after the assassination of Nadir Shah – to incite Persia against Russia. The Russian territorial gains following their victory over Persia and their increased influence at the Persian court began to worry the British, who tried to persuade the Persians to fight the Russians, and at the same time signed a treaty of mutual assistance with Shah Shuja, the son of Timur Shah, who succeeded to the Kabul throne in 1803. But Shah Shuja was unable to hold Kabul and was deposed in 1809, the same year the treaty was signed. His successor, his half-brother Shah Mahmud, was himself deposed in 1818 and a civil war broke out which lasted until 1826, when another member of the Durrani tribe, Dost Muhammad Khan, was recognized as titular head of the tribe. He ruled from 1826-39, but was never effectively in control of anything except Kabul and Ghazni. When the Russians put out feelers to Dost Muhammad, the British decided to sponsor an alliance between the deposed Shah Shuja and the Sikh government in the Punjab. The Tripartite treaty, signed in July 1838, aimed at restoring Shah Shuja to the throne. A military campaign was planned whereby Shah Shuja, with British financial and military aid, should march on Kandahar, while the Sikh force should march on Kabul. In April 1839 the British Army crossed into Afghan territory from Quetta, took Kandahar and Ghazni and, on August 6th, arrived at Kabul. The Sikhs, on the whole, failed to support the campaign.

Dost Muhammad fled from Kabul to Bukhara and Shah Shuja, after thirty years of exile, started the second period of his reign. His kingdom included Kabul, Jalalabad, Kandahar and Bamiyan; the rest of the country consisted of independent tribal principalities.

The British move into Afghanistan was countered by an abortive Russian expedition against the Khanate of Khiva in 1839. Dost Muhammad attempted a comeback in 1840, but eventually gave himself up and was granted refuge in India. Gradually, the tribal chiefs united against the British and their protégé king and in the winter of 1841 the British were forced to negotiate their retreat. Following the murder of the envoy and several officers, the withdrawal began in January 1842, under highly unfavourable circumstances. On the way to Jalalabad, the convoy of some 16,500 people was massacred by tribesmen. Only a handful were taken prisoner. Shah Shuja survived the departure of his protectors by only three months.

While the British garrison in Kandahar held out against the attacks of the Ghilzai, a punitive expedition under General Pollock came up the Khyber Pass. When the power struggle in Kabul reached civil war proportions, General Pollock moved to the city where he linked up with the garrison from Kandahar. As a token punishment the great bazaar in Kabul was blown up. The family of Shah Shuja was driven into exile and Muhammad Akbar Khan, the son of Dost Muhammad, held the throne vacant pending his father's return. Dost Muhammad was duly freed and shortly afterwards welcomed by the people as the amir of Kabul. Under his rule, most of Afghan Turkestan was reconquered. Kandahar, which for a time had been an independent principality, was annexed following the death of its ruler. Herat, which was held by a local potentate, continued to be a trouble spot; Persia occupied it in 1856 and, although soon forced to evacuate it, the oasis remained under Persian influence until Dost Muhammad annexed it definitively in 1863, just nine days before his death.

By then the Russians, who had held a bridgehead on the east coast of the Caspian since the 1830s, were pushing eastwards from it along the Kopet Dagh mountains, and at the same time south from Siberia towards the Syr Darya. After the Crimean War they began systematically penetrating into the Central Asian khanates of Khiva, Bukhara and Kokand which occupied the territory between the Amu Darya and the Syr Darya. They took Tashkent in 1867, a year later occupied Samarkand and in 1869 the amir of Bukhara accepted the suzerainty of the tsar. Kokand was taken in 1871, in 1876 the khan was deposed and the khanate incorporated into the Governorate General; and two years later it was the turn of Khiva. The conquest

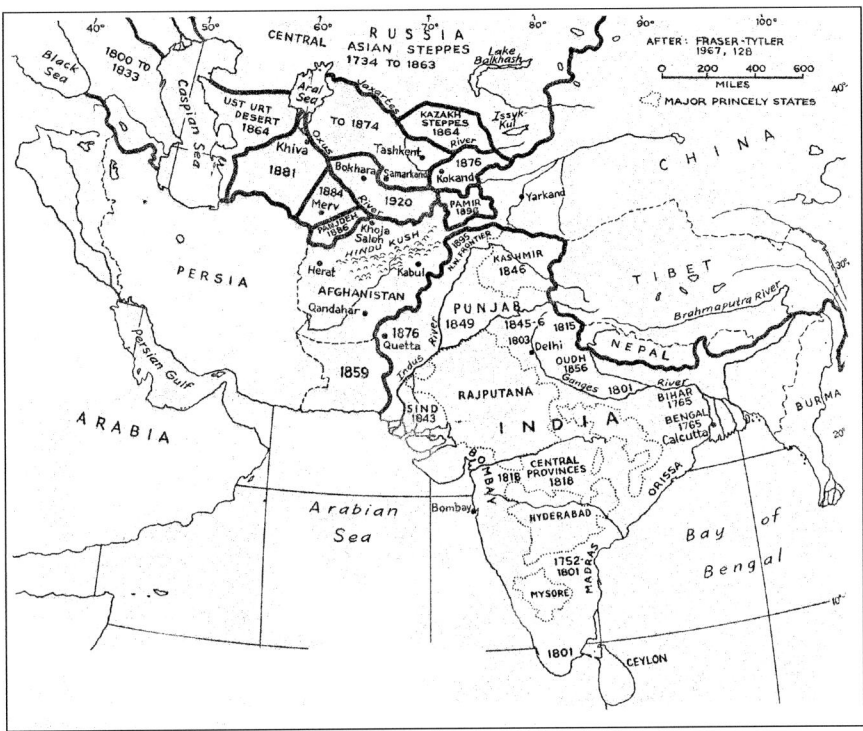

18 Russian advances in Central Asia. Dupree/Fraser-Tytler (1967)

of the whole area was completed by the defeat of the Turkomans in 1881 and the occupation of the Merv oasis in 1884. Thus the Russian forces of Trans-Caspia and Turkestan were brought into direct contact. The construction of a railway enabled them to concentrate rapidly on the Afghan frontier which, naturally, was regarded by the British as highly unfavourable for the security of India.

The death of Dost Muhammad was followed by fratricidal fighting among his sons and grandsons which lasted nearly six years. One of his younger sons, Shir Ali, finally emerged as the new amir. Supported by British money, arms and ammunition, he managed to retain power until his death in 1879. However, when in 1878 he received a Russian mission in Kabul, the British reacted strongly and Shir Ali was forced to leave the city and flee to Balkh. Yakub Khan, his son, then signed the Treaty of Gandamak in May 1879, under which Britain was given control of Afghanistan's foreign affairs and a British mission was to be set up in Kabul. The amir also ceded certain tribal areas bordering on the North-West Frontier territory, in return for which he was given financial assistance.

The British mission had been in Kabul for barely six weeks when some Afghan troops mutinied and massacred all its staff. British troops moved into Kabul and Yakub Khan abdicated. Prompted by these events Dost Muhammad's grandson, Abdurrahman, crossed the Amu Darya in 1880, after a ten-year exile in Russian-

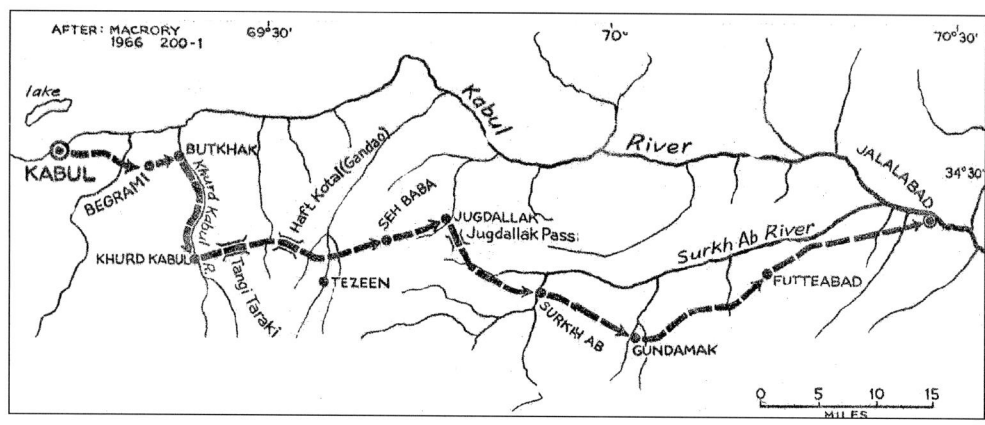

19   British retreat route: Kabul to Jalalabad, January 1842. Dupree/Macrory (1966)

occupied Samarkand, with arms, ammunition and money provided by the Russians. Nevertheless the British decided to support his claims to the throne and in July 1880 Abdurrahman was proclaimed amir of Kabul.

However, the fighting was not yet over. A British detachment was defeated at Maiwand near Kandahar, and Kandahar itself was besieged by hostile Afghans until a relief column arrived from Kabul. British troops were then withdrawn but Abdurrahman still had to fight for the possession of Herat and Kandahar which were held by his cousin, Ayub Khan.

The twenty-one year rule of Amir Abdurrahman was marked by three major events. One was the unification of the country under one law and one ruler. It took sixteen years to accomplish this task, which involved breaking up the tribal system and eliminating all petty chiefs and local strongmen. The Kafirs of Nuristan were the last to submit, in 1895-6; still pagan at that time, they were then forcibly converted to Islam.

The second event was an international crisis precipitated by Russian advances in Central Asia and their occupation of Merv in 1884, which brought them into the immediate vicinity of Afghanistan. A dispute broke out over the Panjdeh oasis, southeast of Merv, which had been claimed by the Afghans but was inhabited by Turkomans, whom the Russians wished to incorporate into their empire. Russian troops moved into the oasis in 1885 and a battle took place in which the Afghans were defeated and forced to withdraw. Both Britain and the amir became worried about the possibility of a Russian advance on Herat. The city's defences were hastily strengthened and it was in the course of these works that the order was given to blow up the remnants of the famous Musalla. The issue was finally defused by the establishment of a joint boundary commission, which fixed the frontier between the Hari Rud and the Amu Darya.

The third important event was the demarcation of the country. The northern frontier of Afghanistan had already been fixed by a previous agreement between Britain and Russia, along a stretch of the Amu Darya; following the Panjdeh crisis, the western frontier was laid down as far as the Hari Rud. The eastern boundary between Afghanistan and India was negotiated with the amir by Sir Mortimer Durand in 1893 and was subsequently properly demarcated and mapped all the way from the Pamirs to the Persian frontier in the south-west by Udny's and McMahon's boundary commissions, in the years 1894-6. The Wakhan Valley in the Pamirs presented something of a problem. The amir originally refused to retain it but was eventually persuaded to do so by Durand, who was anxious to establish a buffer between Russia and India. The Russians had previously penetrated into the Valley, then a territory somewhat disputed between China and Afghanistan, and massacred its Afghan garrison. The Pamir question was finally settled in 1895. The last stretch of frontier to be fixed was in the western part of the country, between Sistan and the Hari Rud. In 1872 the Goldsmid Commission divided the Sistan oasis, awarding the left bank of the Helmand to Persia, and the right to Afghanistan. In 1903 the second McMahon commission mapped the area. The stretch north of Sistan as far as the Hari Rud was definitely fixed only in 1935.

Habibullah, the eldest son of Abdurrahman, was proclaimed amir in October 1901. Tough negotiations with the British, who demanded a new and more far-reaching treaty, ended only in 1905 with a new draft based largely on the previous agreement. Meanwhile, the Russians continued their attempts to penetrate Afghanistan both politically and commercially; in Persia their activity also increased and in the Pamirs they pushed forward steadily. As Britain was trying at the same time to secure a foothold in Tibet, the two powers found themselves again in close competition. A convention was eventually concluded in 1907 which divided the whole region into spheres of influence. Persia was divided between the Russian zone in the north, and the British zone in the south and east. Each party obtained the right to occupy its zone if threatened by a third party (this provision was applied in the Second World War, when Iran was occupied by the two powers). Both parties recognized Chinese control of Tibet and agreed not to interfere in this area. Afghanistan was recognized as being outside the Russian sphere of influence, but Britain was not to occupy or annex any part of it nor to interfere in any way in its internal affairs.

During the First World War a Turco-German mission was active in Kabul in 1915-16, but Habibullah refused to be drawn into the fighting while at the same time, naturally, demanding substantial concessions from the British for his neutrality. Habibullah was murdered on 20 February, 1919, and his throne was seized by his third son, Amanullah. To unite the army behind him, the new amir hoped to exploit the unrest in the Punjab and elsewhere in India and launched an unprovoked campaign against Britain. The Afghans invaded Indian territory, but an attempted uprising in the Punjab was quickly extinguished, the invading columns were brought to a halt and after bombing raids on Jalalabad and Kabul, the amir demanded an armistice. The whole action lasted less than a month.

In the peace treaty which was signed on 8 August, 1919, Britain acknowledged that Afghanistan was officially free and independent in its internal and external affairs. (This concession must be seen in the light of the post-war chaos in Bolshevik Russia which, as far as could then be seen, removed all threats to Afghanistan and India.) Nevertheless, the amir soon despatched a mission to Moscow and invited a

Bolshevik envoy to visit Kabul. The arrival of the Russian mission inaugurated a Soviet-Afghan relationship which continued somewhat uneasily after the Soviets had destroyed the Central Asian khanates of Khiva and Bukhara, incorporated them into the USSR and forced the amir of Bukhara to seek refuge in Afghanistan.

A Soviet-Afghan treaty was signed on 26 May 1921, followed by a treaty with Britain signed on 22 November of the same year. Treaties with Turkey, France and Italy followed in close succession, and a rapid modernisation of the country was now embarked on. The DAFA (*Délégation archéologique française en Afghanistan*) was founded in 1922, the French lycée and a German college in 1923 and an English college in 1928. The first legislative assembly, the Jirga, was established in 1928 with 150 members, women were encouraged to remove their veil, girls' schools were opened and all Afghans in Kabul were made to wear western clothing.

These and other reforms provoked widespread reaction and in the end led to a revolt. In November 1928, an illiterate Tajik called Bacha Sakkao – Son of a Water-Carrier – entered Kabul at the head of a brigand army, deposed Amanullah and ruled Kabul and central Afghanistan for nine bloody months. Chaos broke out elsewhere in the country, from which Muhammad Nadir Shah, a senior member of the Durrani clan, emerged as leader. In October 1929 he captured Kabul and was proclaimed king.

Some of Amanullah's reforms were rescinded and the constitution which Nadir Shah promulgated in 1931 was in many ways more conservative and more favourable to Islam than the Amanullah constitution of 1923. It created a façade of parliamentary government while leaving all effective control in the hands of the royal family, kept the judiciary primarily under religious leaders, and created a semi-socialist economic framework. Kabul University was founded in 1932.

A new treaty of neutrality and non-aggression was signed with the Soviet Union in 1931, following a serious border incident of 1929, when the Red Army pursued Muslim guerrillas across the border and penetrated some 60km into Afghanistan.

King Nadir Shah was assassinated by a student on 8 November, 1933. His son, Muhammad Zahir Shah, was proclaimed king and was able to stay in power for forty years, until his deposition in 1973. During his reign Afghanistan joined the League of Nations (1934), signed the first treaty with the United States (1936) and agreed to accept aid from Germany, Italy and Japan (1935). Although prior to 1939 the Germans had become the most important foreign community in Kabul, Afghanistan remained neutral in the Second World War.

After the war, during the time of the partition of British India between India and Pakistan, the Afghans challenged the validity of the Durand line as an international boundary and supported the idea of an independent tribal state, 'Pushtunistan' on the territory of the North-West Frontier Province, which could eventually become part of Afghanistan. The problem of 'Pushtunistan' has been a bone of contention between Pakistan and Afghanistan ever since. Frustrated by both this issue and the increased United States aid to Pakistan, the Afghans turned once more to the Soviet Union. A trade agreement was signed in 1950 which made Afghanistan partly dependent on the USSR for many items formerly imported from the West. A Soviet trade representation was opened in Kabul and a certain number of Soviet technicians began to operate in the country.

On the internal political level a reformist 'liberal' parliament was elected in 1949. Laws were passed to permit freedom of the press and a campaign for a more liberal government ensued. Conservative circles, especially religious ones, were alarmed by this trend and a reaction quickly followed. In 1952 all non-government newspapers were closed and many leading liberals arrested. However, the younger members of the royal family and contemporaries of the king, who disagreed with the conservative attitude of the older generation, challenged the king's two uncles (who held the real power in the country), and effected a bloodless coup on 20 September 1953. The king's cousin, Daoud Khan, became prime minister but no liberalisation followed. In the ten years of Daoud's premiership, economic progress was slow but steady. Large irrigation programmes, not always successful or well organised, were undertaken with foreign help in the Helmand and Arghandab valleys, and attempts were made in these areas and in the north around Kunduz and Balkh to resettle farmers and introduce settlement programmes for the nomads.

Relations with the USSR continued to develop. In 1955 the trade agreement of 1950 had been extended by a further five years, and the 1931 treaty of neutrality and non-aggression by ten years. A large economic development loan was granted in 1956, which included such projects as the road from the Amu Darya port of Kizil Kala to Kabul, airport construction, irrigation dams and canals, and a fertilizer factory. With the assistance of Soviet advisers a Five-Year Plan was launched in 1956; and furthermore, a contract was signed in the same year for imports of arms from the Soviet bloc countries. On the other hand, mistrust towards the Soviets had been deeply rooted in the Afghans since the early 1920s and 1930s, when many of the anti-Soviet guerilla fled to Afghanistan, and the Muslims in Central Asia were subjected to the brutalities of collectivisation and Russification.

By the late 1950s, substantial numbers of Afghan officers were being trained in the USSR, and Soviet personnel served as advisers to Afghan military schools. The question of 'Pushtunistan' continued to plague the relations between Afghanistan and Pakistan. In 1961 a crisis arose over this issue after Afghan troops had invaded Pushtun territory. Diplomatic relations were broken off and, by decision of Daoud, the border was closed, leaving Afghanistan wholly dependent on the Soviet Union for all its imports and exports. The self-imposed blockade lasted for over a year until Daoud submitted his resignation to the king, on 9 March 1963.

A period of genuine constitutional government followed. A constitutional Assembly, partly appointed and partly elected, was convened in 1964, in which all the ethnic elements of the country were represented. Elections to the new bicameral parliament were held the following year, the first free Afghan elections ever. No political parties existed, however. A press law was promulgated in 1965 under which a number of journals began to appear. One of them was the leftist Khalk (The Masses of the People) published by Nur Muhammad Taraki. It appeared only six times before the government closed it down, allegedly for its anti-Islamic, anti-constitutionist sentiments.

On July 17, 1973, King Zahir's experiment with constitutional monarchy came to an abrupt end. While the king was in Europe, the former prime minister Muhammad Daoud, supported by the army, declared a republic and assumed the offices of president and prime minister. In his first period of power Daoud had been largely responsible for bringing in massive Soviet assistance, but now, in his second period, he seemed to lean more towards the West. In the end, the army which brought Daoud to power proved, after only five years, to be also the main instrument of his final and disastrous defeat; on April 27, 1978, a group of Moscow-trained army officers brought down Daoud's government in a bloody coup in which Daoud himself, his whole family and a part of his guard regiment were massacred.

Nur Muhammad Taraki, the former publisher of *Khalk*, emerged as the new strongman. Taraki himself revealed the programme of his government in an interview published on May 3: 'This Revolution took place on the instruction and under the leadership of the People's Democratic Party of Afghanistan . . . our government is devoted to the interest of the oppressed classes of Afghanistan . . .' (*The Kabul Times*).

The Taraki coup ended the Durrani supremacy in Afghanistan, which had lasted for over two hundred years. Taraki himself belonged to the Taraki Ghilzai tribe, and the coup may well have been basically an internal, tribal affair in which one party asked for, and obtained, the support of the USSR in return for an appropriate orientation of the country's policies. The Soviet Union was the first foreign country to recognize the new regime, and Taraki's first foreign visit was to Moscow. In December of the same year, Afghanistan signed a treaty of friendship and co-operation with the USSR, on the same pattern as Vietnam and Ethiopia shortly before.

On September 4, 1979, Taraki was killed in another coup, engineered by his right-hand man, Hafizullah Amin, who had been prime minister since March that year. The resistance against the harsh Amin régime began to take a rising toll in the provinces which the government seemed unable to control. After only three months, on December 27, 1979, the Russians invaded Afghanistan with massive forces. Hafizullah Amin and his henchmen were massacred in Kabul and a new president, Babrak Karmal, was installed by the Russians. This brought about a protracted guerrilla war fought by ill-organised and ill-equipped resistance groups, mainly Muslim traditionalists, against government troops and their Russian backers. In less than two years nearly two million refugees fled the country to Pakistan and to Iran.

Under the Russian occupation a puppet-government headed by President Najibullah ruled the country until the Russian withdrawal in 1989. Najibullah was killed in 1993 and various guerrilla forces began to fight each other. Their split was due partly to Islamic fundamentalism, partly to ethnic and tribal rivalries. In the civil war the Tajik and Uzbeks from the north and north-east fought the mainly Pushtun Islamists who call themselves 'taliban' (students). Heavily supported by Pakistan, the Taliban occupied most of the country with the exception of the mountain valleys in the north-east, where the guerillas, under Ahmad Shah Masud (killed in 2001), were getting some help from the Russians (or via Russia) and from some ex-Soviet

Central Asian Republics who were worried about the possible spread of militant Islamism into their own territories.

The National Museum of Kabul seems to have survived the Soviet occupation rather well, but had the misfortune to find itself in the firing line between the warring factions in the civil war. It was hit by an anti-tank rocket, caught fire and partially burned down. Some 80 per cent of its collections was either destroyed or subsequently looted. Disappeared, among others, were some 30,000 coins, the famous ivories of Begram and other priceless treasures, including the gold artefacts from Tilla Tepe.

The anarchy raging during the civil war, between 1992 and 1996, reached such proportions that the Taliban movement, which promised the introduction and strict observance of the *shari'a* (coranic law), was welcomed by the population as a guarantee of order and security. Their ideology was based on the Sunni philosophies of Saudi Arabia and the Indian sub-continent, the Wahhabism and the Deobandism. Wahhabism originated in the eighteenth century in the Arabian penisula with the teaching of Muhammad ibn Abd al-Wahhab, a puritan who criticised the religious rites as too lax. Deobandism, named after a village near Delhi, developed in the nineteenth century as a pan-Islamic orthodoxy and, after the creation of Pakistan in 1947, became stricter and more radical through the influence of a preacher, Abul Al'a Maududi, who insisted that the Qu'ran should be followed in every detail. According to Maududi, Islam is perfect and does not need any interpretation by the faithful. Qu'ranic law takes precedence over state law.

In Afghanistan however this teaching met with local traditions in many ways stricter still. For example the traditional code of conduct, the *pushtunwali*, required punishment for adultery based on simple rumour, while the Qu'ran needs the visual testimony of at least two witnesses. A radical strand of Islamic thinking thus came into being, the basic ideology of which originated outside Afghanistan.

A complicated game ensued in which Pakistan, anxious to have a safe backyard in case of a conflict with India, supplied the Taliban with arms and provisions and provided religious schooling – or indoctrination – for Pashtun youths in its *madrasas*. Saudi Arabia and the Gulf sheikdoms provided the money. Volunteer fighters from Libya, Algeria, Chechnya and other countries arrived in increasing numbers. On the other hand, more and more refugees were leaving the country, most of them for Pakistan, but also for Iran and Central Asia. It is estimated that because of the war and emigration, Afghanistan may have lost almost a third of its population.

International terrorist groups targeting Western and mainly American interests operated from bases in Afghanistan. In March 2001 the Taliban, as a gesture of defiance, blew up the Bamiyan Buddhas; on September ninth Ahmad Shah Masud was assassinated, and on September eleventh the World Trade Center and the Pentagon were blown up by Islamist suicide bombers, believed to be guided from Afghanistan. On October seventh, the bombing of Kabul, Kandahar and other Taliban targets by American and British forces began. In the words of *The Economist*:

Flooded with millions of weapons, infected with the worst sort of religious fundamentalism and plumbing the depths of human misery, Afghanistan has become the world's saddest and most dangerous example of a failed state.

Now, at the end of 2010 and after nine years of fighting, the bleak prophecy of Ahmed Rashid seems to be confirmed.[6] The central government is weak and its writ does not extend far beyond the Kabul area which may be the reason why most recent archaeological work has been done in this area. Although Kabul is slowly rising from 'the miles of rubble', it had been at the turn of the century, the infrastructure that can sustain society is still rather chaotic. The economy is still too dependent on poppy and drugs and tribal chiefs are still calling the shots in the provinces, preventing the realization of any large state-wide reconstruction project. The building of security forces, the army and the police, is proceeding at a snail's pace with many setbacks, and the Taliban, still finding refuge and supplies in Pakistan's Tribal territories, are in fact gaining ground, not only in the south, but also in the east and north-east. The main supply-line of the allied forces, the Peshawar-Jalalabad-Kabul road, is frequently disrupted or blocked, whereas the Taliban supplies can get into the country by the Quetta-Kandahar road mostly undisturbed. The interior situation in Pakistan and the Iran-Pakistan differences over the Sunni-Shia relations are beyond the scope of this book, but their repercussions contribute in no insignificant way to the rising sectarianism in Afghan society. Seen in this way, a fragmentation or even partition of the country remains a possibility. Its unification under Amir Abdurrahman thus looks like an exceptional event in its history.

January 2011

3 Notes on architecture

Early Iranian Architecture

The towns of the Achaemenian period provide the earliest models for the eastern Iranian provinces – Drangiana, Arachosia and others. Some elements from even earlier civilisations with developed urban centres (Egypt, Eastern Mediterranean, Mesopotamia or the Indus Valley) have also left their mark, in urban design as well as in some features of the monumental buildings, temples, palaces, gates or ramparts.

The earliest towns were most probably built according to three basic considerations: security, defence and the supply of water, to which trade may be added as the fourth. Fiscal aspects also played their part, so a town would be founded, or would grow more or less spontaneously, where an easily defensible spot with a good supply of water lay on or near a trade route, so that tolls and taxes could be levied. The town thus functioned as a garrison, as an administrative centre, as a refuge for the surrounding population in time of war and, also, as a market place – even if, in many cases, the actual markets were outside the walls.

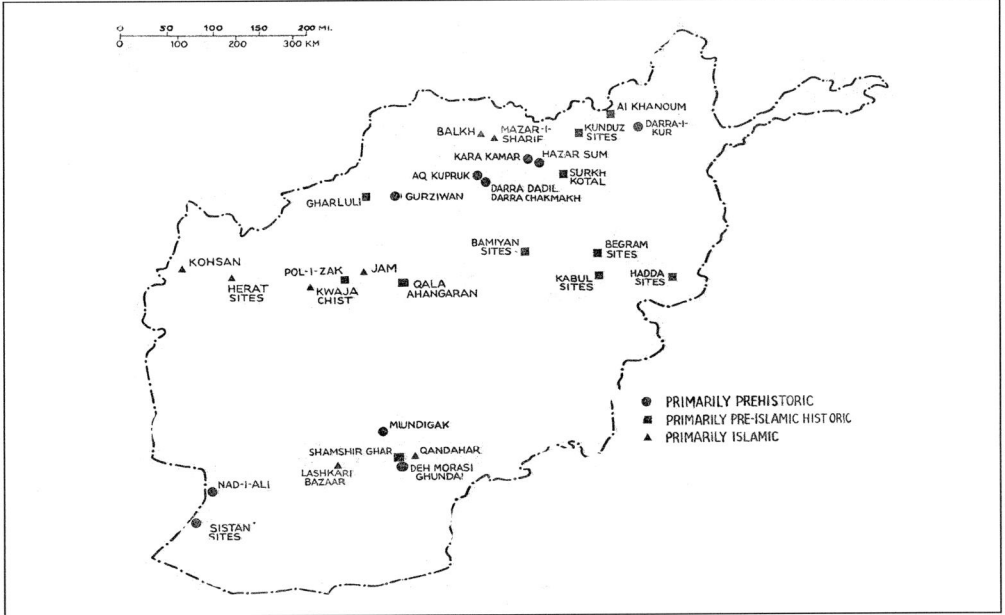

20 *Archaeological sites*

21   Ancient Balkh, the citadel

The supply of water often dictated the location of the town, within easy reach of a stream with permanent water; the layout of streets and squares was conditioned in most cases by the system of water conduits which had to follow the shape of the terrain. The main surface canals were usually aligned with streets and converged in, or led to, a water tank or pool around which a square formed. The *bridge*, another type of ancient building, was not necessarily part of the town,

The position of the *gates* (which may have been adorned with statues) and *walls* were likewise dictated by the terrain and by the contemporary fighting and defence techinque. The *citadel* (usually containing or linked to the *prison*) was always built on a strategically suitable place and, if no such place was available, the terrain was conveniently altered and an artificial mound was raised, a river arm diverted, etc. The architecture of the citadel, the gates and the ramparts had to correspond to both the requirements of defence and the contemporary technique of warfare and so be constantly updated, which led to frequent reconstructions, alterations, and even relocations.

Sometimes, a town may have developed from a military stronghold, or camp, surrounded by a wall and functioning also as an administrative centre. Within its precinct were palaces and temples. The central part of the palace was the audience chamber, or *apadana*; this was a *hypostyle* hall, usually square, the roof of which was supported by columns and pilasters with decorative capitals and bases. It was one of the main features of an Iranian city and, apparently, had its origins in Egypt. The temple consisted of a cube-shaped structure, the *cella*, raised on a terrace and accessible by a monumental staircase. Assyrian, Hittite, Babylonian and Egyptian elements can be discerned in its architecture.

The town's commercial activity centered on the *bazaar*, which combined crafts and trading and more often than not took place in one or more ordinary streets. In later periods bazaar buildings were constructed, such as the vaulted structures covering street crossings, which still can be seen in Bukhara and other Central Asian towns.

The *maydan* was originally not a market place but merely an open space located within or outside the walls where military parades and training could take place. It was also used for cattle, horse and camel markets, and as a place for caravans to discharge their goods, and so on. *Gardens* were another creation of urban design, though the earliest formal gardens that have come down to us date from the late Timurid period only.

The town of Susa, built by Darius, consisted of a citadel on the acropolis, a palace and an *apadana* on a neighbouring mound, as well as the city proper, which was separated by a broad avenue. The whole complex was surrounded by a strong wall of unbaked bricks, which had projecting towers and was protected by a moat.[1] The palace still showed a strong Babylonian influence.

> The plan consisted of interior courts which opened on to the rooms and living quarters; these again were surrounded by long corridors that permitted the guards to watch every movement. The walls of unbaked bricks were also decorated in Babylonian style.[2] The throne room itself, known as the *apadana*, was a hall, the roof of which was supported by six columns nearly twenty metres in height, surmounted by capitals with protomes of bulls; on the north, east and west the hall was surrounded by three peristyles of twelve columns . . . It was approached by three wide stairways . . . Some of the capitals were simple imposts . . . in others the *protomes* rested on *volutes*.[3]

The *apadana* of Darius at Persepolis was built on the same principles; his palace there was built of unbaked bricks, with door and window frames of stone, surmounted by Egyptian lintels.

It may be noted in this connection that the palace of Pasargadae was laid out like a tent camp of the nomads; it consisted, unlike the Babylonian and Assyrian palaces, of several structures grouped informally and serving different purposes – living quarter, audience hall and so on – to which was added an *apadana* and an entrance hall. In Persepolis the *apadanas* of Darius and Xerxes dominate the lay-out and screen off the private apartments. The tradition of a nomadic tent camp may still be discerned in the lay-out of the Moghul forts in Delhi, Lahore and Agra as well as the Top Kapi Saray in Istanbul.

After the invasion of Alexander, the Greek influence on the Iranian plateau became much stronger. The temple retained its classical Iranian shape, but in some structures Greek motifs can be found in the decoration of capitals and, to some extent, in the general plan of the building. Statues are the main manifestation of Hellenistic art (generally considered to be inferior to that of the classical period), although it is difficult to determine how much they were used as architectural decoration. The Greek contribution to the urban design was the *agora*, a city square designed as an integral part of the city centre.

There seems to be a difference of opinion among scholars about the origins of the *iwan*. This was a great vaulted space open to the court and wholly or partially enclosed on three sides, which supplanted the *apadana* as a dominant element in Iranian art. According to Ghirshman, a *triple iwan* can be found already on the terrace of Masjid-i Suleiman in southern Iran, dating from earlier than Persepolis.[4] On the other hand, Tadgell sees this as a Parthian contribution, which would date it some five centuries later.[5] It should be noted in this context that the earliest known vault found at Haft Tepe in southern Iran dates from the Elamite period, 1500 BC.

Early Buddhist architecture

Iranian influence made itself felt in India in some buildings of the Mauryan period. The palaces, gardens and *hypostyle* halls of Pataliputra, described by Megastehenes in the early third century BC, 'excelled the *apadanas* of Susa and Ecbatana.'[6] Some decorative motives also betray Iranian and West Asian influence, while the Ashoka columns, or pillars (referred to later in the text) were most probably also the work of Persian craftsmen.

The three main structures of the early Buddhist architecture were the *stupa*, the *temple* and the *monastery*. The *stupa* probably originated at the time of Ashoka (third century BC) and developed from a Vedic burial mound. Its function was commemorative at first, with holy relics contained in the mound, but later it became an object of worship in itself.

The mound was of earth and rubble with a brick surface, and was surrounded by a wooden fence. Although primarily a religious structure, the *stupa* was a monument for every purpose. There were funerary *stupas*, *stupas* as reliquaries or cenotaphs, memorial *stupas*, and so on. In the course of time the mound differentiated into a square base surmounted by a hemispheric cupola. On top of it was a square railing, or a box-like structure, called the *harmika*, from which rose a shaft of metal or wood supporting a number of umbrellas, usually seven, symbolising the stages of heaven. The building material was usually brick or stone – in Kushan times often the so-called *diaper masonry*, which consisted of thin layers of schist or slate interspersed with large blocks of different coloured stone.

Inside, the *stupa* was filled with earth or rubble except for a small chamber containing the relic. Brick-built *stupas* without decoration seem to have been the earliest; the later examples, built of schist or a mixture of schist and brick, often had pilasters with decorated capitals.

The whole structure stood either in a courtyard or on a terrace to permit ritual circumambulation. The terrace itself was sometimes raised, with one or more monumental staircases leading to it. The umbrellas were often painted gold and carried bells, so that the edifice could be seen and heard from afar. Franz[7] sees in the simple tumulus *stupa* a continuation of the Bactrian heritage going back to the nomad *kurgans*, or tumulus graves, whereas the combination of a square base and a round or cyclical superstructure contains both Hellenistic and Iranian elements. The earliest *stupas* with a square base, which were the Hellenistic transformation of the Indian *stupa*, were found in Taxila-Sirkap. They date from the end of the first century BC, when, with the end of the Mauryan empire, Greek influence increased considerably.

In later periods the structure became more sophisticated. The *stupas* were composed of square and cylindrical parts in various combinations; an octagonal part was exceptional. The base was often star- or cross-shaped, raised on several superimposed terraces. The cupola rested on a high and richly-decorated *drum*. The main *stupa* was surrounded by a number of small votive *stupas*.

The architectural decoration was fairly simple: false columns with capitals, cornices, false arches, etc. The main decorations, however, were *sculptures*. Traces of colossal statues, 5-8m high, have been found on several sites. Large statues stood in niches either at the base, or in the walls surrounding the courtyard, while smaller sculptures were ranged in several rows or tiers on all sides of the base. Paintings were sometimes used to decorate the niches or the flat surfaces between them.

Early in the fifth century, in the Gupta period, the *stupa* lost its importance and was overshadowed by the temple built to house the image of the Buddha. These images, replacing the empty throne of the earlier period, depicted him either freestanding, seated cross-legged or enthroned.

The earliest Buddhist *temples* may have been circular. To the round sanctum a rectangular assembly hall was added, and the two together formed what K. Fischer calls *Apsidenhalle* (Hall with apse).[8] The basic form of the temple became the *cella*, round or square, harbouring a statue, and the hall, along with a terrace, either open or covered. In later periods the terraces became more numerous, staircases were added and the roof was raised into a tower.

Towards the end of the Gupta period the temple acquired an ambulatory and a vestibule, and an open or closed hall for ritual dancing. The portico became more prominent and subsidiary porches and balconies were also added. Pillars were at first square, but later were divided into zones alternatively octagonal, sixteen-sided or circular.[9]

The general feature of the *vihara*, or monastery, was a fortress-like structure reminiscent of the Greek and Syrian fort (*hydreuma*). It was square for the most part, with or without towers and with a surrounding wall. The rooms or cells backed onto the wall on the inside, and there was one or more courtyards and a principal *stupa* with a number of smaller *stupas* either in front of it or surrounding it. The entrance was always opposite the main *stupa*. The whole complex did not always face the same way; it seems that the direction the main *stupa* was facing was set with regard to a certain position of the sun.[10]

Originally, the *vihara* was a secular building, but often a *stupa* was incorporated into it to give it a sacred character. Sometimes the *stupa* occupied a separate courtyard connected with the *vihara* by a corridor. Some *viharas* were hewn from the rock-side, making a fairly complex troglodyte dwelling like the famous rock monasteries of Aibak, Bamiyan and Foladi. The cave *viharas* often imitated in rock certain features of Indian wooden architecture – for example balconies, lattice-screen walls, dormer and bay-windows, and the so-called *lantern ceiling*, which consisted of wooden beams put across the angles of a square, stage by stage, until the square was filled.[11] The *vihara* cells could be isolated or grouped around either an assembly hall or a communal room with a portico, reminiscent of the Hindu *ashrama* surrounded by huts.[12]

Imitations of the Persian domical *cupola* and the *squinch* can be found in later caves. The open-air monastery of the later period used the Persian principles of the *four-iwan* court, domed ceilings, barrel-vaulted corridors, and so on.

The art of Gandhara

The Indian Buddhist influence radiated from the great Buddhist centres in the province of Gandhara – now eastern Afghanistan and the northern Punjab – and by mixing with the Greco-Bactrian and later Roman elements produced an art which became known as the *art of Gandhara*. This had both a religious and a secular, or dynastic, side; it reached its peak under the Kushan empire with its capital in Begram, or Kapisa, just north of Kabul, and dominated the area from the first century AD until the invasion of the Hephthalites in the fifth century.

The earlier non-theistic tradition had been gradually abandoned and a new development called *Mahayana* took place, probably in connection with the patronage of the rulers. Shrines were erected for the lay devotees and Buddha's images were adopted as objects of worship. The *stupa* as a symbolic representation of the Buddha became the principal object of veneration, and the *vihara* also ceased to be only residential and became a place of worship. The excavations at Begram and Hadda brought to light a great number of Gandharan statues, as well as other objects of that period. The Gandharan artists found their inspiration in the sculptures of the Hellenistic period, through the intermediary of Seleucid craftsmen and Bactrian Greeks.[13]

The art of Gandhara was characterised mainly by its sculpture, whether in schist, stucco or moulded clay. No buildings in the Gandhara style have surived, unless we include in its heritage some foundations and fragments of wall uncovered in archaeological sites. The frescoes that survived in the niches of the Bamiyan Buddhas and in the cave temples in Xinjiang may have Gandharan appearance but they are of later origin, and there is no agreement among specialists over whether they can be attributed to the period. The main feature of the Gandhara sculptures was the representation of the *Buddha* in human form. Previously, these representations had only been symbolic. The Gandharan sculptures mostly represented scenes and legends connected with the life of the Buddha. Their subjects were, apart from purely symbolic elements, the images of the Buddha, the *bodhisattvas*, donors, soldiers and demons. The Gandhara Buddha was sometimes seen as an orientalised version of Apollo, although the statues were mostly treated in the traditional way, with idealised faces, motionless expressions and perfectly balanced features. Greek influence was also present in the *bodhisattvas* which often imitated idealised features of Greek models, such as Aphrodite or Alexander. The *donors* and *soldiers* were evidently inspired by real people and reflect different ethnic types, dresses, hairstyles and weapons. The *demons*, on the contrary, were grotesque, anthropomorphic or zoomorphic creatures, not unlike their counterpart in European Romanesque art.

Gradually over the centuries the Greek influence weakened and with the increased influence of Sasanian Persia the Iranian element, never totally absent, became more pronounced. Created in this period, the frescoes of Bamiyan and Xinjiang show a mixture of Iranian and Indian elements. Buddhist figures are clad in Iranian costumes, have Persian facial features and wear Iranian adornments and weapons. The Indian components can be traced to the Gupta period.

Archaeological discoveries on both sides of the Oxus, as well as Italian excavations in the Swat Valley in north-west Pakistan, tend to accentuate the regional diversities of Greco-Bactrian art, and its relationship with the art of Gandhara, Mathura and also Parthia. This led D. Schlumberger to coin the term *Greco-Iranian* or *Kushan* art, of which the products of Bactria, Gandhara and Mathura would represent only regional variations.[14]

The later period of the art of Gandhara is sometimes called *Indo-Afghan*.[15] Politically, it coincided with the rule of the so-called Kidara-Kushans who came to the Punjab from Bactria at the end of the fourth century AD. Its main characteristic is the use of terracotta and stucco in sculpture, as opposed to the older school which used almost exclusively stone. The best examples are the sculptures of Mohra Moradu and Jaulian at Taxila, as well as Shotorak in Afghanistan.

The Parthian and Sasanian architecture

The Parthian empire was founded by the Parni, who included the Parthian tribes. Headed by the clan of the Arsacids, they arrived from Khorasan in the mid-thirteenth century BC, won Iran from the Seleucids and in the early centuries AD positioned themselves between the Kushans in the east and the Romans in the West. They succumbed in the early third century AD to the rising power of the Sasanians.

The artistic production of the Parthians was on the whole not outstanding. However, very little Parthian has been found in Iran, and most of that in the outlying provinces, both east and west. There is a mixture of Greek and Iranian elements in Parthian art – but not much original inspiration. On the whole, it may be said that the Parthian civilisation did suppress the Iranian tendencies for a time, but gradually these came back to life and created what is known as neo-Iranian art. According to some scholars, the Parthians thus provided a link between the Achaemenian and the Sasanian art, and therefore the latter cannot be properly understood without taking into account the Parthian contribution.

In relation to urban design, some Parthian towns were laid out in the circular form which, according to some authorities, went back to an old urban tradition in Western Asia, and perhaps to the form of Assyrian military camps.[16] The inner city of Balkh, the Erg-Kala in Merv (which dates from the Achaemenian period) and the site of Koy-Krylgan-Kala in Khorezm were all laid out to this system. In domestic architecture, some houses were no doubt built around a courtyard, which was a form derived from Mesopotamia, as found in Dura Europos and elsewhere.

In the Parthian capital Nisa (or Nysa), in what is now Turkmenistan, the palace consisted of a warren of walled chambers around several courtyards; one of them, which may have served as an audience-hall, was dominated by a raised iwan-like hall.[17] The Achaemenian *cella* still survived as a four-square domed chamber in Zoroastrian fire temples, but it was separated from the exterior by an ambulatory, while the external staircase was now built into the wall and led up to the roof, where the sacred fire burned.[18] The material was rubble and pebbles with mortar rather than stone, and the decoration consisted of stone sculpture, moulded stucco and frescoes. The motifs, apart from some geometrical ornaments showing Assyrian traditions, were acanthus leaves, musicians, divinities and royal personages.

The Sasanians revived the rectangular town shape based on Greek models, with two main streets bisecting the rectangle and meeting at right angles in the centre. The town of Bishapur is the best preserved example of this type. The invention of the *large arch*, which first appeared in the Parthian period, had a profound effect on the adaptations of earlier architectural forms. Thus the *iwan*, while still retaining its function as a reception hall, was transformed into a vaulted archway, with relief decoration executed mainly in stucco covering all the walls.

The introduction of the *cupola*, or *dome*, which was the logical consequence of the arch, entirely transformed the whole concept of roofing. The problem of how to put a circular dome on a square base led to the invention of the *squinch* which was to become one of the basic features of Iranian architecture. It was, in principle, an arch built across corners to enable the transition from a square base to a round dome. The earliest surviving *squinches* probably appeared in the early third century AD. One of the first may be seen in the palace of Firuzabad, while the palace of Shapur I at Bishapur shows, perhaps for the first time, the *four-iwan* courtyard on a cruciform plan, another basic feature of Iranian architecture. (It is sometimes argued that the great hall of the Bishapur palace was covered with a cupola, but this cannot be taken for certain).

The decoration of Sasanian palaces was in stucco, fresco painting and, later, stone. The subjects included hunting scenes, banquets and religious feasts. Mosaic pavements were found in Bishapur, showing Roman subjects and executed in Roman technique, with Iranian elements only discernible in details.

Round towers appear at Bishapur and Taxila[19] and found widespread use as minarets in the Islamic period. The Sasanian temple, as described by Ghirshman[20] consisted of the traditional *cella* enclosed by four corridors. In Firuzabad, a tower stood next to the temple, on top of which a fire was lit during the ceremonies. These ceremonies centered around pavilions open on all four sides, with four pillars supporting four arches surmounted by a cupola.

The Kushan and late Buddhist architecture

The influence of Buddhism was weakened but not eliminated by the Hephthalite conquest. The deterioration of Buddhist art, however, as manifested by sites ranging from Bamiyan to Tepe Sardar, is obvious. Colossal-sized statues replaced sophistication of forms and attention to details. Static postures, crude composition and cheap materials confirm the picture of general decline.

The Iranian influence became stronger again when the Hephthalite empire disintegrated and the Sasanians re-established their suzerainty over the local princelings, but it was stronger north of the Oxus than south of it, where the Buddhist tradition remained dominant. The rock paintings of Dokhtar-i Nushirwan are an isolated manifestation of the Iranian spirit in a country which knew no parallel to the secular works of art comparable to the frescoes of Pendzhikent, Varakhsha or Balalyk-Tepe, or secular buildings of the *kushk* type.

Examples of the composite character of the Kushan empire – which included Afghanistan as well as Soghd, Khorezm, Bactria and other provinces – are given by Frumkin:

> The Indian-style Kara-Tepe with Iranian sculptures and Hellenistic features was Buddhist; Khalchayan with its Hellenistic sculptures and wall-paintings was not. The Kushan Toprak-Kala was a huge Khorezmian castle, neither Buddhist nor apparently devoted to any of the major religions, but probably connected with dynastic worship. Liyavandak (Bukhara) showed Hellenistic features, but there is no reason to believe that it was Buddhist. The same applies to Afrasiab and Tali-Barzu. Whereas a small building of Surkh-Kotal was a Buddhist shrine, the main shrine was presumably devoted to dynastic worship.[21]

The evidence of Bamiyan, the greatest Buddhist centre, is inconclusive but it seems that it remained Buddhist until the ninth century, and perhaps even later.[22]

It may be concluded, therefore, that although weak and artistically decadent, Buddhism survived in the eastern parts of Afghanistan and Transoxania until the arrival of the Arabs. Considering the Hindu (Brahmin) presence in Eastern Afghanistan, as documented by the excavations at Khair Khane, eastern Afghanistan was not properly secured for Islam until the end of the ninth or, more probably, the tenth century.[23] The rest of the country, Khorasan and Sistan were already Islamised in the seventh century.

Early Islamic architecture

General terms

The Iranian architectural principles, such as the *apadana*, the *iwan*, the arch and the cupola, were all incorporated in some form into early Muslim architecture (although there is no agreement over the extent and the timing of these adaptations).

The first Arab *mosques*, perhaps simple imitations of the Prophet's house, were apparently rectilinear, forum-like enclosures with a flat roof supported by rows of columns or arches reminiscent of the Greek *stoa* or Achaemenian *apadana*. The *kibla* (qibla) wall, which was oriented towards Mecca, contained the mihrab or prayer-niche, usually framed with ornamental decoration. The service was conducted from a raised pulpit or *minbar*. This was the *hypostyle*, or congregational, mosque.[24]

However, large congregational mosques were not the only type of the building. Small sanctuaries destined for private devotion no doubt existed alongside them, and the fact that we know little about these may be due simply to the fact that they were built of lighter and cheaper material and did not survive. Some mosques of that kind, with wooden ceilings, columns and wooden arcades on the outside, still exist dating from the sixteenth century or later (for example, Masjid-i Baland in Bukhara), and there is nothing to suggest that this was a late Islamic innovation.

Another style originating in the west took the form of an open pavilion, square or rectangular, standing either alone or within the precinct of an Arab-type mosque. Local contributions brought about the adaptation of the Sasanian fire-temple, open on three sides, which resulted in two other types of mosque – one with a domed pavilion, and the other with an *iwan* opening into an enclosure.

The original position or function of the *iwan* is also not clear. Thus Vogt-Göknil[25] argues persuasively that in ancient Iran the *iwan* as an audience hall was oriented towards the outside (to the façade) and not into the courtyard. An analogy in Christian architecture would be the crossing of the transept, a sort of 'throne room' of Christ. Similarly, in the mosque the *iwan*'s function was that of a threshold, a *'lieu de passage'* analogous to the portal of a cathedral. In a *madrasa* it served as an auditorium, while in a *caravanserai* it was used as a common room by the travellers. Its function as an entrance, or entrance hall, came as late as the Safavid period (sixteenth century). Before this, the entrance was behind any one of the four *iwans* (although most frequently the northern one). Vogt-Göknil also maintains that the central concept which determined the design of the façades and the *iwans* was that of the courtyards, and not the interior arrangement of the mosque. The courtyard was more important than the *mihrab* room. In contrast to the sobriety and simplicity of the North African mosques (for example Ibn Tulun), the Persian mosque displayed an undeniable quest for beauty and grandeur.

Other religious buildings constructed on the same principles as the mosque were the *madrasa* and the *khaniga* (khangah). The former, a religious college, was usually an arcaded building constructed around a court and housing, on one or two storeys, lecture rooms and living quarters for teachers and students. A *khaniga* was originally a kind of Sufi monastery designed for meditation, which later developed into a complex of buildings comprising a mosque, a mausoleum, a hostel for pilgrims and students, a kitchen and so on. Buddhist monasteries with a courtyard lined with cells may have been a model for both types.

The *caravanserais*, particularly those built in open country, were often constructed like fortresses, with protective towers in the corners, bastions and so on. Their courtyard was much larger, in order to accommodate animals, and the domed chamber was often missing. The outer walls were usually bare and featureless, although there are some cases of architectural decoration (pilasters, blind arches) being used. These buildings were founded by the Seljuks and their predecessors in order to stimulate trade and to protect caravans; they also served as royal post-houses. There are similarities between their lay-out and that of some palaces; semi-cylindrical corner towers, monumental projecting entrances, and *four-iwan* courts were common to both, for example, as was the presence of a domed chamber behind the *iwan*, and two-storey buildings with apartments on the upper floor.[26]

The *mausoleum* was either a square domed chamber, or a tomb tower which could be round, square or polygonal and was topped by a round or conical cupola. Over the chamber was an inner dome and there was often a *mihrab* inside; the tomb was placed on the floor of the chamber or in a crypt below. At a later stage an ornamental portal or *iwan* was added to the original structure. According to Grabar[27] the *mausoleums* were among the first buildings to acquire monumental gates.

The *minaret* was a tower, whose purpose was to mark a religious building and make its presence visible from afar. Minarets were of various shapes and heights ranging from the circular and conical Transoxanian type to the star-shaped towers of Ghazni or the gigantic three-storey minaret of Jam. The earliest Persian minarets seem to have been square, at least at their lower levels. By the early eleventh century elaborately decorated brick shafts became the usual form. Spiral minarets in Cairo or in Kairouan were no doubt built on Sasanian models going back to the Babylonian *zigurrat*. Some minarets were free-standing, others were connected to the mosque. In Seljuk times and under the influence of Iran, two minarets were used to flank the entrance gate in order to enhance the monumental aspect of the building. By the same token, the number of minarets was sometimes increased to four, six or even more. In some places in Iran, Anatolia and Egypt, the function of the minaret was fulfilled by a small baldachined platform on the roof of the mosque.

The earliest Persian minarets seem to have been square, at least in their lower levels. By the early eleventh century elaborately decorated brick shafts became the usual form. Building in brick was an old tradition in the East whereas stone buildings belong rather to Anatolian, in particular, Armenian traditions. Stone-built Seljuk mosques may therefore have been built by Armenian master builders.[28]

Various types of *vaults* were used for roofing. *Iwans* had been roofed by barrel vaults since Parthian times; and in the early mosques the same system had been used to cover the bays behind the court arcades. Square or rectangular premises in the corners of the court posed certain problems which required new types of vaulting to be devised, most of them structural variations of the barrel-vault principle.

Another ancient type of roofing which passed into Islamic architecture was the *dome* or *cupola*. The single dome was a direct development of the Sasanian version. Some time in the twelfth century the double dome appeared, but it did not become widely used until the Timurid period.

Other changes saw the *iwan* eventually become a more or less shallow recess set in a tall *pishtak* (pishtaq) portal screen; while the *squinch*, already known from Parthian and Sasanian times, now became used in an astonishing variety of shapes and forms. If necessary, small arches could be built higher up to bridge the corners of the octagon, thus producing a 16-sided figure which nearly approximated the ring of the dome. In the earliest examples of this type of construction, the *squinch* was rather crude and compressed, and the arch created a small trumpet-shaped hollow in each corner of the angle which had to be filled or masked. Various ingenious ways to do this were devised.

The *mukarnas* or stalactite vault has probably developed from a tripartite *squinch*, and may have had a structural function in the early period, although later it became a purely decorative device. It consisted of clusters and tiers of cells that softened and enriched the broad expanses and simple contours of buildings. This feature became used almost universally although, in Pope's words, it was difficult to describe or record, and its planning was a baffling task. Briefly, it was formed by 'rows of superimposed out-curving panels, generally miniature quarter-domes, the apices apparently leaning on empty space, the point of each support being the dividing line of the row above'.[29]

Architectural decoration

Architectural decoration in carved stone goes back to Achaemenian times, but it was more often designed to fill the surface of the wall than to become part of its fabric. Brick decoration, on the other hand, was more likely to ensure that the decorated surfaces became parts of architectural volumes (walls, towers, arches) of brick constructions. Variations in brickwork could emphasise architectural lines and distinguish surfaces which were to be decorated, just as visual designs could be obtained by the very way in which the bricks were laid. According to Grabar[30] brick decoration spread from Central Asia to Iran and Anatolia.

Stucco (plaster) was used to fill gaps between bricks, and stucco panels were eventually used as part of brick ornaments. The material was known in pre-Islamic times (and was found for example in the palaces of Ctesiphon and Varakhsha); and early Iranian motifs can be found depicted in stucco on Umayyad palaces,[31] while pre-Islamic motifs can be discerned on the decorative slabs from the early eleventh-century palace of Termez, on some of the ninth- to tenth-century panels from Afrasiab (Samarkand) and in the eleventh-century mausoleum Nasr ben Ali in Uzkend, as well as on the mosques of Samarra, Nayin and Noh Gumbad.

22　*The tower of Masud III, Ghazni. Detail*

23   The tower of Bahramshah, Ghazni. Detail

The use of *terracotta* – ceramic fragments formed to fit certain areas or to create patterns – was also known in Central Asia in Parthian times, its motifs no doubt inspired by stucco patterns. According to Grabar, the technique 'reappeared in Uzkend and Bost'.[32] It further developed into '*mosaic faience*', which became widely used from the fourteenth century onwards, when 'stucco and brick began to lose their effectiveness'.[33]

Small glazed bricks were manufactured mainly in the town of Kashan in Iran, using mixtures of metallic oxides with cobalt, sulphur and arsenic. They were best suited to inscriptions or epigraphic friezes. One of the earliest is believed to be in the town of Damghan, dating from the eleventh century. Small ornamental bands can also be seen on the Central Asian minarets in Bukhara and Vabkent, dating from the twelfth century. *Kufic* inscriptions and geometrical ornaments could easily be executed in this technique. A different mode was required for vegetal and floral patterns and for the more flexible scripts, like *naskhi* and *thuluth*. Larger ceramic tiles, or panels, were therefore made with the decoration either painted or carved under glaze. Such panels were suitable for filling large surfaces with ornamental designs. The first area decorated in mosaic faience is believed to be on the Sircali Madrasa in Konya, and dates from the early thirteenth century.

In Central Asia architectural decoration was, with a few exceptions, unglazed and monochrome until after the Mongol occupation. The use of glazed tiles became

24 The mosque Noh Gumbad. Detail of ornament

virtually universal in the fourteenth and fifteenth centuries, with an ever-increasing range of colours (the first shades were turquoise, royal blue and white). The peak of mosaic faience technique came in the late fourteenth century in Samarkand, a little later in Herat and Balkh; after which a decline set in, the quality deteriorated and the range of colours shrank again.

Glazed tiles were first used to decorate the *mihrab* and the entrance gate. Bands of decoration, ornamental or epigraphic, were used on minarets from earlier times (at Jam, Kalan-Bukhara, Vabkent, Dawlatabad and Ghazni amongst others). Large surfaces, domes, drums and *pishtak* walls followed when appropriate techniques were developed.

The ornamental motifs were classified by Grabar[34] into five categories. Human and animal features were rare, with stucco figures now existing only in museums; there seemed to be a limited range of figural wall paintings although many more appeared in manuscripts, thus responding both to the Iranian and Indian traditions. At a later stage some highly stylised bird and animal shapes appeared, probably under Chinese influence, on some buildings in Samarkand and elsewhere. Architectural elements – columns, pilasters, blind arches, cornices, capitals and bases – were more frequent. The *muqarnas* (mentioned above) would fall into this category. Geometrical ornaments originally consisted of simple forms and patterns, usually combinations of squares, triangles and circles, with more sophisticated examples in the form of knots (*girikh*) appearing later. Floral and vegetal ornament on its own

25 Alabaster carved panel from the palace of Afrasiab, Samarkand. Tenth to eleventh century. Rempel (1961)

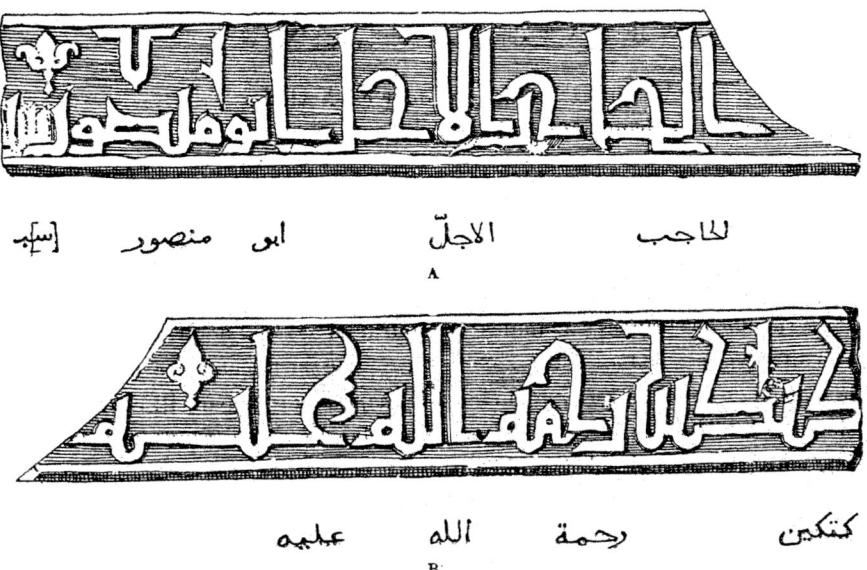

26 Ghaznavid calligraphy. Flury (1925)

was rare before the Mongol period; vegetal motifs were mainly used as a background to inscriptions, and only at a later stage did they form independent panels and patterns. Finally, some abstract designs may be discerned, especially in the form of *medallions*, and sometimes incorporating pre-Islamic symbols and signs. Three-dimensional abstract designs composed of bevelled curved lines were used in Iraq in the ninth century, carved into stones, stucco and wood. Later they were also used in Iran and Central Asia.[35] There was, no doubt, a close connection between ornamental motifs used in architecture, in carpets, in book illumination and in various other crafts, such as pottery, metalware etc., although it is not easy to determine their mutual influence. It seems that in certain periods architectural decoration was inspired by motifs used in carpets or pottery, whereas at other times the inspiration flowed in the opposite direction.

As for other mediums of decoration, very few wall-paintings have survived (although in those from Lashkar-i Bazar Schlumberger finds a strong influence of Buddhist art)[36]; wood carving was, no doubt, extensively used, but only a few specimens have survived, among them the well known 'Somnath door' at Agra. In the early mosaics, Greek and Roman inspiration predominates; Sasanian motifs do occur, but the geometrical forms and interlace which later became the main feature of Islamic decoration do not yet appear.[37]

Islamic calligraphy
The need to record the Qur'an precisely compelled the Arabs to reform and beautify their earlier script. Several calligraphic variants were developed from this

27 The façade at Hadda. Barthoux (1930)

script (called *Jazm*); in the course of time, the two main forms became the angular, monumental and hieratic *Kufic* (developed in Kufa in Irak), and the cursive, inscriptional *naskhi*.

The *Kufic* script, which has a relatively low vertical profile with extended horizontal strokes, came to be used mainly on surfaces where the height was less than the width. The early, austere *Kufic* developed into more decorative styles; ornamental *Kufic* (the best examples of which can be seen in Ghazni), floral *Kufic*, foliated and plaited *Kufic* and so on. An angular version developed in Herat in the fourteenth century is sometimes called *Herati Kufic*.

The cursive scripts, which appear in several ornamental forms (but mainly *naskhi* and *thuluth*), began to be used in manuscripts, religious as well as secular; and in the field of epigraphy competed successfully with *Kufic*. The extensive use of calligraphy gave rise to special styles of *naskhi* and *thuluth*, and both also developed their Indian varieties; Indian influences can be found in some decorative elements in inscriptions, such as those on the tombs of Mahmud of Ghazna and, later, of the sultans Masud and Ibrahim. An elegant and lighter variety of script, called *nastalik* (*nastaliq*), was later developed in Persia.

The Samanid, Ghaznavid and Ghorid architecture

Although there are few monuments surviving from this period, mention must be made of the mausoleums of Ismail Samanid in Bukhara and Arab Ata at Tim, both in Uzbekistan (cf Central Asia, p.117), and, in Afghanistan, the palace of Lashkar-i Bazar and the towers of Ghazni.

28 Ornament at Balkh, Noh Gumbad. Pugachenkova (1970)

New architectural elements appeared, some ingredients of the later classical Persian mosque were utilised and altered, and different types of tombs emerged (such as those in the form of a centrally planned polygon with a conical roof). A minaret which used to be a simple cylinder now acquired a star form, while the earlier type of palace has been given a crucifrom shape; but the most important innovation was the emphasis on monochrome brick decoration, which was to become the hallmark of Seljuk architecture in the centuries that followed.[38]

From the Ghorid period several important monuments survived in India, but only one in Afghanistan: the minaret of Jam (see below, p.127). Otherwise, there is only the so-called Ghorid portal, inside the Friday mosque in Herat.

The Seljuk architecture

From the Seljuk period, again, not many monuments survived the impact either of the Mongols, or of Timur one-and-a-half centuries later.

The *four-iwan* mosque now became a square building with four wide arches covered by a dome, to which sometimes *hypostyle* halls or colonades were added. This structure was combined with the *four-iwan* courtyard already known from Iranian palaces since Bishapur, with one *iwan* in the middle of each side of the rectangular courtyard. The *iwan* opposite the entrance, which was usually rather shallow, opened into the domed chamber in front of the *mihrab*. Another type of Seljuk mosque was the so-called mosquée-kiosque, a cube-shaped structure again inspired by the fire-temple, being open on three sides, usually through triple portals.

The *madrasa* became an important instrument of state policy: an institution for the training of state officials, for spreading the Sunni orthodoxy and for combating heresy. The Seljuk *madrasa* also had a similar lay-out to the palaces and *caravanserais*; a square or rectangular plan with four iwans and a domed chamber.[39]

Tombs were usually brick-built octagonal towers. The brickwork was rich and varied, though still largely monochrome. The roof was – or may have been – a double dome, a feature already in use for some time. *Mukarnas squinches* and *stucco* carvings were used for interior decoration.

It was in this period that glazed tiles appear, the first of these probably being used in the early twelfth century. Inscriptions in turquoise and white glazed bricks can still be seen on the minarets of Vabkent and Bukhara in Uzbekistan, both structures dating to this era.

Although all artistic activity in the territory of Afghanistan was interrupted by the Mongol invasion, the *Ghaznavid*, *Ghorid* and *Seljuk* architectural tradition lived on in India under the rule of the Sultans of Ghor. A series of remarkable buildings were erected in Delhi in particular, and these provide an interesting blend of Iranian Muslim and local Hindu features.

Timurid and late Islamic architecture

General

In the words of J.D. Hoag 'there has probably never been a period in the history of world architecture when color and form achieve such a perfect balance of design and meaning as they did under the Timurids during the reign of Shah Rukh'.[40] It can be argued, of course, that a generation earlier the architecture and decoration of Samarkand, Shahrisabz and elsewhere drew from the same inspiration and can equal, if not occasionally surpass, that of Shahrukh and Husayin Baykara in both design and form, if not always in materials and techniques. Unfortunately, most monuments reach us in a state of advanced dilapidation, and the current war and bombardment, together with the absence of maintenance, could only have added to the sad state of one of the most glorious chapters of Afghanistan's cultural heritage.

The Mongol invasion and the half-century or so that followed marked a profound interruption in the country's cultural continuity. Hardly any new buildings were constructed throughout the enormous area between western Iran, India and the border of China. A long period of inactivity resulted in the disappearance, or at least deterioration, of specialised crafts and skills. When some building activity was at last resumed towards the end of the thirteenth century, skilled craftsmen had to be sought in the only area unaffected by Mongol destruction: southern Iran, where builders, masons, ceramists, ornamentalists and other craftsmen contributed to the resurgence of Iranian influence in the whole of Central Asia. However, the pace of recovery was uneven. In Transoxania there were a few buildings constructed in the middle of the fourteenth century, but in the last quarter building activity was already in full swing under Timur's personal patronage.

In Afghanistan, with the exception of the reconstruction in the early fourteenth century of the Great Mosque in Herat, virtually no monumental building was carried out until the reign of Shahrukh at the beginning of the fifteenth century. It seems that the eastern Islamic outpost in the Sultanate of Delhi, where some remarkable buildings were constructed in the fourteenth and fifteenth centuries, had little to contribute to the artistic revival of Afghanistan. The gap here was almost two centuries and it may be assumed that, with the revival of craftsmanship in Transoxania, some of Shahrukh's architects and craftsmen were also recruited in Samarkand. Nevertheless, the contribution of Shiraz could still be significant because the city had been occupied by Timur in 1393 and all its artists and craftsmen were deported to Samarkand.

The ideas and models of pre-Mongol Seljuk architecture that were still used in fourteenth-century Iran thus became an inspiration for the construction of Timur's Samarkand which, in turn, served as a model for Shahrukh's Herat.

Architectural forms

There was not much change in architectural forms since before the Mongols. The two basic elements, the *dome* and the *iwan*, continued to be used, although their appearance and function changed considerably. The *double dome* now became frequently used, with the two domes usually displaying quite different profiles. As a rule the outer one was raised much higher than the inner, in order to enhance the exterior effect of the building; and to increase this effect still further, the outer dome was given a bulbous shape and raised on a high drum. The drum, which in earlier times was hardly more than a zone of transition between the base and the dome, now helped to enlarge the interior covered by the dome. The drum as such was well known in Buddhist architecture, where it was used to raise the cupola of the stupa; but in Islamic usage it acquired real significance only in the Timurid period. An isolated innovation was the *triple dome* used in the mausoleum of Gawhar Shad in Herat; but the added inner dome was purely decorative, with no structural purpose.

The *iwan* developed into a monumental entrance hall. Two *iwans* were usually erected back to back, one facing into the courtyard, the other turned outwards. An *iwan* standing in the middle of a long, beautifully decorated façade enhanced the outer appearance of the building. In addition, some constructions were made even more impressive by their colossal dimensions. Indeed, this emphasis on the colossal and the conspicuous became the charateristic feature of the Timurid period, often to the detriment of the quality of construction or the attention to detail – although some scholars find this combination of architectural massiveness, decorative designs and colour combinations to be in perfect balance.⁴¹ While this may be true of some of the smaller and more intimate buildings in Samarkand (Ishrat Khana or Shah-i Zinda), it can hardly apply to such rambling structures as the Bibi Khanum Mosque, and even less to the much cruder buildings and their decoration in Herat or in Balkh.

The tendency towards the colossal continued for some time under the Uzbek khans in Transoxania, where a notable addition to the previous style was the presence of an exceedingly high *pishtak* wall (the front wall of the *iwan*). However, these buildings were on the whole of inferior quality, both in design and decoration, to the contemporary Safavid monuments in Iran.

In *urban design* the Timurid and post-Timurid era contributed the notion of the monumental square; an open space surrounded by large, impressive buildings and conveying a sense of proportion and harmony, as well as greatness. The Registan in Samarkand, the somewhat later Labi-Hauz complex in Bukhara and the Maydan-i Shah in Isfahan (laid out in 1598) were expressions of the same idea. Meanwhile, the Persian tradition of enclosed *gardens* and garden pavilions seems to have been revitalised by a new influx of nomads in Timur's time, as is attested both by Clavijo and Babur.⁴² The Timurid gardens were based on the Iranian principle of the *Chahar Bagh* (Four Gardens): symmetrically laid out squares divided by water channels, with straight rows of trees and shrubs lined with flower beds. They can still be seen in the Babur Gardens in Kabul and in their later imitations in Srinagar, Lahore, and elsewhere in India.

Finally, a special *bazaar* building made its appearance in this period. Its standard plan was the so-called *Chahar-Su* (Four rivers); two passageways intersecting each other at right angles, covered by a dome at the crossing. Small apertures in the vaulted roof let in sufficient light, yet kept out the intense heat in summer and retained warmth in winter. Buildings of this kind seemed to have a long tradition in the area.

Apart from this, not much new architecture appeared in this period: after *mosquée-kiosque* and the *four-iwan* mosque achieved their final refinement, no new ideas appeared, and decline in the execution of the old soon became apparent. Only pavilions, like the Chehel Sotun in Isfahan, survived in a fair condition and allow a valuable insight into the splendour of earlier palaces and gardens.

In the Indian architecture, Central Asian ideas rather than Persian ones seem to predominate in the Moghul period; under Akbar, an increased Hindu influence made itself felt and where Islamic motifs appear they signal a return to the Timurid period rather than to the Safavid.⁴³

Architectural decoration

In contrast to architecture, the *decoration* and in particular the *ornament* changed considerably. The main innovation was the introduction of glazed tiles. The small bricks used for the composition of large ornaments (*banai technique*) were now glazed and polychrome. More sophisticated ornaments were composed of mosaic panels made of a number of small particles of various shapes and sizes. The terracotta, incised or carved, which was monochrome in the Seljuk period, was also glazed and polychrome. Large epigraphic bands in *Kufic* and geometrical ornaments were made in the *banai technique* while, on spherical surfaces, complicated *girikhs* (knots) appeared based on intertwined geometrical patterns, pentagons, hexagons and octagons. Floral motifs were widely used on arches, vaults and spandrels. Chinese motifs, stylised dragons, clouds and mountains sometimes appeared among purely vegetal ornaments. Another important innovation was the ever increasing range of colours; turquoise, royal blue, and white, the three basics, were followed by black, red and yellow, as well as other shades of green and blue: 'In the orchestration of colour . . . nothing has been built in the West so dependent upon nor so adroit in the application of colour . . . '[44]

Nevertheless, although the range of colours and the variety of techniques used in making glazed tiles reached an unprecedented level of perfection, it has to be admitted that the architectural form and the geometrical design which covered these tiles were sometimes not in perfect harmony. Painted decoration was fairly rare, and few specimens have been preserved; there are some in Samarkand, in the Masjid-i Shah in Mashhad and in the Zarnigar Khana of Gazurgah (Herat), all dating from the second half of the fifteenth and the first half of the sixteenth century. The motifs were mainly floral, in medallion and band form, with some affinity to carpet design and miniature painting.

Important inspiration was sometimes derived from Chinese art. Trade relations with Ming China were lively in Shahrukh's time, and Timurid artists frequently adapted motifs from Chinese textiles and ceramics for their ornament and design.

The trend seems to have been reversed in the origin of the motifs. Whereas in the previous period architectural ornaments were often imitated in other crafts (pottery, textiles and so on), it now seems as though architecture preferred to use motifs already developed elsewhere, especially in carpet-knotting and book decoration. Totally flat decoration inspired by book illustration dominated the field. To quote Melikian-Chirvani[45] the decoration became 'totally independent from architecture itself . . . in accordance with the general tendency of the Timurid century where art of the book prevailed over all other arts'. It was the surface alone that mattered, and this had to be flat. Consequently, purely architectural decoration almost disappeared, apart from some examples of corner colonettes with capitals, blank arches and panels which can be seen on the Timurid mausoleums in Samarkand and, in a much cruder form, on the Green Mosque in Balkh.

Calligraphy and carpets

In *calligraphy* the highly decorative *thuluth* style was added to the *Kufic* and *naskhi*; but in general the inscriptions of this period are inferior to the elegance and variety of the monochrome bands of the previous age.

Timur paid special interest to the art of calligraphy, and was directly responsible for the creation of a new style of illumination which was named after him. In contrast to the earlier style, which aimed to achieve grandeur by means of monumental script with bold and geometrically structured illumination of the text, the Timurid style aimed to create a balance between beauty and grandeur by combining a clearly written script with extremely delicate, intricate and softly coloured illumination of floral patterns integrated with ornamental *Kufic* so fine as to be almost invisible.

Naskhi was used to a lesser extent, but given a greater clarity and purity of line. Although the practice of using various styles and different sizes of script on the same page dates back perhaps to the tenth century, the Timurids were probably the first to extend it to the Qur'an. The Qur'ans of the Timurid period are probably the largest ever produced.

Timur's successors continued in this tradition. Shahrukh held calligraphy in very high esteem, and one of his sons even became an outstanding calligrapher, while another ranks among the world's greatest bibliophiles. The Timurid school of book production, which developed mainly in Herat, was marked by its elegant style, superb illuminated Qur'ans and splendid volumes of Persian epics with exquisite miniature paintings and other illuminations.[46]

Under Shahrukh and Husayin Baykara, the art of *miniature* and book illumination reached its peak, with the famous Bihzad as its supreme master. After Herat fell to the Uzbeks in 1507, Bihzad moved to Tabriz and the court of Shah Tahmasp who, as a boy, had spent several years in Herat. Tabriz had for some time been the home of a rival miniaturist school, that of the Turkomans, which was considerably influenced by Chinese art. Under the shah, who became acquainted with its artists and himself became a keen painter during his stay in Herat, the refined classical Timurid style coexisted in Tabriz with the much wilder and rougher Turkoman idiom. Eventually, a synthesis of the two styles emerged in the work of Sultan Muhammad, a Tabriz painter whose pictures might even surpass Bihzad's in their refinement as psychological characterisation.[47]

Muslim calligraphers in India were directly influenced by their Persian counterparts. In Afghanistan and some parts of India a slightly different *naskhi* was used, characterised by heavier, bolder and more widely spaced letters, more perfectly rounded curves and a resulting higher solidity than in ordinary *naskhi*. The *thuluth* developed along similar lines.[48]

Little is known about *carpet-knotting* and design in the Herat period. However, the arrival of Shah Tahmasp in Tabriz brought about changes in traditional carpet patterns which were in many ways similar to those in the art of the miniature. It seems that all carpets woven before the end of the fifteenth century have vanished and all our knowledge of them is derived from their representations in miniature paintings, where rugs are portrayed as supports and canopies of thrones or provide decorative settings in gardens, at hunts or on country outings. The geometrical, primitively abstract ornament of early carpets tried to break out of the limited space available by a repetition of the same motif. Abstract patterns which dominated all rug design up to the end of the fifteenth century were, in Turkish carpets, enlivened by floral ornaments, while in Iran they were replaced by figurative and floral motifs forming an arabesque around a central medallion. The style was created not by the weavers but rather by the paintings and illuminations of the court school. The large characteristic central medallions served to give the rugs a monumental character. Some of them were of supreme simplicity and austerity, while others were more elaborate, with a great variety of decorative motifs. The carpet design was often taken from drawings by well-known painters; it may be assumed that with high-quality carpets the designs must have been drawn in the fashionable style of the period by expert artists, and transferred to worksheets by copyists. Persian workshops were producing carpets with magnificent compositions, sumptuous decor and dazzling colours in which the subject became more and more important. Hunting carpets and animal carpets developed at that time, showing scenes of animals fighting among trees and plants or chased by hunters.

The sumptuous illuminations of manuscripts produced in Herat in the fifteenth century depict lotus blossoms and leaves, pomegranates, scrolls and palmettes combined with geometrical arabesques and cloud bands. Animal and human figures are portrayed in some, while others are entirely floral. The miniature paintings indicate that the craft of *carpet making* reached a high level of development in Herat; there was a great variety of geometrical patterns, interlaced ornaments and floral motifs. The distinctive style of Herat was introduced at the Safavid court in Tabriz by Bihzad and his disciples, and the sixteenth-century carpets recall both the patterns of spiralling floral stems of the Timurid period, and their characteristic brilliant colours. They are generally assigned to Herat not necessarily because they originated there but rather to indicate that they were made in the grand manner of the Herat school. Technically, the warps were usually in silk, and the wefts in cotton, a combination of cotton and silk or pure silk, with three shoots per row of knots. The pile was wool and knotted in the Persian knot, open to the left with a count of approximately 290 per square inch.[49]

Late Islamic period

When Babur became the first Moghul emperor of India, Kabul and eastern Afghanistan were open to an ever increasing Indian influence. This lasted until the invasion of the Persian Nadir Shah in the eighteenth century, after which the local Turco-Iranian traditions again prevailed. The Moghuls were obsessed by flowers and water, and Babur himself was a man of acute aesthetic feeling, and an admirer of Timurid and Safavid architecture. Consequently, in the garden he laid out in Kabul – the first of the great Moghul gardens which later adorned Agra, Lahore, Srinagar and other cities – water was the most important element. His successors, too, emulated the works of their Timurid ancestors in combining native and imported architectural and decorative features.

Apart from the Babur Gardens in Kabul, little of historical interest remains. In architecture the most remarkable building showing strong Indian influence is the mausoleum of Hazret Ali in Mazar-i Sharif. It was originally built in the Timurid style, but acquired an increasingly Indian appearance as a result of the subsequent additions, restorations and rebuilding which have continued until recently.

In the seventeenth century, *wall paintings* with subjects such as landscapes and buildings appeared alongside purely ornamental motifs, with the holy places of Islam apparently the favourite subject. Golombek[50] distinguished between two different styles, one from the mid-seventeenth, the other from the eighteenth or even early nineteenth century, the main difference being the emphasis on line in the first, and on area colour in the second. Paintings of both styles have been preserved in the shrine of Gazurgah in Herat; but although in the nineteenth century Khiva *wood carving* on doors and wooden support columns of the traditional *ayvan* (*iwan*) was of very high quality, few comparable specimens can be found in contemporary Afghanistan.

Although the Afghan period, from the middle of the eighteenth century onwards, may be regarded as a period of national independence, culturally it was an era of decadence. The tribal oligarchy which ruled the country had neither the financial means nor the cultural background to foster artistic activity of any significance. The mosques of Kabul and the palaces of Amir Abdurrahman, all built in the nineteenth century, partly abandoned the traditional idiom but failed to introduce any innovation of substance except for the orientation of the palace towards the exterior, showing a Western influence in contrast to the traditional way of opening into either the courtyard or the garden. In general, they lag behind the older buildings in technique, in style of decoration and in overall taste and harmony. Although not in any way outstanding, the mosque of Takht-i Pol with its Indianised architecture and interior decoration is the most interesting building from that period.

The origins of Gandharan art

The interesting mixture of Indian and steppe elements, which can be discerned mainly in the head-gear of personalities portrayed on the late Kushan coins, led to different appreciation by different schools of archaeology. The British prefer to identify it with Buddhism and Greek Bactria, using terms like 'Graeco-Bactrian', 'Graeco-Indian' or 'Indo-Afghan', while some French scholars coined the term 'Hephthalo-Buddhist', accentuating the contribution of the steppe.

The reconstruction of Ay-Khanum

The site of Ay-Khanum at the banks of the Oxus (see below), has been systematically looted and pillaged for years. Even heavy earth-moving equipment has been brought in by looters. The destruction of the city thus being nearly complete, a reconstruction in 3D has been attempted by a franco-japanese team inspired by the Japanese film *The Illusive Alexandrias,* shown in 2003.[51]

The fate of the Kabul Museum artefacts

Although the museum itself was bombed, destroyed and looted, the gold treasure of Tilla Tepe, some of the gold objects and ivories and coins, were found in 2003 in the underground vault of the National Bank. The key to the vault was lost and some sealed tin containers found there could only be opened later. Nevertheless, some stolen objects from the museum still appear on the world art markets and auctions. Despite this some renowned museums in Europe and North America and now the British Museum were able to mount an impressive exhibition of artefacts that remained or were recovered.[52]

SITES AND MONUMENTS
4 Pre-Islamic

Mundigak and Deh Morasi Ghundai

In their earliest period, some 4000-5000 years ago, both sites were probably peasant settlements based on an economy that was a mixture of farming and animal husbandry. Deh Morasi Ghundai seems to have remained until the end of its existence a small semi-sedentary village growing wheat and barley and breeding sheep, goats and cattle. Mundigak developed into an urban centre comparable to those of the Indus valley civilisation, and it is highly probable that both sites had connections with that civilisation. Mundigak's position as the urban centre in south-east Afghanistan ended when Kandahar took over in pre-Achaemenian times, while Deh Morasi Ghundai ceased to exist some time after 1500 BC.

The site of Deh Morasi Ghundai is some 6.5m high and 50m long, while Mundigak is 20m high and 170m long. Seven successive layers of habitation were uncovered at **Mundigak**.[1] The first two periods seem to belong to a village-type settlement, whereas Period III (approximately 3000-2750 BC) has a much higher density of habitation and Period IV already shows a fully-fledged town, with ramparts consisting of two parallel walls of sun-baked bricks, a large palace with a number of courtyards and premises, and a substantial structure consisting of several rooms grouped around an inner courtyard which is believed to have been a temple. One small, low-lying room seems to have been the sanctum with tables for offerings and sacrifices; a raised fireplace nearby could have been an altar. The town seems to have been destroyed at this point, but three more layers within the same period are again urban (IV 2, 3 and 4). The fifth period, probably with a different population, shows a mysterious truncated pyramid with several terraces, of unknown purpose. In Periods VI and VII the site appears to have been occupied only sporadically. The Bronze Age objects from Mundigak could be seen in the Museum of Kabul.

Ay Khanum

Ay Khanum, or the Moon Lady, is the site of a Greek town in the region of Kunduz, discovered in 1963 by French archaeologists at the confluence of the Amu Darya and the Kokcha. The site, which can be dated to between the fourth and second centuries BC, is situated on the left bank of the Amu Darya and comprises an upper town with a huge citadel in its northern part, and a lower town based on a regular grid of broad, straight streets with residential and administrative areas, including a palace with a peristylar courtyard, a Greek-style gymnasium, a large private house, an oriental temple and other buildings.[2] It also had gates and ramparts with rectangular towers more than 20m wide, and water was brought from the river by canals.

The site can be compared to Dura Europos, the Greek city in Syria described by Rostovtzeff in 1943.³ The ceramics and terracotta roof tiles resemble those found in other Hellenistic cities from the same period in Western Asia and on the Greek mainland, with Persian-style column bases and Corinthian capitals providing evidence of the coexistence of the two civilisations. Two important Greek inscriptions in stone have been found, which confirm the overall 'Greekness' of the site, as does the discovery of a sculpture of a Greek deity, which was displayed in the Museum in Kabul. The city was destroyed by fire, most probably when the area was invaded by nomads some time at the end of the second century BC, and has never been reoccupied, the most likely explanation for this being that the destruction of the irrigation system rendered the region uninhabitable. In recent years the site has undergone extensive pillage.

In **Shortugai**, 25km east of Ay Khanum, a Harappan trades seal was found which confirms that the Indus valley cities traded this far north. Trade objects were manufactured in Shortugai.

Surkh Kotal

Surkh Kotal, some 15km north of Pul-i Khumri and within sight of the main road to Mazar-i Sharif, is the location of a Kushan temple from the second century AD. It was discovered in the course of road-building in 1951, and was excavated systematically by the French archaeological expedition from 1952 to 1963. The excavations revealed a hilltop complex consisting of the main temple, a secondary temple and a monumental staircase leading down the hill. The main temple, standing on a brick platform faced with a stone revetment decorated with pilasters, contained a square central room surrounded by corridors on three sides, with three entrances facing east. In the centre was a stone platform with a huge column in each corner; the bases of these columns are still *in situ*. The temple building stood in the centre of a large paved courtyard, with porticoes and numerous niches in the walls where large painted statues once stood. From the outside the whole complex looked like a fortress, with solid, thick walls, a series of towers and narrow entrances. The secondary temple, beyond the outer wall on the north side, contained a square fire altar, surrounded by a passage for ritual circumambulation, representing a difference from the Greek temple model, where the object of worship, a statue of divinity, was hidden in a shrine at the far end of the building. The 7m wide staircase starts from a huge terrace on the east side of the main temple. As the archaeologists followed it downhill, they discovered that it consisted of five flights and five terraces.

In 1957, a large limestone slab covered with Greek letters in an unknown language was unearthed on the fourth terrace. It has been subsequently found that the 25-line inscription, 'probably the most important single specimen from Surkh Kotal'⁴ is in the eastern Iranian or Bactrian language. It has not yet been fully deciphered but it mentions King Kanishka and refers to the repairs of the sanctuary. There seems to have been a fire during the reign of Kanishka's immediate successor, and it can be assumed that these restorations and repairs were undertaken soon after that fire, which would place the inscription – and the fire – in the latter half of the second century AD. The

29 The site of Surkh Kotal

inscription also includes the word 'Bagolango', which was the Old Iranian word for 'temple or sanctuary', and is easily recognizable in the present-day name of Baghlan. In the Middle Ages, Baghlan was the name of the whole district, thus meaning 'district of the sanctuary'. The original temple of Kanishka extended down to the third terrace; the fourth was the work of the restorers and the fifth was probably added between the third and the fifth century AD, after the Sasanians had succeeded the Kushans.

Although Surkh Kotal was built in the peak period of Buddhism, it was certainly not a Buddhist temple, but is instead assumed to be a dynastic temple dedicated by Kanishka to his own divinity. A huge headless statue was found here which could represent King Kanishka himself, and it is possible that this sculpture, which was in the Museum of Kabul, was a cardinal deity in the temple. On the other hand, a stone platform like that found in the central room was typical of Iranian fire temples, and the secondary temple did contain a fire altar. There is little doubt therefore that the cult of fire played a leading role in the rites practised here; but Buddhism was not far away. Excavations at **Kuhna Masjid**, a hill just opposite Surkh Kotal, have revealed a Sasanian settlement and 2km away, directly in front of the main staircase, are the remnants of a Buddhist sanctuary, a square platform adorned with 40 pilasters once supporting colossal statues. Twenty-five capitals have been found here and on one of them is a turban, which was a symbol of the Buddha in early Gandharan art. Yet, like Ay Khanum, Surkh Kotal is not a Greco-Buddhist site (or to use another terminology, Indo-Greek). It is a mixture of Greek and Persian elements, and thus provides proof that the traditions of Achaemenian Persia were still strong several centuries after its disappearance.

Culturally, Surkh Kotal provides the earliest evidence of an indigenous Bactrian art, and contributes substantially to the understanding of Gandharan art. It may be assumed from the Surkh Kotal finds that a Bactrian style composed of eastern Iranian and Hellenistic elements developed already before the heyday of the Silk Route trade, and represents therefore a native contribution to the Greco-Bactrian art style.

Robatak, 40km north of Pul-i Khumri and east of Aibak, was linked with Surkh Kotal by an ancient road. An inscription was found here which could throw a new light on the Kushan dynasty and modify the Kanishka dating.

Samangan-Aibak

Samangan, on the road between Tashkurgan and Pul-i Khumri, is a modern town but was mentioned by medieval authors up to the fourteenth century under the name of Siminjan or Saminkan. Mukaddasi speaks of it as a larger town than Khulm, and Yakut describes it as lying in a maze of valleys which were peopled by Arabs. Mustawfi in the fourteenth century says it was already in ruins but corn, cotton and grapes were much cultivated here. According to some sources, Samangan means 'cave-dwellers' in the local dialect; and indeed, some 2km from the town is the site of **Takht-i Rustam** or **Aibak**, formerly a Buddhist monastery consisting of a number of caves and a *stupa* dating from the fourth or the fifth century AD. It was visited by several travellers in the nineteenth century, but was first explored systematically by Foucher in 1923, and then by Mizuno in 1959 and 1960.[5] The monastery stands at the bottom of the hill and has five caves. The

30 The monastery at Aibak

31 The stupa *at Aibak*

first of these consists of an anteroom and a large circular room, with a ceiling decorated with the carving of a huge lotus in full bloom – a highly unusual technique. The only other example can be found in one of the monasteries of Taxila, but on a much smaller scale. In the back wall are two niches, one above the other, which were probably used for statues (although nothing remains of them). The second cave is a long double corridor with a vaulted ceiling, two entrances and individual cells for the monks. The third cave, similar to the first, also has an anteroom, but the ceiling is not decorated. There are *squinch* arches in the corners, and one large niche for a statue. The fourth cave was utilitarian, and consisted of four rooms; the central one has benches along three walls and a square water tank in the centre. It was most probably used as a bathhouse, especially as the fifth cave, next to it, has numerous features indicating that it was a lavatory. On top of the hill, across from this complex, is a *stupa* which again has a unique feature: it looks as if it had been sunk into a large pit. In fact it stands in an open-topped cave which has been hewn out of solid rock around it, and the top of the *stupa* shows out of the cave. On it is a *harmika*, also hewn out of the rock (the *harmika* was originally a support for the pole holding the *chatra*, or umbrella). This contains a round and domed room which housed the reliquary. It is possible to enter the cave at the base of the *stupa* through a tunnel and to walk around it. The passage around the *stupa* is approximately 2m wide; the *stupa* itself, made of polished limestone, is 28m across and 8m high.

32 Interior of the monastery at Aibak

Kandahar: Shahr-i Kuhna

The Old City, which lies about 4km west of the modern town, is dominated by the tall mound of the citadel, the Kasr-i Naranj. On the north side, it is flanked by the Kaital range, on the summit of which a ruined Buddhist *stupa* can be seen. There are also remnants of two imposing cisterns and some fortifications dating from the Islamic period. Next to the citadel stands a small Muslim sanctuary, the Ziyarat-i Mir Sahib.

The site was excavated by the British Institute of Afghan Studies in 1974 and 1975. A trench in the city wall revealed layers of five periods, of which the first roughly corresponds to that of Mundigak VI and VII and may be as early as the first half of the first millennium BC. It is possible that the *pakhsa* wall of period II defended the Achaemenian city of Harakuwatis. Period III is characterized by unbaked bricks and was most probably Greek, while the defences of Period IV, which consisted of a solid brick wall, are believed to be Kushan. The layer of Period V is Islamic. The excavations within the walled enclosure had as one of their objectives to seek the solution of the problem of Alexandria of the Arachosians, or Alexandropolis, which might have been the Greek city of Old Kandahar; and although no evidence of the Alexander period was recovered, the finds of coins, pottery and some architectural remains would suggest that a Greek colony, or quarter, was added to the pre-existing settlement. This evidence of a Greek presence at Kandahar certainly strengthens the hypothesis that Alexandria of the Arachosians was located at Shahr-i Kuhna.[6]

Three inscriptions from the time of Ashoka were discovered here in 1957 and 1963. The *stupa* and the monastery next to it were partly constructed in the *diaper* masonry, and can be dated to the Kushan period. On the site of the *stupa* traces of an ambulatory and two drums have been found, decorated with pilasters with bases and capitals and a frieze as well as some mouldings; one of these was made of *stucco*, while others were of stone or fired bricks covered with plaster. The Buddhist remains were later incorporated into Islamic fortifications. The dominant part of the city was the citadel which rises 35m above the surrounding level, and may have been one of the earliest buildings of ancient Kandahar (although some estimates date it to the sixth or seventh century AD). The cisterns and canals were built in the early eighteenth century.

Buried Treasures

In 1946 at Khisht Tepe, some 90km from Kunduz on the bank of the Amu Darya, the frontier guards from the district of Kala-i Zal found an earthenware vase full of coins when digging foundations for a new stable. There were 628 Bactrian coins of various sizes and denominations with the names, in Greek, of 22 rulers. This find, which became known as the **hoard of Kunduz**, provided some useful information for the dating and history of the last decades of the Bactrian kingdom. It is now accepted that these coins date from the second century BC; the latest of them come from the last two decades of that century, from the period immediately preceding the invasion of the Yue-che and the establishment of the Kushan empire.

The **hoard of Tepe Fullol** dating from the Bronze Age, was found in 1966 in the province of Badakhshan. It consisted of five gold and 12 silver vessels from different periods and different localities. The motifs and the techniques used were a mixture of Indian, Iranian, Central Asian and Mesopotamian elements. On this evidence it seems probable that most objects could be dated to *c.*2500 BC.

Another two important hoards of coins were found in 1948 and 1992 respectively, at the site of **Mir Zakah** in the Gardez region.

Ashoka's inscriptions

Ashoka (c.270-32) had edicts carved in rocks throughout his empire. These were primarily concerned with defining the order of his state and ensuring its unity by promoting Buddhism, which was seen as the principal instrument in achieving this aim. A number of pillars inscribed with religious exhortations and legal and administrative orders were erected in various parts of the empire. The languages used in them reflect relations with Persia and the Hellenistic West.

A rock edict of Emperor Ashoka was found near Chehel Sina in 1958. It is a stone slab, 55 x 50cm, with 14 lines of text in Greek and eight lines in Aramaic, which until the finds of Surkh Kotal and Ay Khanum was the easternmost Greek inscription, and also the only one attributed to Ashoka. Another fragment of a Greek inscription came to light in the Kandahar bazaar in 1963, which contained 22 lines on a limestone block measuring 45 x 70 cm, and can also be attributed to Ashoka. It comes, presumably, from Shahr-i Kuhna, the Old City of Kandahar. In the same year, an inscription in Prakrit and Aramaic was also found in the bazaar. It had seven lines of script on a block of 24 x 19cm. A further four Ashoka inscriptions were found in the Laghman area in 1969; three of them were in Prakrit, or another Indian language, and one in Aramaic.

Begram-Kapisa

Near the village of Begram, some 60km north-east of Kabul, lies a long mound encircled by high ruined ramparts, at the confluence of the Panjshir and Ghorband rivers. This was **Kapisa**, the summer capital of the Kushan kings. It was excavated twice, in the late 1930s and the early 1940s, and the stratigraphic sequence established by Ghirshman in 1941-2 shows three major occupation periods:

1. Second century BC to second century AD, which coincides with the Indo-Parthian level of Taxila.[7] This was perhaps the capital of the last Indo-Greek (Greco-Buddhist) kingdom.
2. Second to third century AD, a Kushan city probably destroyed by the Sasanian King Shapur in 241.
3. Third to fifth century AD, the period up to the Hephthalite invasion. This invasion was, of course, not the end of Kapisa, for Suen Tsang, when he visited it in the seventh century, found it a very lively place, although a little rough.

> The Kingdom of Kia-pi-che has a circumference of about four thousand *li*. In the north, it leans on the snowy mountains; on the other three sides it is surrounded by black mountains. The distance around the capital is about ten *li*. The country is well suited for the cultivation of cereals and wheat; there is a great number of fruit trees . . . The climate is cold and windy. The character of the inhabitants is cruel and rude. Their language is low and coarse and their marriage is just a shameful mixing of the sexes . . . The inhabitants wear dresses of wool, sometimes lined with fur. In trade they use gold and silver coins and small bits of copper the size and shape of which is different than in other kingdoms. Their king . . . rules over a dozen kingdoms. He loves and protects his people; he respects and honours the Three Jewels. Every year he has a silver statue of Buddha made, eighteen feet high, and then he calls the Grand assembly in which he dispenses grants to the needy and alms to widowed men and women . . . there are a good hundred monasteries there with more than six thousand monks who all study the doctrine of the Great Vehicle (*Mahayana*) . . . There are several dozen temples of various deities and a thousand heretics. Some of them go naked, others rub themselves with ashes or make bonnets of skull-bones and wear them on their heads . . . The princes of various kingdoms in India return in summer to Kia-pi-che; in spring and autumn they stay in the kingdom of Kien-to-lo (Gandhara). This is why, in each place where these hostages stay for three seasons, there was a monastery built for them. This one, which we describe, has been built as their summer residence. This is why, on all the walls, they have painted the portraits of these hostages whose faces and dress resemble those of the men from the East (sc from China).[8]

The excavations of Hackin (1936 to 1940) yielded some of the most spectacular museum pieces found in the last century. In the so-called 'new royal city' two rooms were found which were probably a rich merchant's treasury or warehouse. They were filled with luxury goods and rare Buddhist objects, carved ivories from India, vases and lacquerware from China, classical Greco-Roman sunken reliefs, Greco-Egyptian bronzes, Phoenician glassware. There was jewellery from India, Rome, Egypt and Central Asia. Some specimens even resembled those found in Sarmatian tombs in the Russian steppe.

The objects show, on the one hand, the extent of the trade along the Silk Route at that period, and the variety and high value of the goods traded and, on the other, the refined and elaborate taste of the buying public. The treasure used to be shown in the Begram rooms of the Kabul Museum, in 15 cases containing ivories, Hellenistic bronzes, pottery and marble, Kushan figurines from the first to the third century, Alexandrian glass from the same period, plaster medallions from the second century, plaster casts taken from classical Greek silver salvers, crystal and glassware. Their present whereabouts are not known.

The wealth and commercial importance of Kapisa is thus well documented. This was based on the city's position at the crossroads of important trade routes, one linking Balkh with Peshawar and Taxila and the other leading up the Panjshir valley to Badakhshan and Chinese Turkestan.

There is little to be seen at Begram nowadays. The rooms where the famous treasure was found are situated on the southern edge of the mound, at the end of a long trench which was the bazaar, at a point near a tower in the city wall. The large mound which was the citadel, and a vast area of hillocks and mounds which was the city, are easily discernible.

Shotorak and Paitava

Two Buddhist monasteries were excavated to the east of the site of Begram, dating probably from the first to the third century AD. One of them, **Shotorak** (Baby Camel), was the monastery built for the Chinese hostages taken by the Kushans. The most romantic of these dead monasteries is the Shahzade-i Chin: 'The Chinese Princess'. It is, in fact, the place where a clutch of distinguished Chinese hostages was held, in honourable confinement, by the Kushan emperor Kanishka. The emperor is said to have paid his prisoners the compliment of sharing their monastery-prison with them for a month[9]; and these were the 'men from the East' whose portraits on the walls Suen Tsang saw some five centuries later. The complex consisted of two courtyards and ten *stupas*. The '*sangharama*' or monastery was a two- or possibly three-storey building surrounding the courtyard and built of clay. The ceilings were probably made of matting covered with clay and supported by wooden columns. No traces of a dome were discovered. The main *stupa* in the first courtyard was made of stone and measured eight square metres. Inside was found a terracotta vase filled with earth. No other relics were found and it is possible that the earth came from some holy spot connected with the life of the Buddha and was itself a relic.

There were four small *stupas* in front of the main one, some one and a half metres square. None had a cupola. All show certain similarities to the *stupas* at Mohra Moradu, Jaulian and Takht-i Bhai in north Pakistan. The *stupas* were decorated with bas-reliefs in schist depicting scenes from the life of the Buddha. A number of statues also in schist were found here, most of them depicting similar motifs.

The style of the bas-reliefs, which probably date from the third to fifth century AD, belongs to the latest period of Gandharan art, but the reliefs are heavier, more rigid and more schematic. Among other sculptures, which also used to be in the Museum of Kabul, the most remarkable find was a throne supported by two lions.

It should be noted that schist was a rare material in Afghanistan, and Shotorak was one of the few places where deposits of it existed. It seems that the rough-hewn blocks were brought to the site and worked on the spot. According to Meunié[10] the plain of Kapisa was the northern limit of Gandharan sculpture in this material.

No sculpture dates from before the reign of Kanishka. According to some scholars, the second century AD was the peak period of Shotorak. The other site, **Paitava**, about 8km south of Begram, is a *stupa* which yielded several Buddhist stucco heads with Parthian elements and bas-reliefs in schist dating from the third and fourth century AD. Another *stupa* in the area is at Koh-i Mori.

Sites and monuments in the Kabul area

Khair Khane, just outside Kabul on the road to Charikar, is the site of a Brahmin temple dating probably from the period of the Hindushahi rulers of Kabul, and was excavated in 1935-6. On a terrace built over an older temple stood three newer temples next to each other. Living premises, kitchens and so on were built on a lower level before the temple, and a number of statues in white marble have been found. Some authorities believe that the temple was dedicated to an Iranian deity, and date it to the third to fourth century AD.[11] A marble statue of the Sun god, which could be either Surya or Mithras (and used to be in the Kabul museum), has been found here, showing a mixture of Kushano-Sasanian and early Hindu motifs.

Tepe Darra, some 58km north by the same road, is a Buddhist *stupa*, part of a Kushan monastery. The **Tepe Khazana** (Treasure Hill), south of the city, is a Buddhist site from the Kushano-Sasanian period. Fragments of sculptures found here in the 1930s show a mixture of styles, from Hellenistic to mature Gupta. It is difficult to date them; suggestions vary between the fifth and seventh century AD. Nearby is a water canal built in the fifteenth century, which is still in use.

Tepe Maranjan, a hill topped by the blue-domed mausoleum of King Nadir Shah (1929-33), is the site of a Buddhist monastery from the third and fourth century AD. Excavations in 1933 yielded a number of statues of painted clay, and a hoard of Kushano-Sasanian gold coins, and fourth-century AD Sasanian silver drachmas. It is likely that a *stupa* stood above the monastery. The mausoleum is now in ruins.

South of Kabul, two Buddhist *stupas* can be seen on the way to Gardez and the Logar valley. The **Guldara** *stupa*, in desolate countryside about 4km from the village

33 The *Guldara* stupa

34 The Guldara stupa

of the same name, stands on a square platform on a high rocky spur. Below, in a sheltered corner, a spring with a single tree catches the eye, the only refreshing sight in stony desert. The *stupa* has a square base, a two-tier drum, and a dome which has collapsed, leaving only part of it still in position. The square base is an unusual feature, as most Buddhist *stupas* in Afghanistan have only a high cylindrical drum. The base is decorated on three sides with a row of false columns and a central niche; on the south-west side, a staircase leads to the platform on top of the base. The decoration of the lower part of the drum is fairly simple, but the upper part shows elaborate ornamental ledges which form a false arcade of alternating half-circles and half-hexagons. In between is a motif symbolizing the umbrella mast. According to some authorities,[12] this is a motif of a console carrying ornamental stucco eagles with spread wings, painted gold. The masonry, both on the base and on the drum, is of the *diaper* kind, typical of the Kushan period. The layers of *schist* which make the wall-facing are interspersed with large blocks of stone of a different colour, achieving a pronounced ornamental effect.

Gold Kushan coins and several other gold objects were found in the reliquary chamber inside the drum. The *stupa* (which was partly restored) was part of a monastery complex, the main building of which was excavated in 1963-4. There was a figure of a seated Buddha at the end of the entrance passage, flanked by a standing *bodhisattva* and an elephant. A central corridor ran around the entire building, lined with a number of cells with domed ceilings. The middle part of the monastery was occupied by a square open courtyard with a round tower in each corner. The buildings were probably on two floors, but the second floor has disappeared completely. Another small *stupa* stands on the side of the hill.

The **Shewaki** *stupa*, situated on the Kabul side of the mountain, has a typical squat cylindrical drum with a high dome, partly in ruins. The décor consists of a single line of false arches with a symbolic umbrella mast, similar to that on the Guldara *stupa*. The arches are supported by false columns, with what might have been Corinthian capitals.

The **Minar-i Chakri** was 'an enigmatic monument'.[13] It was over 20m high, with masonry in the typical Kushan *diaper* style, and the top was crowned with a Maurya-style bell-shaped lantern, the upper part of which was missing. It can therefore be safely dated as belonging to the early centuries AD, but 'whatever the date of the column may be, it was a child of a marriage of Greek with Persian architecture'. The capital was reminiscent of Persian examples from the Achaemenian age, such as those which can be seen at Persepolis. The Greek element in the column's parentage was represented by the triple bands of decoration – entablature, frieze and cornice – that surround the column at intervals.

Another opinion holds that this was a Buddhist tower, erected on the crest of the Takht-i Shah mountain to mark the mountain pass on the old caravan route from Kabul to Gardez. Franz[14] sees it as an over-sized Buddhist religious column, with some relief ornaments derived from the Gandhara school. Overhanging lotus leaves decorated the capital; also present were the symbolic three wheels representing wisdom, monasticism and the Buddha, as well as a pair of gazelles, which are frequently found in the Gandharan Buddhist imagery. End of the first/early second century AD seems the most probable date of its origin. It collapsed in 1998 from lack of maintenance.

Hadda

East of Kabul, the most important site is **Hadda**. It is the modern name of a group of Buddhist monasteries, *stupas* and *caravanserais*, situated on the outskirts of the ancient city of Nagarahara (which corresponds to the present-day Jalalabad). The site is 8km south of Jalalabad, on what used to be one of the main caravan roads linking the Punjab and the Kabul area. It dates from the late first to the seventh century AD, when the Jalalabad area was among the most sacred in the Buddhist world. There were reputedly as many as a thousand *stupas* in the land of Hilo, which is how the Chinese chroniclers referred to Hadda. So far, the French archaeological mission has explored more than 500 of them.

There are seven main groups of ruins in the area. The most important of them is the site of **Tepe Kalan**; the others are Tepe-i Kafariha, Bagh-Gai (1.5km from Tepe Kalan), Chakhil-i Ghundi (1.3km north-east of Hadda), Prates (on the other side of the Chapriar River), Gar Nao and Deh Ghundi. The excavations concentrating on the Tepe Kalan site have yielded a fantastic number of statues in limestone, schist and stucco which show great similarity with the art of Gandhara and Taxila, although with a slightly provincial touch. Between 1923-8 the French expedition uncovered

35 Hadda, Tepe-i Kafariha. Barthoux (1930)

some 23,000 heads of Buddhas, *bodhisattvas*, various demons, and other figures like donors, soldiers, monks and so on. Apart from the heads, they found bas-reliefs and other sculptures depicting episodes from the Buddhist legend, scenes of offerings, and individual persons, as well as some fragments of secular scenes, and pieces of architectural décor. The art of Hadda comes from two main periods – the second to the third century, and the fifth century – and is a mixture of Bactrian, Greco-Roman and Indian elements. The western influence is particularly visible in the classic profiles, pseudo-Corinthian capitals, vine scrolls and Roman drapery. In particular, the Indo-Corinthian capitals belong to the last phase of the Gandharan period.

Generally speaking, the stone statues, whether in limestone or schist, are of inferior quality to those made from stucco. The proportions are clumsy, the folds of the garment unnatural and rigid, while in contrast the stucco statues are often 'small masterpieces';[15] their proportions, gestures, and folds are completely natural and easy and, although it is obvious that they were produced quickly and in large numbers, they show a technical experience and a mastery of skills as well as a noticeable talent. Meticulous attention is given to minute details in the faces, hair and dress; ink and red paint were used to underline features which were intended to stand out, while hollows were darkened to accentuate the relief effect.

36 *Capitals at Hadda.* Barthoux (1930)

It was in Hadda that the stucco technique reached its peak. The bodies of figures were moulded in mud and covered with decorated gypsum plaster, while the heads were made separately from lime plaster mixed with straw and pebbles and then covered with a shell of stucco, which consisted of lime, sand and marble dust. The figures were painted in bright colours, pink and ochre; the hair was often blue.

Here for the first time, and under the influence of the Mahayana school, a representation of the Buddha in human form was produced, replacing the older symbolic portrayals of the Indian bas-reliefs. Some scholars nevertheless attribute the first images of the Buddha to Greek or Roman influence. At any rate, the art of Hadda shows at least in part Greek influences. Its peak seems to have been in the second to third century AD, and the statues and decorative panels produced, which were used in both *stupas* and monasteries, mostly depicted scenes from the life of the Buddha, miraculous events, and portraits of the faithful who commissioned them.

The faces show western influence in their strong chins, straight noses and finely chiselled mouths, whereas bulging eyes, soft oval cheeks and elongated ears point to oriental origins. The Buddhas were surrounded by a multitude of figures – barbarians, soldiers, monks, deities, donors and demons, as well as fantastic or realistic animals. Frescos were rare in Hadda; one, now in the Musée Guimet, decorated a niche in which stood a small statue of a Buddha.

After the French, the Afghan Institute of Archaeology continued the excavations at another site, the **Tepe-i Shotor**, which was a large monastery active between the second and the fourth century AD. There was a large *stupa* surrounded by smaller votive *stupas*, statue-lined corridors and side-niches for statues of Buddhas. Most of the sculptures found here were left *in situ*.

Numerous ruins of monasteries and *stupas* of a similar kind exist in the Kunar Valley which was another ancient route between Bactria and Gandhara. The upper part of this valley is now the territory of Chitral in north-west Pakistan. The lower part opens out not far north-east of Jalalabad.

Bamiyan and Kakrak

The valley of **Bamiyan**, 233km north of Kabul, with its colossal statues and innumerable caves, has attracted the interest of travellers ever since the Buddhist pilgrims Fa-Sien and Suen Tsang described it (in the fifth and seventh century AD respectively). Bamiyan was, between the sixth and ninth century, the capital of a small kingdom which was part of a confederation of Turkic and Hephthalite principalities between the eastern borders of the Sasanian empire and the Punjab in the south-east.

The valley is 15km long and not more than 3km wide, and lies at an altitude of 2500m. It was conveniently situated halfway between the important cities of Balkh and Kapisa on the caravan route linking India with Bactria and Transoxania, at a place which had probably for centuries before been a natural caravan halt offering a sheltered resting place to traders and pilgrims, well equipped with provisions and repair facilities, grazing grounds and replacement mounts. It was well sheltered from

37 Bamiyan, the valley and the cliff

the winds and had an abundant supply of water. It was in the past, as it still is, an oasis of intensive cultivation and refreshing greenery amid the barren mountainous landscape which surrounds it. In the early stage of the penetration of Buddhism across the Hindukush and into northern Afghanistan, it became the home of a colony of Buddhist monks, who may have preferred this place to others because of the sheer vertical cliff-face of soft rock which was eminently suitable for carving statues and digging cave sanctuaries. There was an established tradition of such sanctuaries in India whence Buddhism came, and no doubt Ellora, Ajanta and others provided the models for the first cave sanctuaries at Bamiyan, just as they were to provide them for the similarly situated sites later developed in Chinese Turkestan, at Miran, Longmen and Yun-Kang.

The first European source to mention Bamiyan was Professor Thomas Hyde's Latin work, *Veterum Persarum et Parthorum et Medorum Religionis Historia*, first published in 1700. It was followed by Captain Francis Wilford's *On Mount Caucasus* in 1798 and Sir Mountstuart Elphinstone's *An Account of the Kingdom of Caubul* in 1815, but these were all second-hand reports based either on other historic sources or on information gathered from local people; none of the authors had actually visited

38 The large Buddha at Bamiyan

the site. The first eyewitness account comes from William Moorcroft and George Trebeck, who travelled in the area in 1824, only to die shortly afterwards, one in Balkh and the other in Mazar-i Sharif. Their joint report appeared in 1841 under the title 'Travels in the Himalayan provinces of Hindustan and the Punjab; in Ladakh and Kashmir; in Peshawar, Kabul, Kunduz and Bokhara, from 1819 to 1825'.

Sir Alexander Burnes, Dr Gerard and J.M. Honingberger were here in 1832, and another Englishman, Charles Masson, visited in 1835.[16] It is mentioned in the notes of Lady Sale and Lt Vincent Eyre, survivors of the massacre of 1842, that British prisoners camped opposite the large Buddha. M.G. Talbot described Bamiyan in detail in 1886,[17] and when in 1922 King Amanullah granted the French a 30-year exclusive right of archaeological exploration in the country, the site became quite naturally the first target of the DAFA (*Délégation archéologique française en Afghanistan*). The valley was briefly visited by the DAFA director, A. Foucher,[18] and in 1924 it was systematically explored and described by J. Hackin and Mr and Mrs A. Godard.[19]

39 The small Buddha at Bamiyan

The most striking features of Bamiyan were the two giant statues of the Buddha, carved in the cliff, one 38m and the other 55m high. Each was surrounded by a number of man-made caves of various sizes and shapes, some of them grouped in elaborate sanctuary complexes. Between them there were other statues of seated Buddhas.

According to Suen Tsang's description, the earliest monastery – which he calls 'the monastery of an ancient king' and which was probably built at the end of the first century AD – stood somewhere at the base of the cliff, between the two Buddhas and nearer to the smaller one. Needless to say, the monastery was earlier than the statues. To the west of the statues, its northern flank protected by the cliff, stood the capital city, of which nothing remains, except perhaps some disused caves. A mound east of the 'small' Buddha, which hides the remnants of a *stupa*, is the only trace of an open-air construction from the Kushan period. The complex of caves surrounding the statue of the smaller Buddha originated as an extension of the monastery into the rock. J. Hackin, during his careful examination, noticed the same inexperienced craftsmanship on the surface of the niche of the Buddha statue and in some of the adjacent caves. This, together with the fact that a certain time was needed for the monks of the monastery to dig their sanctuaries and carve the statue in the rock, and also the Greek hairstyle of the Buddha led him to the conclusion that the 'small' Buddha and the earliest caves around him must have originated later than the monastery. The statue is certainly one of the earliest colossal representations of the Buddha, which would explain its cumbersome and primitive features.

By contrast, the larger statue was more sensibly proportioned, its niche had a more sophisticated, trilobate vault, and the finishing of the surfaces was clearly the work of experienced, accomplished craftsmen. The same applied to the caves in its immediate neighbourhood, which although not forming any groups or complexes were generally of a more sophisticated design. It seems logical, therefore, that the larger statue and its caves should belong to a later period than the smaller one with its surrounding sanctuaries. It was probably built in the fifth to sixth century during the reign of Yabghu Tung Shih-hu, who was an ardent exponent of Buddhism.

The *smaller* of the two Buddhas stood in the eastern part of the cliff in a niche 8m deep. It had a disproportionately large head, wide shoulders and thick-set body. The hair, as mentioned above, was dressed in Greek fashion, and the folds of the garment were stiff and unnatural. The face has been systematically obliterated. The whole statue was hewn out of solid rock with the exception of the folds and the (missing) forearms, which were made of plaster. The statue, which probably dated from the fourth or fifth century AD, was covered with a layer of clay mixed with straw followed by a layer of mortar. This was originally painted, the body in blue, the hands and the face in gold.

The niche was decorated on the inside with frescoes, in parts still clearly visible. They formed a vast composition centred around a lunar, or solar, deity surrounded by two rows of figures – *bodhisattvas*, donors, and so on. There are strong indications that the frescoes, which resemble those found at Kizil and Kumtura in Chinese Turkestan, were of Iranian origin and were probably executed in the fifth or sixth century AD. As a curious detail, some of the figures are remarkably similar to Tibetan female demons as depicted in temples in the region of Kucha, again in Chinese Turkestan. Thus the frescoes of this section at Bamiyan show a mixture of Indian, Iranian and Chinese elements.

By comparison, the statue of the *large* Buddha, which stood 400m farther west, represented a considerable artistic improvement. Its proportions were better balanced and it looks as if the artists modelled their work on certain Hellenistic statues. On the other hand, the ornamental folds of the garment were very shallow and at places barely indicated; this was closer to the schematic arrangement typical of the Gupta period, which differed considerably from the softer and deeper folds of the Hellenistic style.

According to some authorities, the statue never had a face; instead, a metal mask is believed to have been fixed above the chin. The forearms, which were again missing, were not cut out of the rock but, as on the other statue, were made of plaster carried on wooden beams. The legs were damaged by cannonballs fired by Nadir Shah's troops. The folds were modelled in plaster and fixed to the body by wooden

40 The large Buddha at Bamiyan: niche and frescoes

pegs, the holes of which were clearly visible. The body was probably painted red, while the face and the hands might again have been gold. As it was later than its smaller counterpart, the statue most probably originated in the fifth or the sixth century AD, although in some sources an earlier date is given.

An account of the building technique of this colossal statue is given in *The seventy wonders of the world*:

> The Bamiyan Buddha was created by cutting a high-relief figure into the face of the soft conglomerate cliff. It is probable that the niche was carved out first, using scaffolding slotted into holes cut into the cliff, before the ambulatory galleries were carved; the scaffolding later being replaced by a series of permanent wooden ladders, landings and façades. The torso was roughly shaped and the detailing of the folds of the gown was built out by cutting lines of shallow holes for wooden pegs on which were hung ropes coated with thick stucco . . . Arms and face were formed by timber superstructures or armatures covered with sheets of brass or gilded metal; massive metal earrings may have been attached in the deep grooves under the stucco ears . . . Finally, the rough surfaces of the niche, galleries and chapels were thickly coated with clay mixed with vegetable fibres before a thin, white layer of burnt gypsum was applied, to which pigments, bound by animal glue, were than added.[20]

The niche of this statue was also decorated with frescoes, the oldest of which can be seen on the lateral surfaces. There is, for example, a series of five medallions with two female and one male figure in each, surrounded by winged demons reminiscent of Gandharan iconography, and a series of five Buddhas resembling those of Ajanta – although more clumsily depicted – seated under the sacred fig tree with a group of royal donors, all framed by architectural decoration and floral ornaments. There are female figures with Indian faces, semi-nude or thinly veiled in transparent robes, some dancing and others playing musical instruments. A dome or an umbrella of a *stupa* can be seen behind each group. The contours of the figures were drawn in ochre, and indigo blue was used for some surfaces. This, again, points to an Indian origin and, in particular, to the Gupta period. Certain details of dress and hair-style, as well as some decorative elements, show Iranian influence, while the virtuoso brush strokes and the softness of the lines betray a Chinese hand. It seems that these frescoes are somewhat earlier than those in the niche of the older Buddha.

The caves were not spread haphazardly over the rock face. They formed organised units serving definite purposes, and were connected by a wealth of communications, both horizontal and vertical. Steps and staircases were dug in the rock, and horizontal galleries linked caves on the same level so that each complex had it own independent access. The caves were of various types, either rectangular with barrel-vaulted ceilings; round, octagonal or hexagonal with flat ceilings; or square with ceilings which were domed, or imitated a pattern of beams. In later ones there is evidence of the transition from a square base to a round dome by means of *squinches*, a clear imitation of brick construction borrowed from Persian architecture. The so-called *lantern-ceilings* are an interesting imitation of Indian timber architecture. At any rate, all architectural elements in the caves are purely decorative, with no structural function.

The caves around the small Buddha form four complexes marked by Hackin as A, B, C and D.[21] In the assembly room of complex A, the *squinches* were decorated with several rows of tiny Buddhas executed in Sasanian style while, by the entrance, another fresco shows the Buddha, bare-chested and wearing a *dhoti*, Indian style. Two rooms in complex C had frescoes in Sasanian style. An octagonal sanctuary in complex D was also lavishly decorated, with both frescoes and bas-reliefs; a series of medallions painted on clay decorated the ceiling of its anteroom showing (amongst other things) classical Sasanian motifs, such as the head of a wild boar, or two birds holding a pearl necklace. On each side of the statue a staircase connected the caves and led up to a gallery on the level of the head, which was used for ritual circumambulation.

The caves around the larger statue are less interesting by comparison. There are no groups, and no elaborate decorations. Around the statue there are two ambulatories, one on the ground consisting of 11 chapels, the other at the level of the head, which is illuminated by apertures into the niche. The niche and some of the chapels were decorated with paintings of *bodhisattvas*, *apsaras*, royal personages and so on, depicted in a style which shows a mixture of Iranian, Indian and Chinese elements. Two of the chapels are octagonal: one is decorated with high-reliefs and another has a *lantern ceiling*. Access to the gallery on top is by a comfortable outside footpath of recent origin which crosses ancient water-conduits and drains. Above in the rock face is a large cave with an architrave and an ornamental ceiling decorated with a series of hexagons in star-form linked together with geometrical ornaments of triangles and lozenges. The Buddha may have been carved on the instruction of the princeling himself, but the surrounding chapels were created by hundreds of pilgrims, merchants and residents seeking safe passage and success for their expeditions.

In the 400m that separate the two Buddhas are three more niches which once held statues of seated Buddhas. Very little of these remains, but they, too, were decorated with frescoes of mixed Indian and Iranian origin.

It is worth noting that all known early Buddhist wall-paintings are Indian – those of Ajanta (first to seventh century AD), of Sigiriya in Ceylon (Sri Lanka) (fifth century AD) and of Bagh in India (sixth century AD). No paintings from the Gandharan period have ever been found. In Central Asia, the paintings of Miran, in Chinese Turkestan, date from the third century AD; all the others are later than the Bamiyan paintings. However, the artistic quality of the Bamiyan paintings is far inferior to those of Ajanta. The fact that it also seems inferior to the art of the later frescoes of Turkestan, in which the Iranian influence is much stronger, would indicate that the contribution of Iran injected a certain amount of vitality into Buddhist art.

Recently some caves at the base of the large Buddha were used for the storage of arms and ammunition. The concrete supports of the statue were demolished to retrieve metal bracing. Frescoes above the head were destroyed or looted during the fights between the Taliban and the Hazara. One large fresco covered with soot was spattered with shoe-prints in white paint; the small Buddha had its head blown off in 1999, and its head and neck were turned to rubble. Half of the draperies in the upper part of the body have disappeared; there was a gaping hole in the lower part of the body visible from afar, but this seemed to be of an earlier date. Explosions damaged the right knee, the galleries and the staircase around the statue, and almost all frescoes behind the head seem to have disappeared between 1995 and 1999. Both statues were finally blown up in March 2001.

In the valley of **Kakrak**, a short distance to the south-east of the main valley, another giant statue of the Buddha stands 7m high, with its face intact, in a niche amidst a group of cave sanctuaries. The niche was decorated with frescoes and sculptured ornaments. The main fresco, showing a 'king hunter', had in its style elements of Sasanian or Kushano-Sasanian art as well as that of Chinese Turkestan. On the statue itself only a few folds of the garment remain. In one of the sanctuaries a series of wall-paintings was covered with a layer of mud, and has therefore survived undamaged, and these were removed from the wall and taken to the museum in Kabul. The legs and supports of the statue were destroyed in 1996.

Foladi and Fundukistan

About 4km south-west of the township of Bamiyan the valley of **Foladi** hides another group of cave monasteries. The entrance to the valley is guarded by two brick towers, probably from the early Islamic period. Behind them, on the western side, are 14 caves and opposite them, on the eastern side, four more. They are often grouped in pairs, with a common anteroom. The ceilings include domes on squinches, barrel vaults and false beams in lantern shapes. There are no decorations in relief, but some of the wall paintings are very well preserved, among them frescoes of sitting Buddhas, large and small, and of various other figures, painted mostly in green medallions against a background of blue. Most of the frescoes are in the caves on the western side, while on the eastern side only one cave is decorated.

Almost exactly halfway between Kabul and Bamiyan, about 50km from the town of Charikar and 5km from the village of Siyahgerd, lies the site of **Fundukistan**, one of the most important monastic sites in the country. Excavations carried out in 1937 revealed a monastery complex of the seventh century consisting of a square courtyard surrounded by a wall with 12 niches, with a small *stupa* in the centre. The architectural decoration, arcades with foliated scrolls and columns with pseudo-Corinthian capitals, is perhaps less remarkable than the magnificent frescoes reflecting both Indian and Sasanian elements, and the sculptures reminiscent of the Indian Gupta school, which were recovered in a very good state of preservation, the statues intact and the frescoes still vividly coloured. They offer a strange mixture of influences. There is some similarity with the Gupta school of India, but an entirely new mode of expression: 'languid serenity, and inner reverie, the long slim figures posed in graceful elegance'.[22] The statues were placed in small niches against a background of paintings in bright colours, in which the most frequent motifs were arcades with foliated scrolls and columns with pseudo-Corinthian capitals. Their style is close to that of Tumchuk in Chinese Turkestan.

The statues were made of baked clay reinforced by wooden frames and horsehair, then painted. Terracotta moulds were perhaps used, but none were found. This 'last and delicate flowering of Buddhist art'[23] belonged to a peripheral Buddhist culture which survived in Afghanistan while Buddhism in India was slowly dying out.

Balkh

The best view of the ancient city of **Balkh** is from the air. The huge circular mound of yellow clay is clearly visible among the gardens and fields, ringed with the craggy remnants of once formidable ramparts. This is the Bala Hissar, the 'citadel' covering an area of almost 300 acres, with a hillock in its south-eastern part marking the site of the fort. Its history goes back perhaps to the Achaemenian period or even beyond, for Balkh has traditionally been associated with Bactra, or Bakhdi, the legendary birthplace of Zarathustra and one of the earliest outposts of the Aryan civilisation in the area north of the Hindukush. It was the capital of the Persian satrapy of Bactria, was taken by Alexander in his pursuit of Bessus and became not only his base during his four years of campaigning in Transoxania, but also the scene of his marriage to Roxana. After Alexander's reign, it became the centre of the flourishing Greco-Bactrian kingdom. In the Kushan period, it was an important junction of the caravan routes linking Central Asia and China with Persia and India. Like Herat, it was taken in turn by the Hephthalites, the Turks and the Arabs and reached the peak of its fame on the very eve of the Mongol disaster.

Pre-Islamic

41   Aerial view of the site of Balkh

There is, unfortunately, no evidence that Bactra and Balkh were really the same place. French archaeologists explored the site as early as 1924-5[24] and then in two campaigns, in 1947-8 and 1955-6, in which they concentrated mainly on the ramparts of the city and the citadel. No traces of a settlement earlier than the Kushan period have been found. An American expedition cut a trench in the side of the fort, but to no better end.[25] However, in 1995, illegal diggers found fluted columns apparently identical to those found at Ay Khanum.

The most ancient Balkh of all

> is said to have stood to the east of the present city altogether. A mass of mounds and bricks on the road to Mazar mark the site of some old city, and in addition to these there is still standing a considerable portion of old walls. An old Afghan with me described these ruins on the east as the Shahr-i Hinduan . . .[26]

Yate's old Afghan was quite right. *Kala-i Hinduwan* – the castle of the Hindus – was a fortress outside the city restored by Timur. The ruins which Yate saw were most probably those of a former suburb of Balkh called *Naw Bahar*. Here, according to

Masudi, in Sasanian days stood one of the chief fire-temples built in imitation of, and as a rival to, the Ka'bah of Mecca:

> its walls were adorned with precious stones, and brocaded curtains were hung everywhere to cover these, the walls themselves being periodically unguented with perfumes, especially in the spring . . . when pilgrimage was made to the shrine . . . All the lands round Naw Bahar for seven leagues square were the property of the sanctuary . . . [27]

Mazdeism was not the only religion which had its temples in Balkh at that time. In the Kushan period, the city became an important centre of Buddhism and numerous temples, monasteries and hostels catered for the stream of pilgrims constantly on the move between India – or, more precisely, the Punjab – and China. The famous Chinese pilgrim of the seventh century, Suen-Tsang, mentions several of them. Two strange mounds south of the city, on the modern road from Mazar-i Sharif to Akcha, called Tepe Rustam and Takht-i Rustam, which puzzled Major Yate, probably hide the remains of Buddhist *stupas* (see below).

> The kingdom of Poho (Balkh) has approximately eight hundred *li* from east to west and four hundred *li* from south to north. In the north it borders on the river Po-tsou (Oxus, Wakhsh). The circumference of the capital is about twenty *li*. Everybody calls it 'the little royal city'. In spite of being well fortified it contains few inhabitants . . .
>
> . . . Around one hundred monasteries are here with some three thousand monks who study the doctrine of the Lesser Vehicle (Hinayana). Outside the city, in the south-west, is a monastery called Na-po-seng-kia-lan (Nava sangharama) or the New Monastery, built by the first king of this kingdom . . . There is a statue of Buddha in this monastery built of precious materials and the hall in which it stands is decorated with rare objects of a great value.[28]

The walls of the city were examined meticulously by the two French expeditions mentioned above. Their findings confirmed that the **Bala Hissar**, the citadel with the fort, was the most ancient part of the city. South of it was a suburb with its own walls which in one period extended toward the east. Later, this eastern extension was abandoned and the city extended to the west. It is not certain how far back the history of the citadel goes. Pottery sherds dating from the pre-Kushan period were found here, and some authorities are inclined to believe that the earliest fortifications could be older still. If this is right, then Balkh could indeed have been the legendary Bactria, capital of the Greco-Bactrian kingdom of the third to second century BC.

The southern suburb was most probably late Kushan and flourished in the second century AD when Buddhism expanded north of the Hindukush. This would make it contemporary with the two *stupas*, Tepe Rustam and Takht-i Rustam. The walls of this town can still be located under later constructions on the southern and eastern perimeter. An eastern extension, which in all probability was identical with the suburb of Naw Bahar, was added to the town in pre-Islamic or early Islamic times. Some authorities would place it as far back as late Kushan; it is possible that it was actually founded after the Hephthalite invasion in the fifth century. Its southern wall was built partly over the earlier one, while in the west, a new wall was built a little farther afield from the old one.

It should be noted that the theory that the New Monastery of Suen Tsang was a predecessor of the Sasanian temple at Naw Bahar is mere conjecture, based on the assumption that the Persian name 'Naw Bahar' is derived from the Sanscrit *Nava Vihara*, which means New Monastery.[29]

Tepe Rustam and Takht-i Rustam (Balkh)

Just south of Balkh on the main road from Mazar-i Sharif to Akcha, are two substantial mounds with a platform on top showing traces of brickwork, pillars and internal passages. These are the **Tepe Rustam** and the **Takht-i Rustam** which have already been mentioned above. Yate's description still applies:

> To the south of the city lie two most curious structures, known respectively as the Tope-i Rustam and Takht-i Rustam. My old Afghan gave it as his opinion that they were relics of ancient fire-worship, but it seems equally probable that they are of Buddhist origin. The Tope-i-Rustam is a circular building, some 50 yards in diameter at the base, and about 50 feet in height, much weather-worn and damaged by rain, and looking in the distance like a tall mud mound . . . the base of it is built of large unburned bricks, some two feet in length and four or five inches thick . . . There are no signs of mortar in the building, but the bricks are all of the same large size . . . The base of the tope is pierced by four shafts, apparently meeting in the centre; but whether these passages were part of the original building, or whether they were run through afterwards, it is difficult to tell . . . The Takht-i-Rustam is about the same height, but it is wedge-shaped – not circular like the tope. I saw no traces of brick in it, and it seems to have been built of hardened mud, with straight perpendicular sides, say some 100 yards in length north and south, and 60 yards in breadth at the western and 20 yards at the eastern end. The top is perfectly flat, and full of rain holes, but whether the rain runs down into cells inside or not I do not know. There were no inside chambers or entrances visible at any rate.[30]

Schlumberger and Le Berre examined the bricks and found them to be the same as those in the late Kushan fortification. It can be assumed therefore that these were Buddhist *stupas* from that period, probably built alongside the main pilgrim road which passed through Balkh.[31]

42 The site of Tepe Sardar

Tepe Sardar

In 1967, south of the road from Kabul to Kandahar and on top of a high mound called **Tepe Sardar**, Italian archaeologists excavated an important Buddhist temple consisting of a central *stupa* built perhaps on the remains of an earlier one, and surrounded by a number of lesser votive *stupas* and thrones. The base of the main *stupa* was some 22m square and access to it was by a monumental staircase. Both this and the lesser ones were decorated with sculptures in terracotta and moulded clay, some of which were found in a surprisingly good state of preservation. A thin layer of red clay was used as surface finish. There were also some wall paintings, of which very little remains. A huge clay statue of a reclining Buddha has been found next to the main *stupa*, but it was unfortunately not in good condition. The brickwork and the style of the statues point to the late Kushan or early Sasanian period. There seem to have been both Hindu and Buddhist statues in the temple, a highly unusual coexistence. The temple was probably destroyed either in the early Arab raids in the late seventh century, or ultimately by the Saffarids from Sistan in the later ninth century.

Tilla-Tepe, Delbarjin, Dokhtar-i Nushirwan

The last great archaeological discovery before the curtain dropped on Afghanistan was no doubt V. Sarianidi's excavations at **Tilla Tepe**, not far from the village of Shibargan, in the years 1977-8. The aptly named Tilla Tepe (Gold Mound) lies near the site of Yemshi Tepe, a Bactrian city of the Kushan period, where remains of a temple dating probably from the late second millennium BC were first explored. The six tombs excavated at Tilla Tepe, dating from the first century BC to the first century AD, yielded almost 20,000 gold objects, ornaments, jewels and so on, as well as important information about the population of that period. Certain aspects of the funerary rites point to Scythian origins; women's jewels prove that females enjoyed a privileged position in that society, a phenomenon typical of the nomads. The artistic quality of the jewels is inferior to the Hellenistic ones of Greek Bactria and may have been influenced by Parthia. On the other hand, the treatment of animal motifs reflects the Scythian-Sarmatian traditions and an affinity with the Siberian 'animal style'.

There are artefacts pointing to Greco-Bactrian origin, others which may be classified as Greco-Roman, some of local Bactrian style, and some showing a mixture of Greco-Roman and Siberian Altaic influences, while the animal style of Scytho-Sarmatian origin can also be found. The sixth category is that of objects showing local East Persian or Old Bactrian traditions pointing back to the Bronze Age. Here, then, according to Sarianidi,

> nomad art of the steppes made an important contribution by virtue of its dynamic though conventional lines and its naivete of expression . . . It may be suggested that nomad art served to catalyze the interaction of the two old – Greek and Bactrian – art trends . . .[32]

The site has, apparently, been damaged by illegal digging. The chronological gap between the Oxus Treasure and Tilla Tepe has now been filled by the newly found temple treasure at Takht-i Sanghin (S. Tajikistan).[33]

In the valley of the river Surkhan Darya 20km north-east of Akcha is the site of **Delbarjin**, a Kushan city probably destroyed by the Hephthalites. The excavations uncovered a Hellenistic temple, a citadel and a large building which might have been a palace. Terracotta statues of female deities, a Buddhist statue of a rider, and a fresco of an armed king sitting on a throne, were found here.

An entirely different site is **Dokhtar-i Nushirwan** in the valley of the Khulm river, north of Bamiyan, between the villages of Mohi and Roui. The site is somewhat similar to the rock-face at Naksh-i Rustam near Persepolis. In a narrow defile high above the river a niche has been cut above the natural step in the rock, and its wall has been covered by a series of Sasanian paintings. The floor of the niche is a platform 20m long and 2m wide. In the upper part traces of a large composition can be discerned, measuring some 12 x 4m; a central figure of a man with a Sasanian hair-style figures against a background of blue and brown, sitting on a throne surrounded by animal heads reminiscent of the hunting scenes at Taq-i Bostan. There are only a few small remnants in the lower part of the wall, mainly his legs, boots and the hem of his tunic. Certain decorative elements seem to have been borrowed from the Buddhist repertoire, but there are no Buddhas or *bodhisattvas*, and the entire scene is conceived in the traditional Iranian fashion.

According to an unconfirmed report, a Russian bomb has accidentally uncovered another treasure hoard, in the province of Pakhtia. In 1997, diggers found there large quantities of jewels, gold and silver coins as well as several statues.

Kunjakai some 25km west of Kabul, on the ancient road to Ghazni, consists of a stupa, a monastery and niches between the two, dominated by a citadel on the hill opposite. It has been looted since the 9th century, sculptures that were in the niches have now mostly disappeared and the stupa decoration has also been destroyed, probably by the Muslims, (first by the invasion of Yakublais Saffar at the end of the 9th century, and then by Mahmud of Ghazni a century later), it was similar to the stupa of Guldara (see p. 83-84), and was just a little smaller than the stupa of Tepe Maranjan (see p. 82). Its side measured 16.8m, the height was 6.4m. Either side of Kunjakai were found two cemeteries and three archaeological sites, so far unexplored.[34]

Khwaja Safa south of Kabul, near the Bala Hisar, mentioned for the first time by Charles Masson in 1830, was also a monastery with a stupa and a wall with niches, the sculptures of which have disappeared, In its lower part were several chapels some of which contain remnants of statues painted red and ochre and gilded.[35]

Tepe Naranj south of the citadel of Kabul, is a site dating from the 5-6th century and first excavated in 2004. It yielded some pre-Islamic pottery, bricks from the Hephthalite period and fragments of statues of bodhisattvas in Gandharan style. A major discovery was a statue of a sitting Buddha, with, on his right, a bodhisattva Vajrapani, in a style characteristic of the Hephthalite period. A circular meeting room, covered with a layer of ashes, is so far an unique architectural feature. Excavations in 2008 have uncovered traces of a small monastery below the site and another approximately 2km south-east, which seem to confirm an artistic style called by some scholars 'Hephthalo-Buddhist'.[36]

In 2005, traces of a monastery were found in the **Babur Gardens** in Kabul (see above and p. 160-1), linked with the monasteries of Tepe Maranjan, Khair Khane and Tepe Khazana.[37]

Mes-i Aynak is a major site, some 30km south of Kabul, at an altitude of 2500m, in immediate proximity of a giant copper mine owned by the Chinese, which threatens to destroy it in the near future. There were three monasteries and at least two large stupas. Shards of pottery found here indicate that the site was occupied since the 3rd century BC until the 15th. So far, one of the monasteries, near the village of Gul Ahmad, occupied probably until the end of the 10th century has been explored. Two chapels and some monastic cells were uncovered, next to which were found eight large jars buried in the ground which served probably as water reservoirs. A small square stupa had on one side three lions painted red, of which only the front paws can be discerned. A clay statue of a sitting Buddha was also painted in red ochre. Generally, the style of these sculptures, technically more primitive than the sophisticated 'Hephthalo-Buddhist' style at Tepe Naranj, points to the last period of occupation of the site. Most of the paintings and sculptures have disappeared, probably because of a military attack, when the monks tried to protect the site by blocking it with bricks and clay. Ancient copper smelting took place here, as blackened areas of the ground indicate. Some 150 statues have been found.[38]

5 Early Islamic

Medieval Kabul

In the earliest part of its history **Kabul** was overshadowed by Kapisa (Begram), which was the capital and royal residence in the periods of both Greek Bactria and the Kushan empire, and remained the centre of the area under the Sasanians and the Hephthalites. Suen Tsang, the Chinese pilgrim of the seventh century AD, barely mentions Kabul, but describes Kapisa at length and with enthusiasm. Kabul began to play a more important role at the time of the Arab conquest when the victorious advance of Islam was halted by the stubborn resistance of its rulers, the Turkish or Indianized dynasty of the Kabulshahs or Ratbil Shahs, also referred to as the Turk-Shahi. Although Kabul was taken in 644, the Arab occupation did not last long and the Turk-Shahis survived for another 200 years until, around 850, they were replaced by the purely Indian Hindushahis. The definitive victory of Islam came only with the Ghaznavids, who captured Kabul in 977.

A famous *Kuhandiz* or castle once existed here, and the town which was approached by only a single road was well fortified.

> It was the great emporium of Indian trade, indigo being brought here for export to the value of a million gold dinars yearly. Further, most of the precious stuffs of India and China were warehoused here. As early as the tenth century the Moslems, the Jews, and the idolaters had each a separate quarter in Kabul, where the suburbs, the markets and the merchants' warehouses were alike famous.[1]

Kazwini, in the thirteenth century, writes that Kabul was then famous for the breed of she-camels known as Bactrian, the best in all Central Asia. Ibn Battuta who visited in the next century says that the city had by then sunk into a mere village, inhabited by the tribe of Persians known as Afghans.

The **Bala Hissar**, or citadel, stands on a rocky spur where a fortress is known to have stood already in the seventh century. The walls of Kabul, 6m high and almost 4m thick which the Hephthalites are said to have built originally, start here. It was in this citadel that Babur was married and his son and successor Humayun was born. In Moghul times, gardens and palaces were built within the citadel which probably resembled the forts of Lahore, Delhi or Agra. It became a royal residence again at the end of the eighteenth century, under Timur Shah.

Medieval Balkh

According to Yakubi, **Balkh** in the ninth century was the greatest city of all Khorasan. It had three concentric walls and 13 gates and was known as 'Beautiful Balkh'. Outside the town houses extended over an area measuring three miles square. There were 'two scores of Friday mosques in the city'. The houses were built of sun-dried bricks, and the same material was used for the city wall, outside which was a deep moat. The markets and the main Friday mosque stood in the central part of the city. All around Balkh lay gardens producing oranges, grapes and sugar-cane, which were all exported in quantity.[2]

Mukaddasi gives a lively description of its beauty, splendour and riches, its many streams, its cheap living, the abundance of goods, the innumerable broad streets, the Great mosque and many well-built palaces. No wonder Mahmud of Ghazna made it his favourite residence at the close of the tenth century. The first disaster struck with the raid of the Oghuz Turks in 1155, when the city was destroyed; but it was rebuilt close by and soon recovered its former splendour. This is how Yakut found it in the early thirteenth century, immediately before its second, and far more extensive, devastation by the Mongols. It was still in ruins in the fourteenth century when Ibn Battuta passed through:

> We crossed the river Oxus into the land of Khorasan and after a day and a half's march through a sandy uninhabited waste we reached Balkh. It is in utter ruin and uninhabited, but anyone seeing it would think it inhabited on account of the solidity of its construction.[3]

The description by Marco Polo, who came 40 years previously, does not greatly differ:

> Balc is a noble city and great, though it was much greater in former days. But the Tartars and other nations have greatly ravaged and destroyed it. There were formerly many fine palaces and buildings of marble, and the ruins of them still remain. The people of the city tell that it was here that Alexander took to wife the daughter of Darius.[4]

In the fields south-west of Balkh stands a small ruined structure, which has turned out to be the oldest existing building in the area and one of the oldest known monuments of Islam. It is the so-called **Noh Gumbad** mosque (nine cupolas), also known as the Masjid Hadji Piyade or, as Hoag calls it, Masjid-i Tarikh. It is an open pavilion standing alone, rectangular on the inside and measuring 18.3 x 15.5m, and almost square on the outside at a size of 20 x 19.5m, with nine cupolas, 4.1m in diameter, supported by massive columns 1.56m in diameter[5], and joined by low, pointed arches. The cupolas have collapsed and the fallen masonry hides the lower parts of the columns, so that their height cannot be measured. Some of the arches supporting the domes still exist. The *mihrab* was in the centre of the south-western wall. The material used was partly baked bricks and partly mud bricks (*pakhsa*), covered with alabaster stucco. The decoration on the arches and capitals is mostly of incised stucco

43 Mosque Noh Gumbad. Detail

and shows stylized floral motifs, divided into geometrical fields and separated either by meanders or by simple straight or circular bands. There are also geometrical ornaments consisting of circles and half-circles, octagons and four-leaf figures.

Three different architectural elements were combined in the building: the *iwan*, the *apadana* and the Soghdian *kushk*. The three barrel-vaulted and arcaded naves may have been derived from the Iranian *iwan*; the square with four columns in the centre supporting four cross-beams and thus dividing the whole into nine equal parts, points to the *apadana*, while the square structure consisting of nine cells covered with cupolas and divided by walls had its origins in the *kushk*. The dating therefore poses serious problems. Pugachenkova, who based her dating mainly on architectural analysis, found similarities with certain monuments in Iran and Turkestan dating from the tenth century. Nevertheless, it bears no resemblance to the early Arab type of mosque and points directly to pre-Islamic models, for example, to Sasanian palaces and temples. On the other hand, the decoration which is 'of exceptionally high quality', suggests ninth-century origins, and certain elements of tenth-century decoration are lacking. Thus, according to Pugachenkova, the building should be situated at the very beginning of the tenth century; but Melikian-Chirvani[6], analysing the decoration in particular, came to different conclusions. He found striking similarities with the ninth-century stucco panels of Samarra, and as certain architectural elements seemed to point to an even earlier origin, he was inclined to place the mosque in the late eighth century. According to Golombek[7] the 'deep shadow' technique of the stucco carving resembles that of Samarra. Thus the architecture represents a mixture of foreign models imported from the West (Mesopotamia, Iran) and traditional local styles. The fact that local models were used to facilitate the adaptation of the foreign ones would point to a period fairly soon after the conquest of Islam and yet later than the Samarra monuments. It would seem likely, therefore, that the building originated some time in the first half of the ninth century. At any rate, the Noh Gumbad mosque belongs to the transitional period of medieval architecture, when it was still linked with pre-Islamic traditions, but new features already began to emerge, foreshadowing the formation of a new architectural style which would reach its peak between the tenth and twelfth century.

A little cemetery with a few tombstones lies on the north side of the mosque. The style of some of the tombstones links them to the eleventh, fifteenth and seventeenth centuries. Adjacent to the north wall of the mosque is a clay structure of a later period, the tomb of the saint Hadji Piyade (called Khoja Parda by Pugachenkova).

In the environs of Balkh a wall some 36 miles long once surrounded the town and the neighbouring villages. It ceased to exist in the ninth century.

Dawlatabad, Sar-i Pol, Baba Hatim

Within the district of Juzjan, west of Balkh, the village of **Dawlatabad** contains a *minaret* which was first mentioned in 1936, and first described by J. Sourdel-Thomine in 1953.[8] It is a round structure in baked bricks without a base, decorated with ornaments in unglazed bricks and incised stucco and dating from the years 1108-9. The décor is similar to that of the late Ghaznavid monuments such as the tower of Bahramshah in Ghazni and the arch in Kala-i Bost, or, in Turkestan, the minarets in Uzkend, Bukhara or Vabkent.

At the top is a band of *Kufic* inscription in incised stucco or terracotta, followed lower down by bands of geometrical ornaments in brick consisting of octagons filled with medallions decorated with *naskhi* script, then a band of ornamental *naskhi* in incised stucco and, at the bottom, a band of geometrical ornament, again with hexagons and triangles in brick and a rather crude stucco. The type of *naskhi* script used is typical of the twelfth or thirteenth century and represents one of the earliest examples of Iranian inscription of this kind. The *Kufic* comes in three different types, with a floral or plaited frame, or in plaited form.

Two shrines of the Seljukid period described by A.D.H. Bivar[9] can be seen in Juzjan, near the village of **Sar-i Pol**. There were altogether some ten buildings around the village; but only two are still standing. The first, **Imam-i Khurd** (the Lesser Imam) is about 1.5km south-east of the centre of the village. It is a domed structure approximately 3m square with a rectangular ante-chamber; inside, the walls were once decorated with carved stucco which was partly covered with whitewash in a restoration. The *mihrab* is decorated with floral ornaments and *Kufic* inscriptions; and one of the finest *Kufic* inscriptions in the Iranian world encircles the building at the base of the dome. Its content is strongly Shi'ite. The building dates probably from the late eleventh or early twelfth century.

The other extant building, **Imam-i Kalan** (the Greater Imam) is about 1km from the village and less well preserved. The *mihrab* is sadly dilapidated, but still shows some stucco decoration and remains of an inscription in bold and flowing *naskhi*. It is not earlier than the twelfth century.

Melikian-Chirvani discovered a Ghaznavid mausoleum called **Baba Hatim** some 40 miles from Balkh, on the Akcha road.[10] It is a domed structure about 7m square and 10-12m high, with a simple arched doorway of classical tenth-century design. The decoration in unglazed bricks looks earlier than eleventh-century and resembles that of the mausoleum of Arab-Ata in Tim which is dated 978.[11] The calligraphy around the entrance as well as inside is of superior quality, and probably dates from the first half of the eleventh century. Some of the decorative motifs on the *mihrab* wall, in carved stucco, resemble those of the Noh Gumbad mosque. Inside, the dome rests on *squinches* or quarter-vault pendentives. Above the entrance there is an inscription frieze in floral *Kufic*, in incised terracotta, and another, in decorative *Kufic*, is on the drum.

Ghazni

The period of glory of **Ghazna** (Ghazni is a modern spelling) was comparatively short-lived, spanning less than two centuries. Little is known of its history in earlier times except that, after the demise of the Hephthalites (White Huns) some time in the seventh century, it was ruled, together with Kabul, by the Turk-Shahis, a dynasty which introduced a strong Indian influence. The Turk-Shahis were subsequently replaced, in the middle of the ninth century, by the Hindushahi rajas, a dynasty of Indian origin, and, most probably, of Brahmin faith. The Arab raids from Sistan, which became frequent from the end of the seventh century onwards, were aimed more at exacting tribute, plunder and slaves than at establishing a permanent military occupation; and in general, the local rulers were able to preserve their authority. Connections with India were numerous, and there is much evidence of Indian religious and cultural influence until as late as the tenth century.

Samanid control of Ghazna was established when, in 961, their Commander-in-Chief in Khorasan, Alptigin (Tigin, also spelled Tegin or Tagin, is a Turkish military title) wrested the town from the last Hindushahi ruler and was himself appointed governor. By then the power of the Samanids was already in decline and the administration and defence of their outlying provinces was entrusted, to an ever-increasing extent, to Turkish mercenaries and slaves. Alptigin was followed by a series of other Turkish slave governors until the office fell in 977 to Sabuktagin (Sebüktigin), who held it for twenty years ruling virtually autonomously.

The rise to power of his eldest son, Mahmud, was fast and spectacular. After the death of Sabuktagin he concentrated in his hands the governorships of all southern provinces of the Samanid empire and, when their dynasty was extinguished in 1005, he was in absolute control not only of Ghazna, but also of Balkh, Bost, Herat and Termez. In the rest of Khorasan, namely in Merv and Nishapur, his power was challenged by the Turkish Karakhanids who claimed the succession of the Samanids, but he defeated them decisively in 1008 and thus became the undisputed master of an enormous empire stretching from western Iran to the gates of India. Over the next two decades he added to his territories Sistan, Khorezm and the principalities of the upper Oxus. Even before he had consolidated his holdings in Khorasan, he began to invade India, against which he conducted at least 17 campaigns.

There can be little doubt that artisans and craftsmen were imported from the conquered lands, just as were scholars and men of letters. Gradually, during the reigns of Mahmud and Masud I, 'a certain style of building developed which used marble and carved decoration grafted on to the more sober traditional Persian technique of brick construction and moulded brick decoration'.[12] Little has survived of the buildings of this period, the main reasons being, as listed by Bosworth:

> The effects of an extreme climate; natural catastrophes like earthquakes and floods; the ravages of war; the use of comparatively perishable materials like sun-dried brick, for stone and even fired brick were infrequently used; indifferent workmanship; the theft of building materials by the local population: all these combined to make much building work, however splendid and imposing at the time it was put up, impermanent and short-lived.[13]

Unfortunately, 'no adequate description has come down to us of Ghaznah at the time when it was rebuilt and adorned by Mahmud . . .'

A generation prior to this, Istakhri described the place as like Bamiyan, with fine streams but few gardens. He added that no city of that area was richer in merchants and merchandise, for it was the 'port of India'. Mukaddasi gives a long list of the names of its districts and towns, most of which, however, it is impossible to identify at the present day. 'It was about the year 1024 that Mahmud had rebuilt Ghaznah, on his return home laden with the spoils of India, and the city then reached its greatest splendour, which lasted for over a century.'[14] It was really the Ghaznavid sultans who raised Ghazna into the centre of an empire; Babur, who visited it after it had relapsed into insignificance, wondered at this: 'Ghazna is a very humble place; strange indeed it is that rulers in whose hands were Hindustan and Khurasan should have chosen it for their capital!'[15]

After the defeat of Sultan Masud by the Seljuqs in 1040, Khorasan was lost to the Ghaznavids, and the cultural orientation of the remaining empire changed even more towards the east. It acquired a predominantly Indian outlook,[16] which its heartland had no doubt owned even before the arrival of Alptigin and Sabuktagin. Overshadowed by the growing importance of Lahore, the city survived for another century, until the Ghorid sultan Ala-ud-Din took Ghazna by storm in 1149.

The tomb of the great Mahmud in the village of Rauza nevertheless appears to have been spared (unless it was restored), for Ibn Battuta saw it in the fourteenth century. He describes Ghazna at that time as in ruins for the most part, although he adds that formerly it had been an immense city. His contemporary Mustawfi speaks of it as a small town, with a very cold climate due to its great elevation, but he gives no details of any importance.

The **mausoleum of Sultan Mahmud** is less than a kilometre outside Ghazni, on the right-hand side of the road when coming from Kabul. It is a modern building constructed on the site of a palace in a garden which was once called Bagh-i Firuzi (Emerald Garden), and was one of Mahmud's favourite resting places. The tomb inside was in all probability erected by Mahmud's son Masud I, and can be dated to the first half of the eleventh century. It is a marble-faced sarcophagus with a triangular prismatic slab on top; the slab is decorated on one side with a carved two-line inscription band in superb calligraphy, and a smaller band running along the base. On the other side is a three-lobed medallion with six lines of *naskhi* script. In the middle of each side of the sarcophagus is an ornamental medallion framed with a flat *Kufic* inscription. The stone panels of the cenotaph show that the pointed lobate arches were a popular device at that time of the Ghaznavid period. The first good photographs of the tomb were taken by A. Godard in 1923. They were analysed by Flury, who expressed some doubts about the dating of the monument.[17] The carved lettering on the slab, even more than the floral elements, seemed to point to a later period, following the destruction of Ghazna in 1149. The *naskhi* characters, which are more decorative than the usual Ghaznavid calligraphy, would seem to confirm this, but Flury had not seen the inscriptions or the medallions on the sarcophagus, for the tomb was surrounded by a grille in Godard's time, and the sarcophagus could not be photographed. Godard himself believed that the sarcophagus was the original part of the tomb.[18] The prismatic slab, which is of a different kind of marble and merely balanced on top of the sarcophagus without being in any way fixed to it, was probably added at a later date. In Godard's view, the tomb shows the first traces of Indian influence in Islamic art. The bulbous arches in the medallions as well as the naturalism of its floral decoration already show certain tendencies, which crystallized under the later Ghaznavids into what became known as Indo-Muslim art. This is hotly disputed by some scholars,[19] who maintain that nothing here 'is in the style definitely derived from India'.[20]

The tomb has attracted the notice of more travellers than the famous 'Towers of Ghazni':

> Ibn Battutta . . . says it was surmounted by a hospice. Babur looked in of course, and saw the tombs of Sultans Ibrahim and Masud near by. Next came Vigne in 1836, and six years later an English army, which took away the doors of the Tomb because some idiot of a historian . . . had said they were the doors of the Hindu temple of Somnath in Gujerat which Mahmud had stolen when he sacked it. Prodigies of transport . . . were employed to bring them to Agra, while Lord Ellenborough requested the Princes of India to observe how worthy the British Government 'proves itself of your love, when regarding your honour as its own, it asserts the power of its arms to restore to you the gates of the temple of Somnath . . . ' The ridicule that greeted this announcement consigned the doors to permanent obscurity in the Fort of Agra . . . Their wood is that of Afghan deodar, and an inscription on the lintel invokes the forgiveness of God on Abulkasim Mahmud, son of Sabuktagin. Yet the legend of their Hindu origin still persists in school textbooks.[21]

The door of Agra is still regarded as a prime example of Ghaznavid calligraphy and floral décor in carved wood.[22] After the First World War, when Godard visited the tomb, it lay open to the sky. When Byron himself saw it, the present building already existed.

> The virtue of the tomb as a work of art lies in the depth and fullness of the carving, in the glow of the marble where age has caressed it, and above all in the main inscription. Kufic lettering has a functional beauty; regarded as pure design, its extraordinary emphasis seems in itself a form of oratory, a transposition of speech from the audible to the visible . . . none can compare with these tall rhythmic ciphers, involved with dancing foliage, which mourn the loss of Mahmud, the conqueror of India, Persia, and Oxiana, nine centuries after his death, in the capital where he ruled.[23]

The medieval city of Ghazna once stood on the desolate plain between the village and the modern town. In the middle of this area, accessible by a dusty road running westwards from the main road towards the town, stand **two decorated towers**, the most famous monuments of Ghazni and two of the very few surviving examples of Ghaznavid architecture and decoration. This is how Byron described them:

> The difference between them is in breadth, the diameter of the larger, excluding the stone base, about twenty-four feet, and that of the smaller about twenty-two. Both are built of a rich toffee brick tinged with red, and are adorned with carved terracotta of the same colour. In each case, each of the eight recesses between the star-points is divided into eight ornamental zones of varying depths. Between the third and fourth, fifth and sixth and sixth and seventh zones, the brickwork is interrupted by wooden joists. Apart from the zig-zag patterns in which bricks are set, the ornament of the smaller tower is confined to two narrow bands of terracotta in the middle, and to the sixteen panels of bold Kufic lettering at the top . . . The larger tower is richer, its bricks are closer set, and all eight zones are filled with elaborate ornament, sometimes bordered with lesser inscriptions. Another sixteen panels round the top proclaim the titles of Masud; their Kufic is taller and more graceful, standing out from a maze of pattern like soldiers from a crowd . . .[24]

A sketch made by Vigne in 1836 shows that, originally, they were more than twice as high (approximately 140ft). Above the lower octagonal part rose a circular shaft, of which an old photograph was kept in the British Legation in Kabul. Byron, who saw the photograph, described the shaft as follows:

> The first twenty-five feet of this shaft were plain and were probably hidden, when the tower was first built, by a wooden balcony. Thereafter it was divided into ornamental ribs, alternately curved and flat. These were surmounted by eight pairs of elongated niches and by a belt of carving which looks as if it contained a Kufic inscription.[25]

44 The tower of Masud III, Ghazni

There has been much confusion over the founders of these towers. J.A. Rawlinson published their inscriptions in 1843, ascribing the larger and more splendid of the two to Mahmud, son of Sabuktagin.

> But Rawlinson must have mixed his notes; for in 1925, when Flury the epigraphist obtained some photographs, he found that the inscription relating to Mahmud was actually on the smaller tower, while the larger bore the name of his descendant Masud III, son of Ibrahim. The smaller tower, therefore, must date from before 1030, the larger from between 1099 and 1114.[26]

Early Islamic

45 The tower of Bahramshah, Ghazni

But it was Flury the epigraphist who misread the photographs. He was right that the larger tower was built by Masud III, and should be dated between 1099 and 1114; but the smaller tower, with a much simpler decoration, is actually younger rather than older and must be attributed to one of the last Ghaznavids, Bahramshah (1118-52). Yet Flury himself had doubts about his assessment of the 'Tower of Mahmud': 'If there were not a date on it, one would hardly dare to ascribe it to the eleventh century.'[27] He compared the inscription bands, the calligraphy and arabesque decoration of both towers and rightly saw that the apparently simple inscription of 'Mahmud' was in fact highly sophisticated, better proportioned and better balanced than that on the Masud tower.

46 *The tower of Bahramshah, Ghazni*

47 *The tower of Bahramshah, Ghazni. Detail*

48 The tower of Masud III, Ghazni. Detail

A detailed epigraphic analysis of the tower of Bahramshah was made by J. Sourdel-Thomine.[28] This places it firmly under the reign of that last member of the dynasty, who still resided in Ghazna. Architecturally, it belongs to the end of the eleventh century and as such could be compared, for example, with the minaret of Uzkend.[29] The decoration lacks the richness of the arabesque and floral ornament of the older tower, but its geometrical patterns in brick are, like the script, too sophisticated for the building to belong to an earlier period. The base is richly decorated with carved terracotta and brick panels of geometrical patterns which tend to be unfinished towards the bottom. Both towers have lower sections in the form of eight-pointed stars. The superstructures, still visible on Vigne's sketch, have fallen down.[30]

Opinions still differ over whether the towers were built as minarets or as some kind of 'victory towers', like those found in Hindu architecture. Renz,[31] taking into account the distance between them (about 400m), rules out that they could have been minarets belonging to the same mosque. Diez thought their star-shaped plan reminiscent of an ancient Aryan cosmogony: from the 'world ground-plan' rise the towers of victory like 'trees of the world', each of them symbolizing the 'navel of the world', and thus combining under an Islamic guise Irano-Indian and Turkishshamanistic ideas[32] (the minaret of Jam (see p.127) should also be seen as such a 'centrepoint of the world). In Byron's view

> They were built as minarets, commemorative rather than religious, for the ground gives no evidence that there was ever a mosque in the neighbourhood. It was a Sasanian habit to build such towers, and after the coming of Islam the Persians kept it up, till about the fourteenth century . . .[33]

To the north of the road linking the two towers, the crest and slopes of a low range were once a favoured residential area of the Ghaznavid aristocracy. Several villas were excavated here and interesting specimens of lustreware were found, the earliest on Afghan soil. On the slope of the hillock, a modern pavilion houses the **tomb of Sabuktagin**, the founder of the dynasty.

The sarcophagus is simple and stands on a low base with sloping sides; the whole structure stands on a massive marble socle. Godard was shown an old photograph of the tomb, with no socle and with the base broken in two; obviously, some restoration must have taken place early last century. Unlike the tomb of Mahmud, both the form and the décor of this tomb are purely Iranian. A *Kufic* inscription runs around the sarcophagus, and another along the sides of the base; and these were also analysed by Flury[34] who placed them 'most probably' at the end of the tenth century. They would, therefore, rate among the earliest epigraphic documents in Iranian provinces.

On the opposite side of the town, on the old road to Kabul, is a holy shrine, the **Ziyarat-i Mui Mubarak**. Interesting marble tombstones, some perhaps dating from the Ghaznavid period, can be seen in the nearby cemetery. North-east of the city, not far from the towers, are the ruins of a **mausoleum** belonging to **Sultan Ibrahim** and his son **Masud ben Ibrahim**.

To the south of the road, in 1957 the Italian archaeologists discovered the remnants of a **palace** believed to be built by **Masud III** more or less at the same time as the older tower, and usually assigned the date 1111. A large courtyard has been uncovered, measuring 42 x 20m, which was paved with marble, with an *iwan* in the middle of each side, and surrounded by a number of buildings including a mosque, an audience hall, administrative offices and royal apartments. The main entrance was on the north side.

The layout of the palace is similar to that of Lashkar-i Bazar, but the decoration is much richer. The *four-iwan* court was surrounded by butresses, which probably supported arched niches. The carved marble panels show three-lobed arches decorated with palmettes, and scrolls with animals and birds; above these was a *Kufic* inscription in Persian, and higher still more scrolls and inscriptions in stucco and terracotta. Out of 510 epigraphic panels, 44 are (or rather were) left *in situ*, painted blue on a bright red ground. The whole inscription was c.250m long, an eulogy of the Ghaznavid dynasty modelled on the famous epic *Shahname* by Ferdausi and extolling also the beauties of the palace. It is one of the earliest surviving secular inscriptions glorifying both the building and its patron – a form which in the eleventh century may have been common throughout the Islamic world.[35]

The exploits of Masud, especially in his Indian campaigns, were the occasion for the composition of this remarkable panegyric in Persian on the military achievements of the whole line of sultans. 'This was written in the *mutaqarib* metre (that employed by the *Shah-nama*) and inscribed on slabs forming part of a dado round the main courtyard of the palace of Ghazna . . . Here, it would seem, is the Iranian epic genre at last specifically adapted to the greater glory of the Ghaznavid dynasty.'[36]

The decoration in terracotta, stucco and marble consisted of geometrical ornaments, arabesques and inscriptions in *Kufic* and *naskhi*. Most of them had traces of colouring: gold and yellow in the lettering, blue and red on the background, and remains of carved terracotta were found on the walls. Apart from this however the construction of the palace was probably rather flimsy, as can be gathered from the report by Baihaqi (995-1077) about an earlier palace built by Masud I. This had taken four years to complete, cost seven million *dirhams* and was erected by corvée labour; yet it was already dilapidated when Baihaqi wrote his chronicle.[37]

The Italian expedition uncovered thousands of objects in Ghazni, including marble statues of Hindu gods worn smooth by the feet of Muslim worshippers. The sultans had placed the idols under the threshold of the mosques for use as stepping stones.

Lashkar-i Bazar

South of the road from Kandahar to Herat, at the confluence of the rivers Helmand and Arghandab, a vast area of ruins stretching for more than 7km along the Helmand marks the ancient city of **Bost** (Kala-i Bost) and the winter residence of the Ghaznavid sultans, the palaces of **Lashkar-i Bazar**.

Bost, at the southern end of the site, has always been an important place:

> Istakhri mentions that at its gate was the great bridge of boats . . . across which the high road came in from Zaranj. Bust was the second largest city in Sijistan in the tenth century, the people were in easy circumstances, and are described as dressing after the fashion of the men of Irak, and as being for the most part merchants who traded with India. The neighbouring lands were extremely fertile, growing dates and grapes . . . Half-a-league distant, on the Ghaznah road, was Al-Askar, 'the Camp', built like a small city, where the Sultan had his residence. In the thirteenth century Yakut writes that Bust was almost entirely a ruin and he notices the heat of the climate, while mentioning the abundance of its gardens.[38]

Like Ghazna, Bost was first laid low by the Ghorid Sultan Ala-ud Din in 1151, rebuilt and then destroyed again by the Mongols of Chingiz-Khan. At the close of the fourteenth century the site and its environs were yet again devastated by Timur, who destroyed one of the great dams across the Helmand that contained the head of water which served to irrigate all the western lands of Sistan (now the lake has dried up).

The citadel of **Bost** commands an impressive view over the neighbouring countryside, littered far into the steppe with remnants of clay walls and ruined buildings. At the foot of the citadel mound stands an elegant, slightly pointed arch with a 25m span, built of baked bricks and decorated on the inside with geometrical ornament; on the outside are epigraphic bands in flowering *Kufic*, both on the arch itself and on the supporting columns. Its origins can be dated to the late Ghaznavid period, although some elements in its decoration are probably of a somewhat later date than the eleventh century. The arch was heavily restored some 20 years ago but, when it began to show some conspicuous cracks, the Afghan authorities of the day decided to build a supporting structure inside (1978). The horseshoe-shaped blind arches on either side of it are covered with simple geometrical ornament in baked bricks and were probably inspired by India.

The Arabic al-Askar (the Camp) has become the Persian Lashkargah (Soldiers' Place) or **Lashkar-i Bazar** (Soldiers' Bazaar). It is a group of three palaces at the north end of the site on the bank of the Helmand, with courtyards, gardens and a number of auxiliary structures inside the walled enclosure. It was discovered in 1948 by the French archaeological mission and excavated in five successive campaigns which concentrated mainly on the southern palace, the largest of the three. Parts of this palace can be dated to the end of the tenth century, but it seems to have been finally completed by about 1036. If this is correct, the construction was begun by Mahmud and finished by his son Masud I.

A straight avenue about half a kilometre long provided access to the palace from the south. It was obviously the main shopping street, for it was lined on both sides with shops and stalls of which about 100 have been uncovered. The site of the palace is over 500m long. The southern part of it was occupied by a vast rectangular forecourt surrounded by a wall. On one side was a large mosque with an 86m frontage and a portal of 10.5m, built probably in the time of Mahmud and Masud I. Its two aisles, supported on decorated columns, were parallel to the *kibla* wall and joined at the *mihrab* by a domed chamber. On the north side of this forecourt was the entrance, an *iwan* leading to a spacious vestibule in the form of a cross, through which the centre of the palace was reached.

A detailed description is given by Hoag:

> The walls of *adobe* were reinforced with timber and baked brick or stone foundations, and the decoration was of polychromed terracotta and stucco. Frescoes of the sultan's armed guard were in the throne room as well . . . A monumental south entrance led to a cruciform hall of honor, probably domed, from which, through an *iwan*, one entered a court of about 167 by 207 feet. This had east and west *iwans* and, to the north, a larger *iwan* leading to a square throne room, probably once domed.[39]

Private apartments formed the corners, each grouped around a smaller private courtyard. There is a striking similarity between the layout of the palace and that of some *caravanserais*. Both have semicylindrical corner towers, monumental projecting entrances, *four-iwan* courts and pairs of cruciform apartments next to the iwan leading to the domed chamber.

A canal passed through the audience hall and the adjacent rooms carrying running water across the entire width of the palace, and feeding toilets and bathrooms as well as water tanks; the water was lifted into this canal by some kind of mechanism, but the source has not been found. A small mosque richly decorated with stucco ornament was discovered in 1950 inside the great audience hall.[40]

The material of the decoration was carved stucco on the façade facing the forecourt and terracotta on the entrance iwan. There were panels of geometrical ornaments and epigraphic bands dating from the mid- or late twelfth century. Wall paintings were uncovered on the lower parts of the walls of the audience hall. Above them were geometrical ornaments in baked brick. Two large panels on the wall facing the entrance were framed with inscriptions and filled with carved stucco ornament in the same style as the arch of Bost. On the side of the entrance iwan were hexagonal ornaments and calligraphic bands in elongated *Kufic*.

The wall-paintings were removed and placed in the Museum of Kabul. Remnants have been found of some 44 figures out of a total of perhaps 60, all clad in ceremonial robes in lively colours and carrying insignia of rank – it is assumed that they depict the sultan's guard of Turkish slaves. Schlumberger[41] finds traces of Buddhist and Sasanian traditions in this decoration, while the costumes indicate Chinese Turkestan, with a marked influence of the steppe nomads. Such a depiction on the walls of a procession of palace guards was an ancient habit of Oriental rulers which can be traced back to Persepolis and Susa.

The palace was rebuilt several times, both before and after its sack by the Ghorids in 1149. It was finally destroyed by the Mongols in 1221. Further north were two other palaces and a series of walled courts and gardens.

Medieval Herat

The oasis of Herat stretches along the right bank of the Hari Rud, between the river and the foothills of the Safid Kuh range, the ancient Paropamisus, in the north. On the left bank, the green belt is confined to the immediate vicinity of the river bed. The stony and sandy desert begins, abruptly, only a few hundred yards from the river. From the air, it can clearly be seen that the irrigation network extended much farther in the past and that the area of cultivated farmland began much higher up-stream than now. Medieval sources speak of irrigated land and populous villages on the left bank, too, of which there is now no trace. Nevertheless, the mild climate and the fertility of its soil make the province of Herat the wealthiest and most prosperous in the country.

Herat is, no doubt, one of the oldest cities on Afghan soil. When Cyrus the Great of Persia conquered it in the sixth century BC it was already an important stronghold, mentioned in the *Avesta* as Hairava. Alexander took it in 330 BC, rebuilt and strengthened the fort and gave it the name of Alexandria Ariana; it was then held in succession by the Seleucids, Parthians, Kushans and Sasanians. For a period in the fifth and sixth century it was dominated by the Hephthalites, or White Huns, who ruled their empire from the nearby province of Badghiz. At the end of the sixth century it was sacked by the Turks, and in 645 fell to the Arabs; from then on, it remained firmly Muslim, but the story of conquest continued. It was taken by Mahmud of Ghazna in the year 1000, fell to the Seljuks after the defeat of the Ghaznavids in 1040 and to the Ghorids in 1175. Although the Ghorid domination lasted less than half a century, it is the earliest period from which some architectural monuments have been preserved in Herat. For a few years prior to the Mongols, the province was part of the empire of the Khorezmshahs. After the invasion, it was ruled by a local dynasty, the Karts, or Kart-Maliks, which in its turn was deposed by Timur in 1381.

Ibn Hawkal and Mukaddasi have described Herat in the tenth century. It was a great city, measuring half a league square, with a citadel, surrounded by a wall with four gates, at each of which, inside the town, was a market. The great Friday mosque stood in the midst of the chief market and 'no mosque in all Khorasan or Sijistan was its equal in beauty'.[42] Behind it, on the western side, was the prison. The names of the four gates have also come down to us: there was the Bab Saray, or Palace Gate to the north, on the Balkh road; the Bab Ziyad to the west, towards Nishapur; the Firuzabad gate to the south towards Sistan; and to the east was the Bab Khushk in the direction of the Ghor mountains. These four gates were all of wood, except the Bab Saray which, Ibn Hawkal says, was of iron.

The citadel also had four gates, with names corresponding to those of the city gates. Outside the city were extensive suburbs, but the land was irrigated mainly to the south, down to the Hari Rud where 'populous villages lay one after the other, for a day's march or more, along the Sijistan road'.[43] Figs and grapes were the most famous produce of the country. There was irrigated farmland to the east and west as well, but desert to the north towards the mountains.

Shortly before the Mongol invasion, Yakut considered Herat to be 'the richest and largest city he had ever seen'.[44] Slightly later Kazwini noted that 'there might be seen many mills turned by wind, not by water' which was for him an uncommon sight.[45] Some of these curious mills, working on the principle of a vertical shaft revolving in a cylindrical tower, are still in existence, powered now as in the thirteenth century by the energy of the famous 'wind of 120 days' (*bad-i-sad-o-bist ruz*).

It was in the twelfth century, under the Ghorid dynasty, that Herat reached its greatest splendour. According to Mustawfi 'there were 12,000 shops in its markets, 6,000 hot baths and 659 colleges, the population being reckoned at 444,000'.[46] The city recovered quickly after the Mongol disaster, for chroniclers and travellers of the fourteenth century, among them the ubiquitous Ibn Battuta, considered it the most populous city of all Khorasan after Nishapur (this does not necessarily mean much, as the only two other major cities in Khorasan, Merv and Balkh, were in ruins).

The **citadel** (Arg, Bala Hissar) is an imposing building constructed in the ninth or tenth century on the site of an earlier fortress, the origins of which would probably go back to antiquity. It forms a rectangle of approximately 1300 x 1400m and stands on an artificial mound in the north-west corner of the city. No excavations have been carried out here and the hypothesis that this may be the site of Alexander's

49 The citadel, Herat

fort, Alexandria Ariana, still awaits confirmation. The ramparts and the round towers were rebuilt several times, in particular by the Kart dynasty after the Mongol period, and by Shahrukh in the wake of Timur's conquest.

Although the **Friday Mosque** was, after the citadel, the oldest monumental building in Herat, medieval texts contain surprisingly little information about it. According to Ibn Hawkal, it stood in the midst of the chief market, and no mosque in all of Khorasan or Sistan was its equal in beauty. Other sources are even more laconic; a more meaningful description would not appear before the nineteenth century and by then, of course, the original aspect of the building had been altered beyond recognition.

The layout of the building is that of a traditional Iranian *four-iwan* mosque. On the west side – or the south-west, according to some sources – of a courtyard measuring approximately 90 x 58.5m is the main *iwan* with a prayer hall, flanked by two minarets. Opposite is the entrance *iwan* and, in the middle of the longer sides of the rectangle, two lateral *iwans*. All the *iwans* are unusually deep. Inside the arcaded wings enclosing the courtyard are halls of columns concealed behind the façade niches. Each of the courtyard *iwans* has its counterpart in the outer façade. Each of the outer iwans is flanked by two minarets, and there is a small turret in each corner.

Although Isfizari, writing in 1405-6, attributes the founding of the mosque to the Ghorid sultan Ghiyat-ud Din Sam and to his successor Shahab-ud Din and dates it around 1200, it is known that there was an earlier mosque in the same place. The Ghorid structure was probably damaged by the Mongols and was then substantially

50 The Friday Mosque, Herat. Eastern iwan

rebuilt under the Kart dynasty in the early fourteenth century. According to the records the mosque was spared when Timur sacked the city, but reached its full splendour again only under Shahrukh at the turn of the fourteenth and fifteenth century, when Shahrukh was Timur's governor in Herat. Over the next 100 years, however, part of it again became dilapidated and a further restoration took place at the very end of the fifteenth century owing to the efforts of Ali Shir Nevai, the vazir of Husayin Baykara.

The sanctuary behind the main *iwan* was pulled down, massive columns were added on either side of it and the walls around the courtyard were heightened by a screen wall added as a second storey above the vaulted arcades.[47] After another half a century or so, the Safavid shahs of Persia undertook further work on the mosque, the last to be carried out for 300 years. The present state of the building is the result of restoration carried out since the mid-1940s.

The general impression of the building may be Timurid and there are undoubted similarities with other monuments of the same period in the city, for example Gazurgah or the mausoleum of Gawhar Shad, but conspicuous differences point to earlier origins. For example, the pillars in the passages are remarkably strong, the *iwan* vaults have unusual proportions, and the points of the arches differ from the usual Timurid style. Melikian-Chirvani, who has analysed the building, believes these elements are closer to twelfth- (or thirteenth-) century models,[48] and there are at least three distinct items pointing to this period of origin: the low vaulting and its brick pattern right and left of the western *iwan*, in addition to the inscription along the base

51　The Friday Mosque, Herat. Detail

of the vault in the passage leading south from the *iwan*; a large portal on the south side of the eastern façade, half-hidden under a layer of late Timurid decoration; and the remnants, which were still visible some 50 years ago, of a mausoleum incorporated into the northern façade just behind the northern iwan. Additionally, the brick pattern of the vault of the passage by the western *iwan* is similar to the pattern on the tower of Bahramshah in Ghazni,[49] which dates from the twelfth century. The calligraphy – floral *Kufic* executed in incised terracotta – as well as the under lying floral décor are of exceptional quality.

The portal in the eastern façade was 'discovered' only in 1964, although Byron noticed 'a Kufic legend in fancy brick over an arch in the north-east corner'[50] and Wilber described it – with a photograph – in 1937.[51] Earlier glazed and unglazed terracotta decoration has been found under the Timurid tilework. The portal, which originally had a high arch lined with an inscription frieze, was framed by a band of script and flanked with two pillars covered with geometrical ornament. The medallions decorating the spandrels of the arch and the patterns of the columns were executed in incised terracotta. The *Kufic* in the portal, likewise in incised terracotta, was more conservative in design than that in the passage, but also of a very high quality. The motifs in the frame

52 The Friday Mosque, Herat. Detail of inscription on the southern side

are essentially the same as those on the minaret in Dawlatabad,[52] which again dates from the twelfth century; but the geometrical décor on the pillars and side-panels, showing four lotus flowers and eight-ray stars, represents an entirely new type. The only touch of colour in the otherwise monochrome decoration is a knob of turquoise in the centre of each figure. Some authorities believe, however, that this decoration is not as old as the construction and should be dated around 1300.

In Timurid times yet more work was undertaken here. The restorers lowered the arch, or rather incorporated into its crown a lower one with a semi-dome decorated with tiled medallions and a complicated pattern of circles, triangles and spheres. The flanks were plastered over, flattened and covered with tiles, and the pillars were hidden behind a flat surface. Thus a description to be found in travel guides which speaks of 'a Kufic inscription in blue mosaic faience on a background of floral ornament in turquoise blue, etc.' refers only to the decoration of the late fifteenth or early sixteenth century, and probably pre-dates the uncovering of the portal.

The *ziyarat*, or **mausoleum**, behind the northern wall was a domed structure some 17m square, which was supposedly built to house the tomb of Ghiyat-ud-Din Muhammad ben Sam, the founder of the Ghorid dynasty. Unfortunately, according to Melikian-Chirvani – who again refers to Saljuqi – 'the whole building was pulled down and rebuilt by the Afghan authorities'. None of the original decoration survived, but earlier reports confirm that an inscription running at the top of the walls under the dome was an almost *verbatim* copy of the two above mentioned Ghorid inscriptions to be found in the western passage and on the eastern portal.[53] It can be assumed that this part of the building was also built in the first years of the thirteenth

53   The Friday Mosque, Herat. Inscription on the northern side

century, although again some prefer a later dating, such as the period of the Kart restoration in the early fourteenth century.

When Munshi Mohun Lal visited Herat in 1834, several tombs lay inside the mausoleum under a pile of rubble, but none of them could be identified. The main entrance has been walled in. It is now accessible either through the *madrasa* in the north wing of the mosque, or from a corridor in the north-eastern corner.

Thus three separate sections of the mosque lying west, east and north of the courtyard date back to the early thirteenth century, to the reign of the successor of Ghiyat-ud-Din, Abu'l-Fath Muhammad ben Sam, or of his son Mahmud. It can therefore be assumed that the layout of the Ghorid mosque was substantially the same as it is now and that all the subsequent restorations have little affected the inner structure. Only the eastern and western façades show sixteenth-century additions, although the outer façades were, of course, completely reshaped.

However, this view, expressed by Melikian-Chirvani,[54] does leave several questions unanswered. For example, it is hard to reconcile with the completely asymmetrical position of the 'Ghorid portal' in relation to the rest of the building. As for the mausoleum, an interesting observation was made by Frye,[55] who believed that it had originally stood inside a shrine (*Ziyarat*), most of which had been demolished to make the adjoining street wider and to extend the mosque. This is not corroborated by any other source. However, considering that the length of the courtyard is given as 90m and the side of the mausoleum as 17m,[56] the mausoleum should occupy approximately $\frac{1}{5}$ of the entire length of the courtyard. In the sketch provided by Niedermayer, which Wilber considers 'fairly correct', the *Ziyarat* is shown as occupying a little less than half the length of the courtyard; and Zestovsky[57] also gives the dimensions as 45 x 45m. There is, therefore,

54 The cauldron at the Friday Mosque, Herat

a disproportion of 1:2.2 as against 1:5, which may indicate that a much larger building stood next to the northern wall of the mosque. Adding yet another observation by Frye, that the 'Ghorid' *iwan* stood 'opposite the entrance of the shrine', it is possible that an earlier building comprising both the portal and the mausoleum was at some stage incorporated, at least partly, into the structure of the mosque.

Remnants of Timurid decoration dating from the second half of the fifteenth century can be found in the north-west corner of the courtyard of the mosque. Five arches are adorned on the inside with thin horizontal strips of dark blue tilework alternating with wider strips of beige bricks, bordered by black and white tiles. On the bases are floral medallions. Inscriptions from the same period are in the hall to the left of the western *iwan* and on the left-hand side of the iwan itself. Safavid tilework can be found in several places. The rest of the courtyard and the entire outer façade have been restored in modern times.

In the centre of the courtyard a decorated platform covers a disused cistern. To the north of it, a *mihrab* wall in pink and white marble stands next to a *minbar*, and a few marble steps are used as a lectern. The entire north wing of the mosque is used as a *madrasa* accommodating some 50 students.

Until recently, in front of the eastern *iwan* inside the courtyard stood a monumental bronze cauldron, some 1.5m across, cast in two parts and beautifully decorated with arabesques and inscriptions. According to one of these engravings, it was made 'by order of Ghiyat-ad-dunya wa-d-din Muhammad of the Kart dynasty'.[58] This was used on feast days, when it was filled with sherbet (sweet lemonade) for the refreshment of the faithful. The Chinese embassy from the Ming period made a mention of it and it was described by travellers in the nineteenth century. However, when Frye visited Herat in 1944, it was not to be found.[59] In 1978 it was temporarily placed in a side passage, off the entrance corridor in the eastern *iwan*, and is used for collecting alms.

Early Islamic

55   The Pol-i Malan Bridge, Herat

Monuments in the Herat area

The ancient caravan route crossed the Hari Rud on a bridge which, according to tradition, is even older than the Friday mosque. This is the **Pol-i Malan**, the Bridge of Malan, described by Mukaddasi as early as the tenth century. It is a monumental structure wide enough for two lorries, with 26 arches, some pointed, some round, and dating obviously from different periods of its thousand-year existence. Byron[60] thought that it must have been rebuilt many times, but the piers probably rest on the old foundations, which themselves form a weir in the river (last restored in 1995).

In 1970 remains of a medieval madrasa were discovered on the left bank of the river Murghab, in the Jawand area of the province of Badghiz (north of Herat). The building is known as the **madrasa of Shah-i Mashad** and dates from the Ghorid period, around 1175. It is built in the Seljuk style of baked bricks and is decorated with ornaments and inscriptions in relief terracotta, with cut brick decoration similar to that of the minaret of Jam. In the southern façade the pointed arch of the main iwan was in a very fragile state; it was still standing a few years ago but was in danger of imminent collapse, and it seems that by now it has been completely destroyed.

To the east, on the road up the Hari Rud valley and some 150km from Herat in the village of Chisht (Chisht-i Sharif, Khoja Chisht), are **two domed buildings** of uncertain origin sometimes referred to either as mausoleums or shrines, or sometimes as a mosque and a *madrasa*. Renz describes them as 'harmoniously proportioned structures with a double cupola and a façade on which a rich decoration of fired bricks had been partially preserved'.[61] According to Golombek[62] the buildings are usually attributed to the late twelfth century and should be compared with the style of the tombs at Uzkend.[63] They are also mentioned by Melikian-Chirvani, who noticed epigraphic bands in ornamental *naskhi* along the arches and the drum of the dome inside the larger structure. These, he believes, should be dated to the period of the Ghorid sultan Ghiyat ud-Din Sam.[64] Chisht seems to have been an important religious centre in the eleventh and twelfth century; by the mid-eleventh century there was already a shrine of a saint, around which a little 'city of God' developed just as it had done at Gazurgah. There were frequent contacts between the two places, which were competing with each other in theological matters. 'In the late twelfth century monuments were first erected to commemorate the tombs of Ansari's contemporaries at Chisht.'[65]

The Minaret of Jam

About 100km farther east up the valley of the Hari Rud, in the Ghor province, stands one of the most famous monuments of Afghanistan, the minaret of **Jam**. The road is difficult to find and can only be negotiated by jeep or Land Rover. After the village of Shahrak a track to the left leads to the river, where the minaret stands in complete isolation. It was only discovered in 1957 by a French archaeological expedition, although rumours of its existence had been circulating for some time. With its 65m height it ranks second in the Islamic world, after the Kutub Minar in Delhi (73m), and it consists of a low octagonal base some 8m across and three cylindrical stages. The first is decorated with geometrical patterns in fired bricks, arranged in panels separated by vertical bands of *Kufic* inscriptions. A wide horizontal band of blue tiles with a further *Kufic* inscription runs around the top end in which, in a line of *naskhi*, the name of the calligrapher is given as 'Ali'. The second and third stages are decorated with horizontal bands of inscriptions, again in fired bricks. The stages were originally separated by galleries, which have not survived, and the top was closed by a lantern which has also collapsed; an interior staircase leads up to the second stage. The Persian and Central Asian tradition can be seen in its rich ornament of glazed tiles, stucco, the profusion of carved bricks and the use of wooden tie-beams in the structure, which differ from the contemporary Ghorid monuments in India.[66] The inscriptions confirm that the minaret was erected by Sultan Ghiyat ud-Din Muhammad ben Sam, the ruler of Ghor. It was built, in all probability, in 1190 and is often linked with the legendary Ghorid capital, Firuzkuh, which was destroyed by Chingiz-Khan in 1222 and the site of which has never been found. There is no conclusive evidence, however, to support this view. A topographical survey of the site was made by Herberg and Davary,[67] which showed in the immediate neighbourhood of the minaret the ruins of a citadel, a small fort on a hill guarding a side-valley, three watch-towers, a water reservoir on top of the hill above the citadel and the remnants of a bazaar area. However, all these remains seem to be those of a medium-sized fort or a military camp rather than a capital city. Apart from this, the space immediately

56 Shahr-i Zohak

east of the minaret is not large enough to accommodate a mosque. The river valley upstream from the site is impassable by road and no communication between Herat and Kabul could have passed that way. So the minaret remains a mystery; most probably it was a victory tower built to commemorate some forgotten event. The minaret was in danger of collapsing because of the water of the Hari Rud sapping at its base. A rescue operation decided by UNESCO in 1974 started in 1999, and was completed in 2001.

Shahr-i Zohak and Shahr-i Gholghola

Two sites in the valley of Bamiyan must be mentioned. East of the township, the spectacular ruin on a high rocky promontory is the **Shahr-i Zohak**, the *Town of Zohak*, also called the 'Red City' because of the colour of its brick walls. Zohak, or Zahak, was in Iran's national epic (the *Shahname*) a tyrant reigning for a thousand years, while in another epic he was a legitimate king, and the rulers of Ghor traced their ancestry back to this legendary figure. According to Schlumberger,[68] the fortress was originally a Turkish castle dating from the sixth or seventh century AD, which was rebuilt and reused in the Ghaznavid and Ghorid periods. Its origins may go back to the late Kushan, or possibly late Sasanian period, but no archaeological or historical evidence has been found to support this view. Although it cannot be ascertained whether it was built before or after the Hephthalite invasion, it seems certain that its

1 *The Bamiyan Valley*

2　*The Band-i Amir Lakes*

3　*Women at Shahr-i Gholghola*

4 *A Hazara girl*

5 The Pol-i Malan Bridge

6 The Babur Gardens, Kabul

7 The village of Tashkurgan

8 An Afghan family

9 The Mosque Abu Nasr Parsa in Balkh. Detail

10 The Mausoleum Gawhar Shad in Herat. Detail

11 The site of Surkh Kotal

12 The Friday Mosque in Herat. Detail

13 The Mosque Noh Gumbad, Balkh. Detail

14 The Kuh-i Baba range and the valley of Shahr-i Gholghola

15 The citadel, Shahr-i Gholghola

16 The mausoleum Hazret Ali, Mazar-i Sharif

17 The citadel, Tashkurgan

18 The tower of Masud III, Ghazni

19 *The tower of Bahramshah, Ghazni*

20 *Gazurgah, Herat. Detail*

21 Entrance of Gazurgah, Herat

22 A landscape in the Hindukush

23 *Timurid walls, Balkh*

24 The Musalla, Herat. One of the minarets

25 *The Friday Mosque, Herat*

Early Islamic

57 Shahr-i Zohak

58 Shahr-i Gholghola. View from the citadel

Early Islamic

59 *Kala-i Dokhtaran*

origins are pre-Islamic. The ruins of the fortress are one of the most dramatic sights in the whole country. Soaring on inaccessible cliffs, perfectly blended with the natural rock, dominating the fertile valley to the east, north and west with its three-tier ramparts, it was nevertheless conquered and destroyed by the Mongols of Chingiz-Khan.

The same destiny befell the strongly fortified Islamic city of Bamiyan, the ruins of which are now known as the **Shahr-i Gholghola**, the *City of Murmurs* (more exactly, the City of Noise). It was built in the eleventh century on a hillock south of the Bamiyan cliff, in the middle of a well-irrigated plain. The patterns of the bazaar, the mosques, the palaces and the caravanserais of this once prosperous city are still discernible in the maze of the dilapidated clay walls. From the top a beautiful view extends towards the valley of Bamiyan in the north, the valley of Foladi in the southwest, the Kakrak valley due south and the majestic barrier of the Kuh-i Baba on the horizon behind it. At the foot of the mound, a few hundred yards away, the **Kala-i Dokhtaran** is a fortified mansion, or perhaps a roadside fort which once guarded the access to the city. It is now inhabited by local peasants.

6 Timurid and late Islamic

Timurid Herat

After the death of Timur in 1405 and a period of fighting among his sons that ensued, his youngest son Shahrukh emerged victorious. He shifted the capital of the empire from Samarkand to Herat; and this move sparked off a brilliant period of artistic productivity in the city. Under his patronage, artists and craftsmen gathered around the princely court and throughout the fifteenth century creative activities were supported by a succession of art-loving rulers and their courtiers. A period of peace and economic prosperity no doubt contributed to the enterprising spirit and inventiveness of the time, which expressed itself not only in arts but also in science, literature and other fields. Samarkand, where Shahrukh's son Ulughbeg was governor, was not lagging behind Herat. Ulughbeg, himself an astronomer of world repute, was also a keen builder and a number of architectural monuments from his period can still be seen in the city, among them the foundations of his observatory. Shahrukh died at 69 in 1447 and Gawhar Shad, his wife, survived him for another eight years. In the end, when she was more than 80, she was put to death by a pretender to the throne.

Under Shahrukh, the **citadel** of Herat was thoroughly rebuilt to correspond to the military requirements of the time. It was linked to the city fortifications by a bastion constructed between its north-eastern corner and the north side of the city wall creating in this way a single defence complex. Semi-circular towers were added to the ramparts. At the bottom of one of them still remains part of a decorative frieze of glazed bricks with a pseudo-*Kufic* inscription (*Kufi-gung*) and some geometrical patterns. Originally, there was a wide ornamental band framed with dark-blue and pale-blue tiles within which ran a pale-blue line of calligraphy in imitated Arabic script. Above this band was the famous inscription frieze of Hafiz-i Abru, the chronicler of Timur who accompanied Shahrukh to Herat after Timur's death. He composed the text, a panegyric for Shahrukh, for the frieze which once ran around all the walls and towers of the citadel. Nothing, however, has been preserved of it. Below the ornamental band runs the surviving inscription frieze. Contrary to the upper inscription its purpose was purely decorative, with ornaments resembling the *Kufic* script without any meaning.

The alterations and decorative work undertaken on the **Friday Mosque** have been mentioned in the previous chapter.

The site of the Musalla, one of the most famous monuments of Herat, can be reached by a road north of the citadel, past the fifteenth-century **mausoleum of**

Abu'l-Kasim. It is now a vast plain on both sides of an irrigation canal conspicuous from afar by a group of six tall minarets looking rather like a group of factory chimneys. The plain north of the canal is an enormous field of rubble in the middle of which stands – or, rather, stood until the recent fighting – four of the minarets. The remaining two were in the gardens south of the canal. Between them stands a small mausoleum, a beautiful Timurid structure with a ribbed cupola. This is all that remains of what a French traveller, Ferrier, described in 1845 as 'one of the most accomplished, most imposing and most elegant architectural complexes of Asia'. In the fifteenth century Queen Gawhar Shad founded this vast 'University District' which at the end of the century was extended and completed by Sultan Husayin Baykara.

Musalla means '*Space (or place) for prayer*'; in Arabic, the word originally indicated an open space oriented towards Mecca (the same as the Persian word 'Namazgah'). Later, it was used in a wider sense to describe any place intended for religious gatherings. It is known from late fifteenth-century sources (Khondamir, Babur), that Gawhar Shad built a Musalla in Herat – but it is not quite clear what it consisted of. Babur speaks of three buildings – a mosque, a *madrasa* and a mausoleum – while according to Khondamir, the mausoleum was inside the *madrasa*. Major Yate, in 1885, also speaks of three buildings:

> The Musalla consists in reality of the remains of three buildings running north-east and south-west and covering a space of nearly 600 yards from end to end. Of the eastern building – known generally, I believe, as the Madrasah or College – nothing but two high arches facing each other and four minarets remain. The arches must be from 60 to 80 feet in height . . . inside the arches the beautiful mosaic-work is still in many places almost perfect . . . the minarets of this Madrasah appear taller than the rest, and must be between 120 and 150 feet in height.

Then, 'Between the Madrasah and the Musalla 100 yards or so from each other, is a domed building commonly called the tomb of Shah Rukh . . . It is faced on the east by another archway and one solitary minaret.' The third building stood to the west of this 'tomb of Shah Rukh' and was the actual Musalla,

> a huge massive building of burnt brick, almost entirely faced at one time with tiles and mosaic-work . . . The main building consists of a lofty dome some 75 feet in diameter, with a smaller dome behind it, and any number of rooms and buildings around it. The entrance to this dome is through a lofty archway on the east, some 80 feet in height, the face of which is entirely covered with tilework and huge inscriptions in gilt . . . To the east of this arch is a large courtyard some 80 yards square, surrounded with corridors and rooms several storeys in height – all covered with tilework. The main entrance of all this is on the eastern side of this court, through another huge archway, also some 80 feet in height . . . Four minarets, some 120 feet in height, form the four corners of the building . . . [1]

60 The Musalla, Herat

Yate's three buildings are obviously not the same as Babur's. Babur, being a contemporary, meant what he said when he spoke of 'the college of Gawhar Shad Begum, her tomb and her grand mosque'. He did not include what was not hers, that is another *madrasa* built nearby by his cousin Husayin Baykara. This confused Yate who knew Babur's text. 'Where the college was that bore her name I did not hear, neither did I find any trace in Herat of her mosque. Her tombstone alone remains . . . '[2]

He did not realise that the word Musalla could also mean a mosque. The Musalla was, in fact, 'a second madrasa which served also as a Friday mosque'.[3] Another thing that escaped him was that the archway with a solitary minaret could be the only remains of a large building which once surrounded the mausoleum – in other words, Babur's, and Gawhar Shad's, *madrasa*. In Yate's time, therefore, there seemed to be: the (very scanty) remnants of the madrasa of Husayin Baykara; almost no remains – except the arch and the minaret – of Gawhar Shad's *madrasa*; and the Musalla, which must have been the building which so impressed Ferrier, Connolly, Lal and others.

The Musalla was a typical *four-iwan* structure of its time (although the two later iwans may not have existed by the time that the travellers visited the site). It apparently had a minaret in each corner; all four were still standing when Niedermeyer took his famous photograph in 1916. Three of them have since collapsed – two in an earthquake in 1931, and the other in 1951. It is almost certain that there were once more minarets on the site; Connolly, for example, mentions at least 20 and considering the number that still adorns the Friday mosque, this may not be an exaggeration.

Then came the Panjdeh incident of 1885 and the military thinking of the time turned the Musalla into a heap of rubble.

> In the seventies and eighties Herat was incessantly on English lips. It even crops up in one of Queen Victoria's letters. If the Russians took it, as they were expected to do, the low-lying Kandahar road would be theirs for a railway to the Indian border. In 1885 the Panjdeh incident occurred. Though St. Petersburg had already agreed to the joint boundary commission, Russian troops attacked the Afghans south-east of Merv and drove them back. An advance on Herat was expected any day, and Emir Abdurrahman sent orders that the town was to be placed in a state of defence. The Russians would approach from the north. All buildings, therefore, that might give them cover on this side of town must be demolished. For years officers of the Indian Army had been advising on such measures. I suspect this particular order was of British inspiration; though proof must wait till the archives of Delhi and the War Office give up their dead. In any case the most glorious productions of Mohammadan architecture in the fifteenth century, having survived the barbarism of four centuries, were now razed to the ground under the eyes, and with the approval, of the English Commissioners. Nine minarets and the Mausoleum escaped.[4]

There is a sketch made by a British officer just before the demolition of 1885. It shows the portal of the *madrasa* in an advanced state of decay, with only one minaret out of the two; on the right are the arcades of the *madrasa* court, and behind, the *iwan* and the two domes of the Musalla. It was on this sketch that Byron[5] based his description, in which the Musalla had a monumental portal, a square courtyard with two-storey arcades, and four minarets. Opposite the portal, on the west side, was a single *iwan* behind which were two circular chambers with saucer-shaped domes. Adjacent to the north side of the Musalla was the *madrasa*, inside which stood the royal mausoleum.

The **minaret** with one gallery, which now stands inside a modern *madrasa*, stood in the western corner of the courtyard of the Musalla, which according to a reconstruction measured some 117 x 70m. The minaret can be best seen from the garden called Bagh-i Bihzad. Its octagonal base was once covered with exquisitely carved marble panels, and the whole tower was entirely covered with ornaments in mosaic faience in deep blue, azure and purple, with white marble moulding separating the panels and the bands of calligraphy, parts of which survived until recently. The minaret received a direct hit in 1984/5. Only a stump remains.

The other **minaret**, with two galleries and standing to the east of the mausoleum, was probably one of the flanking towers of the entrance iwan of the *madrasa*. The galleries are supported by lavishly decorated stalactite vaults (*mukarnas*). On the tower itself brick ornaments alternated with bands of tilework. It, too, was hit by a rocket and is leaning precariously. Both minarets have lost their tops.

The *madrasa* of Husayin Baykara occupied an area of some 100 x 100m, the outline of which is marked by the **four minarets**. At the time of the author's visit

61 Mausoleum
Gawhar Shad,
Herat. Detail

they were still 30–40m high; but as their tops were missing it can be surmised that originally they were certainly taller. They were decorated with geometrical ornaments, turquoise blue framed with white, in mosac faience. Curiously enough the white mosaic has survived better than the turquoise one, so that in parts bare bricks are laced with a pattern of white tiles. One of them was hit by two rockets, and later repaired by SPACH in 2001.

The **mausoleum**, commonly ascribed to Gawhar Shad, was perhaps one of a pair. It stood in a pine grove not far from the canal. (The grove is now gone but it is expected to be replanted by a SPACH project.) The architecture of the mausoleum offers some important innovations. It is a squat square structure with a bulbous dome on a high drum, some 25m high. It has been almost entirely restored and remnants of the original decoration can be found on the west side only.

The interior between the square base and the dome shows two zones of transition. The square is first made into an octagon by means of four pointed squinches

62 *Mausoleum Gawhar Shad, Herat. Detail of the interior*

and then transformed into a sixteen-sided figure on which the dome rests. This transition is obtained by a band of sixteen mukarnas-niches. The interior of the mausoleum and the dome are two of the most impressive achievements of Islamic architecture. Intersecting pointed arches, which are remotely reminiscent of the Gothic arch, but have nothing in common with it,[6] divide the sphere into various polygons and *mukarnas*-decorated half- and quarter-domes bearing painted ornaments in lapis-blue, gold, ochre and white. The lapis-blue pigment has been obtained from the genuine lapis-lazuli of Badakhshan.

The outside decoration of the drum consists, in the upper part, of a band of rectangular medallions filled with floral ornament, white on a blue background. The middle part carries an inscription frieze, now largely damaged, while on the lower part there are again ornamental rectangles, much larger than at the top. Dark blue hexagons with stylized golden flowers are separated by natural brickwork with blue and white rectangles above and below. The decoration on the dome consists of geometrical ornaments in turquoise, blue and white tiles on the ribs, whereas the space between them is filled with plain turquoise tiles. Medallions of rosettes and stylized lettering form a white-and-blue band at the bottom. Stalactites, again in blue and white provide the transition between the dome and the drum. Byron[7] was obviously not very impressed by this decoration: 'Looked at in detail, the decoration of the Mausoleum is inferior to that of the two minarets.' The drum has also been partly restored but a good deal of the decoration still exists. The dome, on the contrary, is in its original state with a dilapidated top but with the lower part of the rib decoration still in place (a damaged part of

63 Mausoleum Gawhar Shad, Herat. Detail

the top shown on a photograph in Byron has been repaired). The drum bears a high outer dome and itself exceeds the height of the lower, inner dome. The weight of the double dome is thus divided and the pressure of the base is eased. A third, innermost, dome bears the painted interior decoration.

It is not clear how many tombs were originally in the mausoleum. Some sources mention as many as 20; Khanikov could still see nine in the 1860s; Yate saw five and Byron only three. There is nothing unusual in this, for the habit of reusing tombstones was widespread. Strangely enough, where Byron saw three, there are now six. According to Wolfe[8] they belong to Gawhar Shad (d.1457), her son Baisanghur (d.1432 or 1433), his son Ala-ad-daula (d.1459), his grandson Ibrahim (also d.1459) and two other members of the family, Ahmad and Shahrukh ibn Sultan Abu Said (d.1493). As mentioned above, the mausoleum was originally built for Prince Baisanghur, who predeceased his mother; Golombek (and also Saljuqi, *Khiaban*) call it the mausoleum of Baisanghur and Gawhar Shad.[9] However, Pugachenkova believes that as men and women were buried separately under the Timurids, Gawhar Shad could not have been lain next to her son Baisanghur, and that there was probably another tomb elsewhere. It is interesting to speculate that, if Hoag's assumption is right and the mausoleum was one of a pair, the other one could have been the tomb of the women of the family.[10]

Husayin Baykara built a mausoleum for himself nearby, but the building has disappeared completely. Its site, near the bridge across the canal, is marked by a marble slab at the bottom of a cavity. Some sources have it that a mud-brick structure by

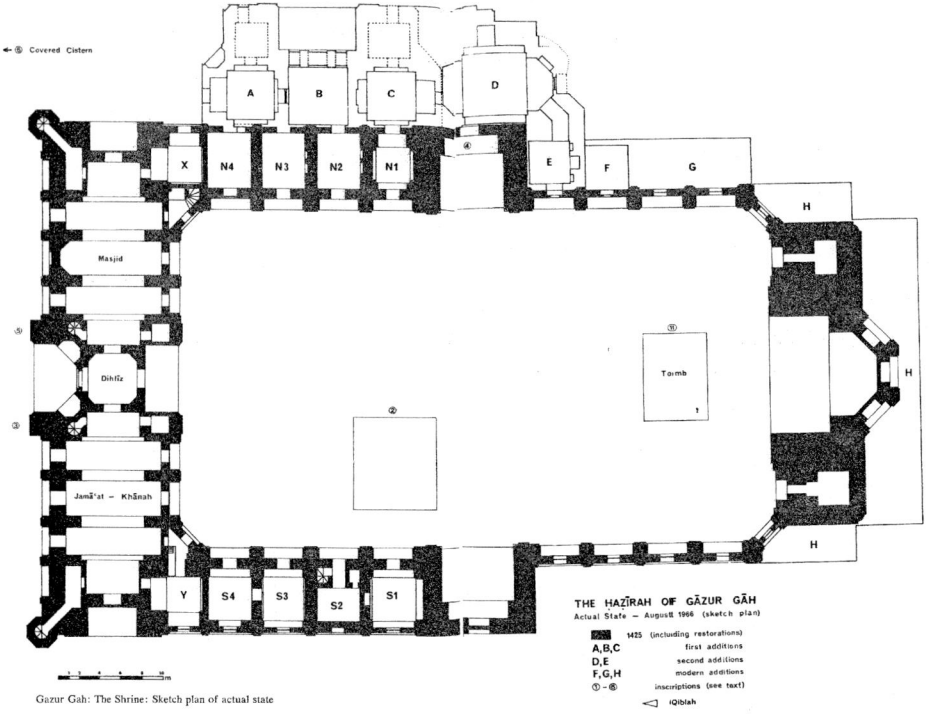

Gazur Gah: The Shrine: Sketch plan of actual state

64 The shrine at Gazurgah. Golombek (1969)

the canal covers the tomb of Mir Ali Shir Nevai, the famous poet and writer, and Husayin Baykara's most influential vazir.

Some 5km north-east from the city and near the village of **Gazurgah** stands the shrine referred to by the same name, built around the tomb of a Muslim saint, the Khoja Abdullah Ansari. Best described in an excellent monograph by L. Golombek[11] the shrine is one of the most complex architectural and artistic monuments in the Islamic world.

Gazurgah means 'bleaching ground', although some authorities would prefer to interpret it as the 'site of a battle'. It lies at the foot of the mountain known as Zanghir Gah which is part of the chain running east to west, along the southern slope of which flows the Hari Rud. Since this part of the oasis has been relatively well watered, it has always been a favourite site for gardens, palaces and burials of prominent Herati personalities. Already before the tenth century medieval historians mention a shrine on the slopes of Zanghir Gah.

A *khaniga* (khanaqah) was founded here by a Sufi sage, Sheikh Amu, who raised it from a minor sanctuary to a flourishing centre of Muslim learning. He died in 1049 and his disciple, Khoja Ansari, became in his turn the leading personality among the Sufis in northern Khorasan; and he became venerated as a saint soon after his death in 1089. He was a philosopher and a mystic; according to legend he died, aged 84, because some boys threw stones at him while he was immersed in prayer. Robert Byron had obviously some sympathy with those boys:

> Even among saints (Ansari) was a prodigious bore. He spoke in the cradle; he began to preach at fourteen; during his life he held intercourse with 1,000 sheikhs, learnt 100,000 verses by heart (some say 1,200,000) and composed as many more. He doted on cats.[12]

According to literary sources, a *madrasa* was built at Gazurgah in the Ghorid period, in the late twelfth and early thirteenth century, and there was at least one royal burial at the site. No remains of these buildings have survived although a small underground chamber in the western slope of Zanghir Gah – a *chillah-khana* or meditation-cell – may well be from that period or even older. The site was developed when Shahrukh moved his residence just south of the shrine. The second period again followed the transfer of a royal residence when Sultan Husayin Baykara chose the Bagh-i Murad, close to his place of birth, as his seat; at this point the place was renamed Bagh-i Jahan Aray and a large palace was built here.[13]

Most of the present shrine goes back to these two periods in the fifteenth century. Originally built by Shahrukh in the years 1425-6, it was heavily damaged in a disastrous flood in 1493; Ali Shir Nevai, the vazir of Husayin Baykara, repaired and rebuilt it in 1499. Some later additions were made under the Safavids, while the Chingizid Khans in the seventeenth century added some interior decoration and restored and reconstructed parts of the complex.

The visitor, entering from the north, comes first into a vast forecourt; on his right lies a rectangular garden with many tall pine trees, on the shorter side of which there is a twelve-sided kiosk called *Namakdan* (the Salt-cellar). Remains of a similar kiosk can be found at the far side of the garden, some 100m to the west. Facing the visitor is a low vaulted building housing a cistern; immediately adjacent to it on the west side are the remains of an underground mosque now concealed within a modern structure. Behind it, the southern part of the forecourt houses a cemetery enclosed by a low wall in the south, a recent structure of an oratory in the west and the actual shrine in the east. A domed pavilion, the *Zarnigar Khana* (the Gilded Room) stands in the south-eastern corner linked to the façade of the shrine (see below p.145).

On the left is the shrine itself with a high portal screen of an *iwan*; on each side of it runs an arcade which ends with a corner turret. Behind it, to the east, is a rectangular courtyard. On the north and south side of it are arcaded wings, each with an *iwan* in the centre. The further (eastern) side of the rectangle is enclosed by a monumental iwan with a mammoth portal-screen (*pishtak*) in front of which is the tomb of the Khoja. The entire surface of the courtyard is densely covered with tombstones and as such it is 'one of the richest graveyards in the East'.[14]

Among the tile techniques found at Gazurgah, three types must be mentioned: the *mosaic-faience* (the most dominant here), which consists of small pieces of tile with surface glaze of different colours assembled in the required patterns; the *banai-technique*, which looks like a course of bricks laid in decorative schemes, but

Timurid and late Islamic

65 Gazurgah, Herat. The eastern iwan

are glazed tiles (this technique is used mainly to cover large surfaces of wall); and the *inset-technique*, which consists of a series of plaques made up of mosaic-faience, or majolica tiles. There is however no majolica among the tile revetments found in Gazurgah.

The main part of the **west wing** of the shrine is the entrance complex consisting of two *iwans*, one facing west into the forecourt and the other facing east into the courtyard. There is a vestibule between the two and on each side of it is a large room, a mosque on the north side and an assembly room on the south one. The proportions of these rooms are similiar and each has a direct access from the outside through lesser portals in the outer façade. The five-sided bay of the entrance *iwan* is covered by a semi-dome joined to a *pishtak*. It is decorated with glazed tiles, mainly in turquoise and black, with medallions in mosaic faience. The *pishtak* is framed with a large epigraphic frieze which was added in the seventeenth century. The entire façade above a marble encasement is richly decorated in glazed bricks just above the arches of the arcades. The top of the wall has been reconstructed and left without decoration. Some of the original decoration also remains on the north wall.

66 Gazurgah, Herat. Detail of the southern wall

Inside the square vestibule are doors north and south giving access to the mosque and the assembly room, and similar doors leading to the inner and outer *iwans*. The arches above the doors, the tympana, as well as the vault and walls of the room, are covered with painted decoration, mostly of floral motifs, and on the upper part of the walls drawings of architectural complexes can be discerned. Some can be identified as images of Mecca and Madinah; the significance of others is less clear. The decoration of the wall is geometrical with medallions emanating in rays from the centre.

The architectural decoration inside the mosque and the assembly room is striking in several respects. Their ceilings consist of a complex system of plaster vaults, semi-domes and transverse arches with fan-shaped plaster *mukarnas* in the domes between the arches. The entire interior is white, only the lower parts of the walls are decorated with a wide band of buff-coloured tiles lined with black and blue mosaic faience and set in a simple geometrical pattern.

The *iwan* on the courtyard side has lost its upper part; it was originally the same height as its northern and southern counterparts. Its decoration is heavily damaged; only a part of the inscription frieze, and some panels with floral and geometrical designs have been preserved.

Seen from the courtyard, the **north wing** consists of a central *iwan* flanked on either side by a façade with four arcaded recesses, or niches. This symmetry is purely visual, however, for the niches on the west side give access to rooms, whereas on the east side they are merely part of a curtain wall. The decoration of the *iwan* is pre-

67 Gazurgah, Herat. Detail of the eastern iwan

68 Gazurgah, Herat. Detail of the western iwan

served mainly on the inside wall, and consists of large geometrical patterns in glazed bricks (banai-technique). Parts of an inscription frieze in mosaic faience still exist on the outer wall, and there is a well-preserved panel in the same technique above the entrance. This however is unlikely to be original,[15] because the inscription, which looks as if it is part of it, refers to repairs undertaken by Shah Tahmasp in 1562-3. A carved marble plate inset above the doorway also seems to have been placed here at a later date. The decoration of the façade resembles that of the *iwan* but is in a very poor state of preservation in places.

There are four rooms on the ground floor behind the façade. The walls in the second are entirely covered with paintings, which are similar in style to the architectural scenes in the vestibule. Behind them is an entire wing built subsequently as an addition – or rather a series of additions – to the original structure. In one of the chambers are five tombstones; one of them, exquisitely carved in black stone in the filigree technique known as *haft qalam*, belonged originally to the mother of Husayin Baykara, but it was almost certainly brought here from elsewhere. These rooms appear to have been built at the end of the fifteenth century. Immediately east are two more rooms constructed at a somewhat later date. The tombs in them belong to the Chingizid period, namely the end of the seventeenth or early eighteenth century.

One more room should be mentioned on this side of the courtyard; a mud-brick construction added in modern times which can be entered by a door in the curtain wall east of the *iwan*. Inside is the famous cenotaph of carved black stone known as the *Haft qalam* or 'Seven pens'. According to Golombek, it is 'one of the most intricate and delicate carvings ever created by the Iranian world. Few visitors have failed to marvel at the workmanship of this stone.'[16] It was probably intended for the Sultan Husayin Baykara himself but, when the sultan's favourite son died, the stone went to him. It was, no doubt, transferred to Gazurgah from the Musalla – or the mausoleum of Husayin Baykara – to be reused. Many carved cenotaphs were moved to Gazurgah in this way.

If compared with the north wing, the **south wing** is somewhat less interesting. It, too, has a central *iwan* and an arcaded façade, but all its eastern part is just a curtain wall. In the western part is a series of premises corresponding, more or less, by their size and layout to their counterpart in the north wing – but the buildings on the south side are much more damaged. The rooms and roofs in the south-west corner suffered the most. Inside, no decoration survived and, on the façade, most of it is in a poor state. The interiors of some of the rooms were reconstructed to such an extent that it is difficult to determine the original layout. There were no later additions on this side.

The **eastern iwan** is the most imposing part of the shrine. The portal screen (*pishtak*) some 30m high, is visible from afar. It was originally completely covered with glazed tiles – but unfortunately much of this decoration has disappeared. Inside the *iwan*, however, 'the surfaces have preserved some of the richest and most imaginative glazed tile compositions ever created'.[17] Its complex geometrical figures are composed of many individual plaques decorated in *inset-technique* or *mosaic-faience*. The five-sided bay in the back of the *iwan* is decorated in the lower part with rectangles consisting of an arched panel with a square above it; the middle part is formed by a large

69 Gazurgah, Herat. Detail of the western iwan

inscription frieze in what looks like *Kufic* script but is, in fact, a 'rare example of *naskhi* script executed in *banai-technique*'.[18] The semi-dome above it is filled with stars and polygons, a favourite motif symbolizing the dome of heaven.

The vault of the *iwan* is separated from the bay by an arch decorated with an inscription frieze. The inscription, executed in beautiful two-line *thuluth*, continues horizontally along the sides of the *iwan*. The upper section, or arch, of the *iwan* is covered with a kaleidoscopic design consisting of small geometric units, squares, rhomboids and triangles, centred around a hexagon and fitted together to form a larger design. The hexagons are decorated with floral and arabesque motifs; the rhomboids bear the word 'Allah' in stylized *Kufic*. The lower section is equally remarkable. It consists of squares and rectangles made up of minuscule simulated brick-ends featuring imaginative epigraphic themes in alternating colours. The whole design is framed by a wide band in the same pseudo-*Kufic* script as in the bay, endlessly repeating the same evocation of God. Byron[19] finds Chinese influence in the ornamental patterns of the *iwan* – but this is not corroborated by Golombek.

Parts of a great inscription frieze are all that remains of the decorations of the portal screen. On the floor of the *iwan* are a number of tombstones, some of them dating from the middle of the seventeenth century. Behind the eastern façade are four domed undecorated rooms on two floors, two on each side of the *iwan*. In the courtyard, the most conspicuous structure is the tomb of Khoja Ansari hidden behind a lattice-work in front of the eastern *iwan*. North of it stands a 5m-high ornamental marble column adorned with inscriptions and stucco *mukarnas*, which was

70 Gazurgah, Herat. Detail of the courtyard

erected in 1454. Next to the column is the tomb of Amir Dost Mohammad who died in Herat in 1863, in the course of a military campaign.

Another outstanding structure is a large rectangular platform in front of the southern *iwan*. It is decorated with a pattern of white marble inlaid with black along the sides and is known as the *Takht* or 'Throne'. Built by Husayin Baykara in 1477-8, on the platform itself are six cenotaphs of black marble belonging to the sultan's family (his father, uncle and brothers). Another black marble stone, elaborately carved but undated, lies opposite the north-western corner of the platform.

The main entrance to the **Zarnigar-Khana**, a Timurid-style *khaniga*, is through a large *iwan* on the north side facing the forecourt, in which remains of elaborate decoration in tinted plaster can be seen. The outer façade is bare. Inside is a large domed hall, some 10m square, with a *mihrab* in the western wall. The transition zone between the dome and the walls and the dome itself is covered with gold and blue paintings that are remarkably well preserved.

> So breathtaking is the contrast of its blues and gold, so precise and yet so varied its design that one European who visited the Shrine incredulous that so fine a work could be produced by 'Orientals', claimed to have read the signature of an Italian artist in the dome.[20]

The traveller was, no doubt, Ferrier, the hypothetical signature that of Giraldi, an Italian painter employed by Shah Abbas. Some travel guides repeat this idea while others merely mention a 'restoration carried out under Shah Abbas'. Byron[21] examined the paintings but found no signature, while according to Golombek, 'this fantasy (needs) no further thought, for the painting of vaults was a well established tradition in Islamic architecture and all of the major themes and motifs... can be correlated with examples from other Iranian monuments'.[22]

Some of the floral motifs in the paintings are similar to those found on the carved tombstones of the '*Haft qalam*' type, which were executed in Herat toward the end of the fifteenth century. A common inspiration for both is seen by some scholars in carpet designs which go back at least to the beginning of that century, and in their ultimate source, Chinese silks.[23]

The decoration of the Zarnigar Khana dates in all probability from the very end of the fifteenth century. It is possible that the structure itself was erected somewhat earlier. It now houses a local school.

The **Namakdan** was probably built in the seventeenth century. It is a garden pavilion, twelve-sided on the outside and octagonal on the inside. It is – or was – used as a guest-house by the keeper of the shrine. Its only decoration is a star-vault composed of intersecting plaster ribs on the central octagon inside. A similar pavilion is believed to have stood some 100m farther west.

The **covered cistern** known as 'Zamzam' was probably built by Shahrukh and restored in 1683 or 1684. There is an inscription in the form of a poem which attributes the foundation to Shahrukh, who is believed to have brought water for it from the holy well in Mecca. The cistern is compared with the Zamzam of Mecca; there are also some mentions of shrines in Hebron and Madinah, which also appear in the paintings in the vestibule, and it can be safely assumed that both the paintings and the cistern were executed at the same time. The **underground mosque**, just west of the cistern, consists of a domed chamber and deep recesses leading to small meditation cells. The vault of the chamber is probably of the Timurid or Safavid period.

The description of the site would not be complete without mentioning the statue of a dog in front of the main entrance *iwan*, which was supposed to be the humble symbol marking the tomb of the architect of the shrine. It is not there anymore.

To sum up, the heart of the Gazurgah complex was a funerary enclosure built around the tomb of a venerated saint. Such enclosures were commonplace all over eastern Islam and their model is believed to have been the screen erected around the tomb of the Prophet in the mosque of Madinah, or rather the enclosure thus formed, which later acquired the more general meaning of a 'wall surrounding a tomb'.[24] There were two competing traditions in Islam as far as funerary monuments were concerned: one favouring the building of mausoleums, the other preferring an open space for the tomb and strongly opposed to any roofed structure over it. Thus, for example, the necropolis Shah-i Zinda in Samarkand, dating from the late fourteenth century, consists of a number of mausoleums grouped around one containing a saint's tomb. At Gazurgah, on the contrary, the idea of the open space prevailed.

There is no doubt that Ansari's tomb became the focal point of such an enclosure soon after his death. It is known that in the late twelfth century a *madrasa* was built at Gazurgah by a Ghorid vazir, but no trace of the building remains. Subsequently, the site seems to have fallen somewhat into oblivion until Shahrukh revived popular interest in it. Gradually, facilities for pilgrims and dervishes grew near by: the mosque, the assembly hall, hostels and kitchens, and the cemetery which by then existed around the tomb were incorporated into the compound. In due course some funerary chambers were added behind the north wing and the former residential cells also began to be used for burials. Prestigious tombstones were transferred from elsewhere and reused. Finally, when the original enclosure was filled to capacity, the cemetery spilled over into the forecourt and new outbuildings were constructed around it giving the site its present shape. A new mosque/*madrasa* has been built outside the south wall. It should be added that, at the beginning of the Russo-Afghan fighting, the western part of the city of Herat has been heavily damaged; according to some reports it was almost completely destroyed.

Other monuments in and around Herat

North of the citadel, on the way to the Musalla, is the mausoleum of **the Shahzade Abu'l Kasim**, built around 1492 and recently restored. It is a Timurid structure with an interesting plaster vault, and partly preserved decoration in mosaic faience. Bands of floral ornament line the lateral niches. The sheikh lived in Herat in the ninth century, and his tomb became a place of pilgrimage long before the present mausoleum was built; parts of an earlier structure may have been incorporated into the present one.

Near the mausoleum of Gawhar Shad, another Timurid building is the mausoleum of **Sheikhzade Abdullah** dating from the fifteenth century. It has a large portal with a small prayer room on the left. The hall is covered with a dome (restored) and decorated with paintings of a later period perhaps painted over some earlier ones. Below the dome is a decoration of tile mosaic.

To the north, towards the road-fork where the roads to Iran and Turkmenistan divide, is a small cemetery with a funerary mosque. In the cemetery is a modest undecorated tomb marked only with a marble slab, lying in the shade of a huge pistachio tree which has broken through its cement covering. It is the tomb of the famous Sufi and poet **Jami**, who was buried here in 1492, and is a popular place of pilgrimage, much venerated by the Heratis.

South of the citadel is a crossroads which until 1934 was the centre of the covered bazaars, the **Chahar Su**. Only a section of the bazaar is still covered; the rest has been demolished. On the left of the crossroads, immediately on the right-hand side, is the entrance to an undecorated vaulted building, a former cistern, the **Hauz-i Chahar Su**. It has an interesting brick dome and dates from the seventeenth century.

Outside the city, on the right of the road leading to the river, is a mound on top of which stands another Timurid mausoleum, the **Ziyarat-i Mir Shahid**, built in 1485 by Husayin Baykara over the tomb of a grandson of Ali, who died in 707.

Moving out to the wider environs of Herat, in the village of Ziyarat Gah some 12km west of the airport and accessible only by a difficult road is a Timurid building, the *khaniga* (hostel) of **Mulla Kalan**. The central chamber contains a *mihrab* and serves as a mosque. It has a large entrance portal and is surrounded by two floors of auxiliary rooms. The building can be dated to the last quarter of the fifteenth century and is in many ways similar to the Zarnigar Khana at Gazurgah; this monument has not yet been described in detail.

In the centre of the village is a **Friday Mosque** dating from the time of Shahrukh, with traces of fifteenth-century tilework on the outer wall and two minarets flanking the main *iwan*; there is also another mosque, the **Masjid-i Chehel Sotun**, founded perhaps in the twelfth century, which has a pillared vaulted verandah with a *mihrab* in fifteenth-century *mosaic-faience*. Behind this veranda is a large hall built over an underground meditation cell. Apparently, both buildings were damaged during the war, but whereas Chehel Sotun was almost completely demolished, the Friday Mosque has been to some extent restored.

South-west of Herat, the *khaniga* of **Sheikh Sadr-ud-Din Armani** was built in the Timurid period, most probably before 1484. In the suburb of Ghalwar, 5km to the west of the city, is another Timurid building, the **Masjid-i Hauz-i Karboz**, dating from the second half of the fifteenth century. Its most conspicuous feature is the *mihrab* wall with a pointed arch, the *soffit* of which is decorated with excellent calligraphy in *thuluth*. In the *mihrab* niche are geometrical ornaments of five- and ten-sided stars, and tiled medallions and floral ornaments can also be seen on the wall. This, according to Pugachenkova[25] is one of the rare surviving examples of a richly decorated suburban mosque from the Timurid period. The only other existing mosque of this kind is the Chehel Sotun at Ziyarat Gah.

About 112km west of the city, in the village of Kohsan near Tirpul, is a shrine and a mosque dating from approximately 1440. The shrine, now destroyed and commonly known as the **mausoleum of Gawhar Shad of Kohsan**, was an octagonal brick building with rectangular or semi-octagonal niches covered with a double cupola of glazed bricks. Inside, the transition from the octagon to the circle was achieved by four-stage pendentives and a row of stalactites. The arches and walls of the octagon were decorated with tiled geometrical ornaments and inscriptions in *banai technique*. Some frescoes imitating the style of miniatures could be seen in the niches. Outside, the blue sphero-conical dome rested on a high drum decorated with a *Kufic* inscription in white tiles with black edges on a blue background.[26]

In the village of Azadan, north-west of the city, **the mausoleum of Abu al-Valid** was a Timurid building now almost completely destroyed. The decoration of its vault consisted of medallions and floral bouquets similar to those already seen in the vestibule of Gazurgah and in the shrine of Sheikh Abdullah. On the wall was a painted frieze of architectural images again comparable to those of Gazurgah, and characteristic of the eighteenth to nineteenth centuries. The dome rests on a sixteen-sided band of *mukarnas squinches*. An inscription in elongated *thuluth* runs along the walls.

North of Herat, on the road to the Turkmenistan border, stands an ancient *caravanserai* called **Kushribat** (the falcon caravanserai) which was founded by a high personage at the court of Husayin Baykara, the 'Keeper of the Falcon House', in the last quarter of the fifteenth century. It consists of two parts, a large courtyard (91 x 72m) surrounded by apartments and a rectangular covered area.[27]

The **Tareb khana**, or House of joy, built in the mid-fifteenth century, was an octagonal pavillion with a central two-storey chamber. Babur later built a wooden one in its place. The form, which probably dates back to Seljuk times, is clearly documented only in the Timurid period. Called *hasht-behisht*, it inspired the imperial Moghul tombs and appeared also in the Safavid empire.[28]

Timurid Balkh

After the Mongol destruction the city revived in the late fourteenth and early fifteenth century, but it shrank back in the east to its original boundary while extending in the west, probably due to the marshland which invaded the ruins. Timur rebuilt much of the city, and also restored a fortress outside the walls which became his governor's residence. Clavijo gave this account in 1404:

> This city is very large and it is surrounded by a broad rampart of earth which along the top measures thirty paces across. The retaining wall flanking the rampart is now breached in many places, but inside this last the city proper is enclosed by two walls one within the other, and these protect the settlement. The area between the outer earthen rampart and the first inner wall is not occupied by any houses and no one lives there, the ground being divided up into fields where cotton is grown. In the space between the second and the innermost wall there are houses, but still this part is not very closely crowded. The innermost circle of the city however is densely populated; and unlike the other towns which we had come to in these parts, the two inner walls of Balkh are extremely strong and as yet well preserved.[29]

The late medieval, or Timurid, walls observed by Clavijo are best visible in the south, where again they were raised over the earlier ones as a third layer. They were also built over the ancient ramparts of the citadel and over the eastern wall. Ruins of these walls can still be seen, while in the west only a small stretch, noticed by Yate, has survived. It seems that the citadel was not continuously inhabited, and the findings suggest that there was a long period when it was abandoned, perhaps from the Hephthalite or Arab invasion until the Timurid revival. After its recovery under the Timurids, Balkh faded gradually into oblivion when under the Uzbek domination all commerce of the area gravitated more and more toward the neighbouring Mazar-i Sharif.

The shrine of **Khoja Abu Nasr Parsa**, also known as 'The Green mosque' is neither a mausoleum (for it contains no tomb), nor a mosque; the locals sometimes call it a *madrasa*, and it therefore seems plausible that in reality it had a mosque close to it, a rather common religious institution under the Timurids. The Khoja was a theological lecturer in Herat in Shahrukh's time and died in 1460. The shrine is a typical Timurid building with a large *iwan* flanked by two truncated minarets and, behind it, an octagonal structure under a ribbed dome on a high drum. It bears the date of 1598, but this was probably the date of a restoration or reconstruction. A

71 The shrine of Abu Nasr Parsa, Balkh

72 *The shrine of Abu Nasr Parsa, Balkh. Detail*

recent restoration was carried out in 1974-5. The Khoja's tomb was nearby, on a platform before the north-western *iwan*.

> The colours of the façade are confined to white and dark and light blue, reinforced by discreet touches of black. It is the absence of purple and other warm tints which produces the silvery effect . . . This effect is continued by the dome, whose fat round ribs are covered with tiny bricks glazed with greenish turquoise . . . The building as a whole is unsubstantial and romantic. An unknown force seems to be squeezing it upwards. The result is fantasy, and in some lights, an unearthly beauty.[30]

Byron was certainly a sensitive observer.

The exterior of the building is dominated by an *iwan* with a large portal screen (*pishtak*) flanked by two 'corkscrew pillars' (Byron's term) with vase-shaped bottoms. Immediately behind them stood the minarets of which only the lower parts remain. The tilework on the iwan and the drum is original but that on the dome has been restored. The transition between the dome and the drum is provided by a band of decorated *mukarnas*. The decoration of the drum consists of two lines of *Kufic* inscription in white tiles framed by black on a blue background. In between them are two small bands of highly stylized script in white tiles only. On the *pishtak* there are two vertical bands of elongated *Kufic* each with a floral medallion at the bottom. On the

Timurid and late Islamic

73 *The shrine of Abu Nasr Parsa, Balkh. Detail*

74 *The shrine of Abu Nasr Parsa, Balkh. Detail of* iwan

75 The shrine of Abu Nasr Parsa, Balkh. Detail of the interior

pillars there is a rich decoration of white and blue floral ornament in mosaic faience. Between the vase and the 'corkscrew' is a band of *mukarnas* in the same colours. On the minarets are two different varieties of script, a *Kufic* inscription similar to that on the drum and the pillars, and a cursive *Kufic* or rather a special kind of *nashki* which we have already seen in Herat, on the eastern *iwan* at Gazurgah. There are also geometrical ornaments in panels and bands. The sides and the back of the octagon are bare.

The *iwan* niche has a geometrical decoration on the inside of the arch as well as on the entrance wall. Floral ornaments adorn the spandrels of the arch. Above the entrance is a wide rectangular band of script, again in 'cursive' *Kufic*, framing a pattern of square panels composed of a stylized angular script-like design around an octagonal medallion. Five-sided bays on two floors flank the *iwan* on both sides; the lower ones have been restored. The upper ones are covered with a semi-dome and richly decorated with arched floral medallions and spherical floral ornaments in blue and gold. The inner chamber is square, made into an octagon by means of simple *squinches* turning into a sixteen-sided polygon with eight latticed windows and eight *mukarnas*-filled niche heads. The inner dome rises from a *mukarnas* cornice, consists of 24 flutes and is much lower than the outer dome, whose windows bear no relation to those inside, which are lower and spaced differently.[31]

Inside – where women are not admitted – the dome is carried by a triple band of *mukarnas* and has ribs reproducing those on the outside and painted with repetitive floral motifs. The *squinches* and the stalactite-niches are decorated with inscriptions and floral ornaments in mosaic faience similar to those which adorn the *mihrab* niche. Byron's photographs from the early 1930s show remnants of an arcaded wing next to the *iwan* and, in front of it, a low structure with several doors; both have since disappeared. A new structure was built onto the southern wall in 1995.

76 The mosque Takht-i Pol

According to Golombek,³² beneath the floor of the mosque is a subterranean chamber which is entered from a staircase outside the mosque on the south-east. Its purpose is not clear. In front of the entrance to the mosque lies a funerary platform covered with tombs – the large, unidentified one nearest to the mosque is reputed to be that of the Khoja. Next to it is a modest tomb belonging, allegedly, to **Rabi'a Balkhi**, a woman poet and a member of the princely family of the Samanids who was executed in Balkh for having fallen in love with a Turkish slave, and who is said to have written her last poem in prison with her own blood.

In front of the shrine, on the other side of the small circular park, stands an isolated portal screen with a high arch which is all that remains of the seventeenth-century **madrasa of Sayid Subhan Kuli Khan**. There are just a few traces of tiled decoration on the inside of the arch.

Takht-i Pol

Due east of Balkh, on both sides of the main road and only a few kilometres from Mazar-i Sharif, lie the ruins of Takht-i Pol, a town which in the middle of the last century became the seat of the government of Afghan Turkestan for a short while. It was built on a rectangular plan and protected by a wall with 11 watchtowers, but now has completely disappeared.

Built hastily, mostly of clay, it was settled with the population of Balkh. On the right-hand side of the road coming from Balkh is a **mosque** which is worth a visit,

77 *Mosque Takht-i Pol. Interior*

78 *Mosque Takht-i Pol. Detail of the interior*

79 Aerial view of Mazar-i Sharif

consisting of three domed halls with an *iwan* in front of the central one, but no minaret. The central hall is higher than the lateral ones and contains the *mihrab*. The arrangement of three halls alongside each other indicates Indian influence. The halls have slightly pointed arches with rows of *mukarnas* decoration; the *mihrab* niche has quarter-domes over the two corners. The entire surface of the interior is richly decorated with paintings in a good state of preservation. Floral ornament and arabesques predominate, and the colours are mostly various shades of red and blue, with some green. Their style is a mixture of late Indian and Islamic traditions.

Mazar-i Sharif

Mazar-i Sharif, the present provincial capital, is a modern town centred around the **shrine of Hazret Ali**, one of the holiest places of the Shi'a. Tens of thousands of pilgrims flock here, in particular for the New Year celebrations (Now Ruz, 21 March) to pray to Ali, the son-in-law of the Prophet and the fourth caliph, who was murdered in Kufa in 661. According to legend, his followers put his corpse on a white she-camel and let her loose. She wandered as far as the neighbourhood of Balkh where, some four centuries later, the body of Ali was found intact. A shrine was built over the tomb in 1136 but was destroyed by Chingiz-Khan. The tomb was rediscovered in 1480, and Husayin Baykara erected a new and sumptuous mauso-

80 Mausoleum Hazret Ali, Mazar-i Sharif

leum over it. The building then underwent numerous restorations and reconstructions, so that hardly anything remains of the original Timurid structure, although there are still fragments which hark back to much earlier times, perhaps even to a pre-Islamic Buddhist sanctuary on the site.

The building stands in a large courtyard with three gateways, in the north, south and east. The south gateway is flanked by minarets. Originally, there was a gateway similar to the others in the west side, but its place was later taken by a mosque which incorporated the dome of the gateway. Outlines of innumerable *mihrabs* constitute the pattern of the pavement. They are used by worshippers at prayer time. Non-believers may enter the yard but not the sanctuary.

The main building has two pointed cupolas over an inner and an outer sanctuary. Inside, behind the entrance, is first a carpeted and decorated anteroom in which, near the door to the inner chamber, stands a huge cauldron similar to that already encountered in the mosque of Herat, but with no decoration. The walls and the ceiling of the inner chamber are decorated with painted floral ornament dating from the second half of the nineteenth century. The tomb of Hazret Ali is covered with an embroidered cloth and surrounded by a railing.

Outside, the entire façade is covered with glazed tiles, mostly turquoise and blue, of undistinguished quality and design. Against the walls of the sanctuary is a number of individual shrines; a number of those on the west side belong to the family of Amir Dost Muhammad.

81 Mausoleum Hazret Ali, Mazar-i Sharif. Detail

Byron believed the plan was copied from Gawhar Shad's Musalla in Herat,[33] while Renz sees its model in the funeral mosque of Ahmad Yassevi in the city of Turkestan (USSR – now Kazakhstan).[34]

During the restoration, Indian influence made itself felt quite considerably, so that now the whole building looks more Indian than Iranian. The decoration, although in a good state of preservation, bears witness to the general decline of taste and craftsmanship.

Ghazni

Next to the mausoleum of Mahmud in the village of Rauza is a Timurid building, the **mausoleum of Sultan Abdul Razzak**, built at the beginning of the sixteenth century and restored by an Italian archaeological expedition. Abdul Razzak was a one-time rival and challenger of Babur.

The tomb was originally built for his father Ulugh Beg Miranshah, who died in 1501; Abdul Razzak himself was assassinated in 1513/14. The mausoleum is a plain and modest structure with semi-circular corner towers, probably meant as bases for minarets, and four *iwans* with high *pishtak* walls. Smaller, domed chambers are behind each *iwan* and in the corners of the square. The building materials were bricks, and there is no decoration. The crypt underneath suggests that the building

82   Mausoleum Abdul Razzaq, Ghazni

83   Mausoleum Abdul Razzaq, Ghazni

was originally planned as a dynastic tomb. The central dome was perhaps meant to support an outer one on a drum, but this was never built. It is the last example of a Timurid mausoleum and it provides an important link to the funerary architecture of the Moghul period in India.[35]

The building now houses the Museum of Islamic art in Ghazni with exhibits of Ghaznavid art, found mostly in the excavations of the palace of Masud III, nearby. North-west of it, the mausoleum **Shah-i Shahid** is a ruined Timurid building, most probably from the second half of the fifteenth century. Its plaster vaults decorated with paintings show a certain similarity in design and composition with the back rooms in the north wing of the Shrine of Gazurgah in Herat.[36]

Kandahar

About 4km from the town in the direction of Herat is the so-called Throne of Babur, **Takht-i Babur**, also known as the *Chehel Sina* or Forty Steps. It is a man-made cave guarded by two dilapidated stone lions, accessible by a staircase of 40 steps. At its entrance an inscription commemorates Babur's conquest of Kandahar in 1522, and his other victories. The inscription, which is from the year 1546-7, was probably completed at the order of Babur's son Humayun.

There is little of historical interest in the town itself, except perhaps the mausoleum of **Ahmad Shah Durrani**, a domed octagonal structure, the interior of which is decorated with glazed tiles of no exceptional value. The neighbouring sanctuary, **Ziyarat da-Kherka-i Sharif**, houses a precious relic, the shirt of the Prophet. It is not accessible to non-believers.

The mausoleum of **Mir Wais** stands approximately 10km outside the town, near the road to Herat. It has a blue-tiled dome and was built in the early 1930s over the tomb of the first Afghan leader who declared independence for his tribe, in 1709.

A metal fountain-tank discovered in the old part of the city, in 1925, was decorated with epigraphic bands in Persian and a lotus crown reminding of a Buddhist begging bowl. Two verses signed Jalal ud-Din Muhammad would date it to 1490.

Kabul

In the time of the Timurids, Kabul was already a provincial capital; but the real turning point came when Babur, the young Timurid prince of Ferghana, made it his capital in 1504. It was from here that he departed in 1525 for his celebrated conquest of India, but even after he established his imperial residence in Agra, he kept returning to Kabul. He also wanted to be buried in the beautiful gardens which he had founded. However, unrest following his death in 1530 prevented the immediate fulfilment of his wish, and it was only nine years later that his wife brought his remains to Kabul.

Bagh-i Babur Shah, Babur's Garden, is the first of the famous Moghul gardens of which a number were built by Babur and his successors in Delhi, Lahore, Agra and Srinagar. It follows the traditional Persian principle of the Chahar Bagh or Four Gardens, and consisted of several squares laid on sloping terraces – although it is much neglected, this original layout can still be seen. It must be assumed, however, that only the rather narrow central part of the garden has survived. No doubt the terraces both left and right of the central strip were once larger, but they have since been used for other purposes.

The early nineteenth-century **citadel** consisted of a Lower Fortress with three palaces and an Upper Fortress, on top of the hill, where the armoury and the prison were located. The ruling amirs occupied it for a time, but in 1879 it was damaged by an explosion and in 1880 it was demolished by the British in retaliation for the massacre of the British mission the previous year.

The British explorer and archaeologist, Sir Aurel Stein, died here in 1943. His tomb is in the Christian cemetery.

In the middle of the slope stands the wooden summer pavilion of Amir Abdurrahman, built in 1883, with fine carved and painted ceilings. On the terrace above it is a small elegant mosque, built by the Moghul emperor Shah Jahan in 1646 to commemorate his victory at Balkh. Its present state is the result of restorations carried out in the 1960s. On the terrace above the mosque is **Babur's tomb**, under a pavilion erected in the early 1930s. The marble slab is from the sixteenth century, but it has been considerably restored, and the inscription on the headstone is only a copy of the original tablet set here by the emperor Jahangir in 1607.[37] The two tombs to the right of Babur's tomb belong to members of his family, his son Mirza Hindal and his grandson Hakim Mirza. The marble tablets at the head of these tombs are the originals placed here by Jahangir. The tomb on the left is of a later, eighteenth-century descendant. On the uppermost terrace is yet another tomb, that of Babur's grand-daughter.

Of two Timurid mausoleums, one is a ruin and without a dome, called **Ziyarat-i Sher Sukh** (the Shrine of the Red Lion), built in the late fifteenth century; nearby, in a better condition, is **Seh Oghor** (Three Holes) from the early sixteenth century, with five tombs belonging to the family of Babur's paternal uncle, Ulughbeg.

The only other historical monument of interest is the **mausoleum of Timur Shah**, built at the end of the eighteenth century in Indian Moghul style. It is an octagonal structure with a small dome at each of the eight corners; the central chamber is covered with a dome on a two-tier drum. In it is a plain undecorated sarcophagus, which is merely a cenotaph. The actual tomb of the amir is in the subterranean vault underneath which is not accessible. There are two other tombs beside it; one of them is said to belong to Timur Shah's son Shah Shuja, who was murdered outside the Bala Hissar in 1842.

Of the other sites and monuments in Kabul the following are worth listing. The **Chahr Chatta Bazaar** was built in the seventeenth century, and was blown up in 1842 by General Pollock in reprisal for the massacre of the British army. It was more than 200m long, with four covered arcades linked by open octagonal courtyards with fountains. The walls had stucco decoration studded with mirrors, and whitewashed with a special solution containing bits of mica to make them sparkle.[38] The original layout may still be visible but the building was reduced to rubble during the war.

The **Bagh-i Bala Palace** was built by Amir Abdurrahman at the close of the nineteenth century, and the amir died here in 1901. It was abandoned and almost completely ruined. Restored in 1964, it housed a fashionable restaurant and later served as barracks for the Taliban. Abdurrahman designed his buildings himself; they no longer followed the traditional design centered around the courtyard, but looked out into the garden. His other buildings, **Bostan Serai** and **Gulistan Serai**, were of similar design.

The **Chilsotoon** (Forty Pillars) **Palace** with its attractive gardens was also built originally by Amir Abdurrahman, then redesigned by Habibullah and again by Zahir Shah. It was later rebuilt and enlarged, and used as a state guest-house. The two principal mosques, the **Pul-i Khishti** mosque by the bridge of the same name, and the **Masjid-i Shah Do Shamshira** ('the mosque of the King of Two Swords') are both of recent origin. Of the numerous shrines in the city, the **Ziyarat-i Hazret-i Tamim**, built in 1939, is the most sacred. An Arab spiritual mission under Tamim is believed to have been massacred here around 644 by the Ratbil Shah of Kabul. The **Ziyarat-i Ashukan-o-Arefan**, built in the early nineteenth century, has an interesting wooden corridor, carved doors and pillars and a decorated ceiling. Even before the American bombing, factional fighting in 1994/5 has turned half of the city into a 'lunar landscape'.

The Tashkurgan and Kunduz area

The present town of Tashkurghan, which has recently been given back its ancient name of Khulm, is said to have been founded by Ahmad Shah Durrani in the middle of the eighteenth century, after he had destroyed the old Khulm, which was situated a few miles to the north and of which nothing remains except a huge mound. Arab geographers in the Middle Ages described it as a small town surrounded by many large villages, with a good climate. Suen Tsang also mentions Khulm; but in his time the town probably occupied a different site nearby, known today as the mound of Shul-Tepe.

On the southern edge of Tashkurghan, on the crest of a hill, are the ruins of the citadel, the **Shahr-i Kuhna** (Old city). It was in ruins and uninhabited when Yate visited it. Amir Abdurrahman built a palace here, south of the present road to Mazar-i Sharif, with a wooden gate which shows some high-quality carving. Apart from this the palace with its domed central hall and stained glass windows is more or less a copy of the Bagh-i Bala palace in Kabul.

The main attraction of Tashkurghan however is its bazaar, one of the last genuine covered bazaars still in existence and in active use. In the centre of it a domed structure in brick, 'Tim', built in the style of the traditional Chahar Suq, is decorated on the inside with inset porcelain saucers. This decoration dates from the nineteenth century.

In Kunduz itself, a ruined citadel is of limited interest. A mosque outside its southern wall has minarets decorated with simple geometrical ornaments in gold and blue tiles; its age is unknown. The word Kunduz, which could be an abbreviation of *kuhandiz* (fortress) could perhaps be applied to the medieval castle of Warwaliz, which is mentioned in this area by Arab geographers of the tenth century. Warwaliz appears to have been a large city in those days, but no town of this name now exists.[39]

Notes and references

1 The country and the people

1 Humlum, J., *La géographie de l'Afghanistan*, p.103
2 Dupree, L., *Afghanistan*, p.4
3 Dupree, L., *op. cit.*, p.40

2 History

1 According to Dupree, *op. cit.*, p.299 n. 3, around 130 BC there were seven Indo-Greek kingdoms: Badakhshan, Kabul, Ghazni, Gandhara, Swat, Taxila and Jammu-Sialkot
2 On problems of Kushan chronology, see several contributions in *Abstracts of Papers*. The Robatak inscription, recently found, gives insight into the Kushan dynasty and may permit a new chronology
3 Tolstov, S.P., *Po sledam drevnie-khorezmiiskoy tsivilizatsii*, p.222 (of the Czech edition)
4 Lockhart, L., *The fall of the Safavid dynasty and the Afghan occupation of Persia*, p.165
5 Dupree, L., *op. cit.* p.331
6 Rashid, A., Taliban, p. 207 ff.

3 Notes on architecture

1 Ghirshman, *Iran* p.165
2 *Ibid.*, p.166
3 *Ibid.*, p.167
4 *Ibid.*, p.232
5 Tadgell, p.17
6 *Ibid.*
7 Franz, G.H., 'Der buddhistische Stupa in Afghanistan', *AFG*, 4, 4, 1977 and *AFG*, 5, 1, 1978
8 Fisher, K., *Schöpfungen der Indischen Kunst*
9 Tadgell, p.101
10 Barthoux, J.J., 'Les fouilles de Hadda', *Mém. DAFA IV*, 1933
11 K. Fischer sees in the lantern ceiling an element of Central Asian wooden architecture, cf *Schöpfungen* . . .
12 Tadgell, p.24
13 Tadgell, p.101
14 Frumkin, G., 'Archaeology in Soviet Central Asia', *CAR* XIII, p.253

15 Marshall, J., *Taxila* I, p.75, II, p.520 Paiman, *Archéologia*, 479/2010. Also Ball, p.111 ff.
16 Ghirshman, *op. cit.* p.273
17 Tadgell, p.30
18 Ghirshman. p.276
19 Ghirshman, *op. cit.* p.322
20 *Ibid.*
21 Frumkin *CAR* XIII, p.252
22 Bosworth, *Culture*, p.34
23 *Ibid.*
24 Hoag, p.89
25 Vogt-Göknil, U., *Les grands courant de l'architecture islamique – Mosquées*, p.72
26 Hoag, p.96
27 Grabar, O., *Islamic architecture*, p. 76
28 Vogt-Göknil, *op. cit.*, p.121
29 Pope, *op. cit.*, p.259
30 Grabar, *op. cit.*, p.74
31 Grabar, *ibid.* p.75
32 *Ibid.*
33 *Ibid.*
34 Grabar *op. cit.*, p.77 ff
35 Ettinghausen, *op. cit.*, p.58
36 Schlumberger, D., 'Le Palais Ghaznévide de Lashkari Bazar', *Syria* XXIX, 1952
37 Hoag, p.13
38 Hoag, p.94
39 Hoag, p.98
40 Hoag, p.141
41 Grabar, *op. cit.*, p.75
42 Hoag, p.131
43 Hoag, p.188
44 Hoag, p.141
45 Eastern Iranian Architecture; apropos of the Ghurid parts of the Great Mosque of Herat, *BSOAS* XXXIII, 1970
46 Safadi, p.26ff
47 Welch, S.C., *A King's Book of Kings* (The Shah-Nameh of Shah Tahmasp), p.54
48 Safadi, p.28
49 Lefevre, p.26-7
50 Golombek, L., *The Timurid Shrine at Gazur Gah*, p.67ff
51 *Archéologia*, 420/2005. The article contains also a detailed description of the site
52 *The Economist*, 12/2003; *The Sunday Times* 10/2003

4 Pre-Islamic

1 Dupree, L., *op. cit.*, p.268

2 *Ibid.*, p.289
3 Rostovtzeff, M., *The excavations at Dura Europos*, New Haven, 1943-9
4 Dupree, *op. cit.*, p.292
5 Foucher, A., 'Notes sur les antiquites bouddhiques de Haibak', *JA* July, September, 1924. Mizuno, S., *Haibak and Kashmir-Smast*, Kyoto, 1962
6 Whitehouse, D., 'Excavations at Kandahar, 1974', *Afghan Studies* I, 1978, McNicoll, A., 'Excavations at Kandahar, 1975', *ibid.*
7 See below, p.85
8 Tr. from Julien, S., *Hiuan-Tsiang*, pp.40-42
9 Toybee, A., *Between Oxus and Jumna*, p.128
10 Meunié, J., Shotorak, *Mém. DAFA* X. 1942
11 Dupree, *op. cit.*, p.309n
12 Auboyer, J., *Afghanistan et son art*
13 Toynbee, *op. cit.*, p.122
14 Franz, G.H., *op. cit.*
15 Barthoux, J.J., *op. cit.*
16 Burnes, A., 'On the colossal idols of Bamian', *JASB* II, 1833; Honigberger, J.M., 'Journal of a route from Dera Ghazni Khan, through Vaziri country, to Kabul', *JASB* III, 1834; Masson, C., 'Notes on the antiquities of Bamian', *JASB* V, 1836
17 Sale, Lady F., *A Journal of the disasters in Afghanistan 1841-42*, London 1843; Eyre, V., *The military operations at Cabul,* London 1843; Talbot, M.G., 'The Rock-cut caves and statues of Bamiyan', *JRAS* 1886
18 'Notice archéologique sur la vallée de Bamiyan', *JA* April-June 1923
19 Godard, A., Godard, J., Hackin, J., 'Les antiquités Bouddhiques de Bamiyan', *Mém. DAFA* II, 1928
20 *Seventy wonders*, p.286-8
21 Godard, Godard, Hackin, *op. cit.*
22 Dupree, N.H., *The Kabul museum*, p.99
23 Dupree, N.H., Dupree, L., Motamedi, A.A., *The National Museum of Afghanistan*, p.99
24 Dagens, B., Le Berre, M., Schlumberger, D., 'Monuments préislamiques d'Afghanistan', *Mém. DAFA* XIX, 1964
25 Young, R.S., 'The South Wall of Balkh-Bactra', *AJA* LIX, 1955
26 Yate, *op. cit.* p.257
27 Le Strange, *op. cit.* p.422
28 Suen Tsang, tr. from Julien, *op. cit.* p.29-30
29 Cf also: Caspani, P.E., 'Nau-Bahar of Balkh', *Afg* I, 1947. A detailed analysis of the meaning and history of Naw Bahar is given by Bulliet, R.W., 'Naw Bahar and the survival of Iranian Buddhism', *Iran* XIV, 1976
30 Yate, *op. cit.* p.258-9
31 Le Berre, Schlumberger, *Observations…*
32 Sarianidi, V., *The golden hoard of Bactria*, New York, 1985
33 Litvinski, B. & Pichikian, I., 'Archaeological discoveries in South Tajikistan', *Bulletin of the USSR Academy of Sciences* 1980, No.7; see also *Archéologia* 387, 2002
34 Paiman, *Archéologia* 419/2005, 430/2006, 461/2008, 473/2010

5 Early Islamic

1. Yakubi, cf Le Strange, *op. cit.* p349
2. Le Strange, *op. cit.* p.420
3. Gibb, p.175
4. Yule, p.151
5. Pugachenkova, G.A., *No Gumbad in Balkh*
6. Melikian-Chirvani, 'La plus ancienne mosquée de Balkh', *AA* XX, 1969
7. Golombek, L., 'Abbasid Mosque at Balkh', *OA* XV, 3, 1969
8. 'Deux minarets d'époque seljoukide en Afghanistan', *Syria* XXX, 1953, p.108
9. 'Seljukid Ziyarats of Sar-i Pul', *BSOAS* XXIX, 1966
10. 'Remarques preliminaires sur un mausolée ghaznévide', *AA* XVII, 1968. Baba Hatem, un chef d'oevre inconnu..., *VIith Int. Congress on Iranian Art and Archaeology*, Tehran 1972
11. Pugachenkova, G.A., 'Mazar Arab-Ata v Time', *Sov. arkheologiya*, 1961. Grabar, O., 'The earliest Islamic commemorative structures', *Ars Orientalis*, VI, 1966
12. Bosworth, C.E., *The Ghaznavids*, p.134
13. Bosworth, *op. cit.* p.139
14. Le Strange, *op. cit.* p.348
15. Bosworth, *op. cit.* p36
16. Bosworth, *op. cit.* p.135
17. Byron *op. cit.*
18. Godard, A., 'Ghazni', *Syria* VI, 1925.
19. Scerrato, U., 'The first two excavation campaigns at Ghazni, 1957-1958', *EWX*, 1959. Bombaci, A., 'Introduction to the excavations at Ghazni', *EWX*, 1959
20. Bombaci, *op. cit.*
21. Byron, *op. cit.* p.279
22. Flury, *op. cit.*
23. Byron, *op. cit.* p.280
24. Byron, *Oxiana*, p.278
25. *Ibid.*
26. *Ibid.*
27. Flury, S., 'Le décor epigraphique des monuments de Ghazna', *Syria* VI, 1925
28. Sourdel-Thomine *op.cit.*
29. cf Knobloch, E., *Beyond the Oxus*, p.200
30. Hoag, p.93
31. Renz *op. cit.* p.286
32. Diez, E., 'Die Siegestürme in Ghazna als Weltbilder', *Kunst des Orients* I, 1952, p.37
33. Byron, *op. cit.* p.278
34. Flury, *op. cit.*

35 Hoag, p.94
36 Bosworth, C.E., *The development of Persian culture*, p.42
37 Bosworth, *Ghaznevids*, p.141
38 Le Strange, *op. cit.* p.344-5
39 Hoag, p.93
40 Schlumberger, D., 'Le palais ghaznévide de Lashkari Bazar', *Syria* XXIXX, 1952
41 *Ibid*.
42 Le Strange, *op. cit.* p.408
43 *Ibid*.
44 *Ibid*.
45 *Ibid*.
46 *Ibid*.
47 Byron, R., 'Timurid Monuments in Afghanistan' in *IIIe Congrès International d'art et d'archéologie Iraniens*, 1935
48 'Eastern Iranian Architecture', *BSOAS* XXXIII, 1970
49 See above, p.114
50 Byron, *Oxiana*, p.85
51 *Op. cit.* p.136
52 See above, p.106
53 Wilber, *op. cit.*, Melikian-Chirvani, *op. cit.*
54 Melikian – Chirvani *op. cit.*
55 Frye, R.N., 'Two Timurid Monuments in Herat', *Artibus Asiae*; XI, 1948, p.206
56 Wilber, *op. cit.*
57 Zestovsky, P.I., 'Esquisses d'architecture afghane', *Afg.* 3., 1949
58 The date of 1375 is usually accepted as correct
59 Frye, *op. cit.*
60 Byron, *Oxiana*, p.108
61 Renz, *op. cit.* p.288
62 Golombek, *Gazur Gah* p.81, 96
63 Knobloch, *op. cit.* p.199
64 'Eastern Iranian Architecture', *BSOAS* XXXIII, 1970
65 Golombek, *op. cit.* p.81
66 Hoag, p.142
67 Herberg, W., Davary, D., 'Topografische Feldarbeiten in Ghor – Bericht über Forschungsarbeiten zum Problem Jam-Ferozkoh', *AFJ* 2, 1976
68 Le Berre, M., Schlumberger, D., 'Observations sur les remparts de Bactres, in Monuments préislamiques d'Afghanistan', *Mém. DAFA* XIX, 1964

6 Timurid and late Islamic

1 Yate, C.E., *Northern Afghanistan*, p.30-2
2 *Ibid*.
3 Saljuki, F., *Khiyaban*, p.18 (quotation from Golombek, *Gazur Gah*, p.97 n. 28)
4 Byron, *Oxiana*, p.94-5

5 Byron, *Timurid Monuments*
6 Renz, *op. cit.* p.468
7 Byron, *Oxiana*, p.96
8 Wolfe, N.H., *Herat, A pictorial guide*
9 Golombek, L., *Gazur Gah*, p.90
10 Hoag p.136
11 *The Timurid Shrine at Gazur Gah*, Toronto, 1968
12 Byron, *Oxiana*, p.101
13 Golombek, p.85
14 Golombek, *op. cit.* p.28
15 Golombek, *op. cit.* p.33
16 Golombek, *op. cit.* p.43
17 Golombek, *op. cit.* p.45
18 *Ibid.*
19 *Oxiana*, p.101
20 Saljuki, F., *Gazur Gah*, p.20 (quotation from Golombek, *op.cit.* p.65)
21 *Oxiana*, p.101
22 Golombek, *op. cit.* p.65
23 Golombek, *op. cit.* p.66
24 Golombek, *op. cit.* p.103
25 Pugachenkova, G.A., 'No Gumbad in Balkh', *Sov. Arkheologiya*, 3, 1970
26 Mustamandy, S., 'A building by the name of Gawharshad in Kohsan of Herat', *Afg* 4, 1968. Pugachenkova, G.A., 'A l'étude des monuments timourides d'Afghanistan', *Afg* 4, 1970
27 Golombek p.99
28 Hoag, p.175
29 Le Strange, Clavijo, p.198
30 Byron, *Oxiana*, p.256
31 Hoag, p.137
32 Golombek, *op. cit.* p.115
33 Byron, *Oxiana*, p.247
34 Renz, *op. cit.* p.475
35 Hoag, p.141
36 Pugachenkova, G.A., 'A l'étude des monuments timourides d'Afghanistan', *Afg* 3, 1970. Golombek, L., *Gazur Gah*, p.63, 78
37 Dupree, N.H., *Kabul*, p.78
38 Dupree, N.H., *Kabul*, p.95
39 Le Strange, *op. cit.* p.428

Glossary

Abbasids	Arab caliphs of Baghdad (AD 750-1258)
agora	(Greek) assembly, market-place
aiwan (*iwan*)	vaulted hall or recess opening off a court
ambulatory	curved or polygonal aisle, usually leading round a sanctuary
amir (*emir*)	leader or general, then military govenor
Anahita	'The Immaculate', goddess of the water and fertility
apadana	(Persian) hypostyle hall of Achaemenian palaces usually square in plan, with portico to one or more sides
apsaras	celestial dancing girls
arabesque	interlacing foliate
Aramaic	a tongue indigenous to Syria and Phoenicia, *lingua franca* in Achaemenian Empire
Architrave	horizontal unit supported on columns
Arsacids	Parthian dynasty, founded by Arsaces, *c*.250 BC-AD 224
Ashoka	third emperor of the Maurya dynasty (268-231 BC); converted to Buddhism between 250 and 248 BC
Ateshgah	fire temple sheltering the sacred fire, Zoroastrian
Avalokiteshvara	one of the main *bodhisattvas* of Mahayana Buddhism; personification of charity and compassion
avatar	incarnation
bagh	(Arabic-Persian) garden, usually formal; as in *chahar-bagh*, quadripartite garden with quadrants divided by water channels
banai technique	large geometrical patterns composed of small glazed bricks
barrel vault	see vault
bodhisattva	a previous incarnation of the Buddha; a compassionate spirit
caliph	leader of the Muslims, both spiritual and political
caliphate	Office of Successor of the Prophet
capital	block of stone, usually moulded or carved, that is placed on top of a column and supports the beams of the ceiling or roof
caravansarai	fortified hostel on a trade route
cella	inner sanctum of a temple; principal chamber with the cult statue
chahar-bagh	see *bagh*
chehel sotun	forty-columned pavillion or hall
Chingizid	local dynasty ruling in Heart in the seventeenth and eighteenth century
chinoiserie	selective use of Chinese motifs, both foliate and animal
chowk	palace court

Glossary

cloud-scrolls, bands, collars
    serpentine forms with hooked or imbricated excrescences; a reminiscence of curved and convoluted ribbons from Chinese art.
cuneiform   wedge-shaped writing used in ancient Assyria, Persia etc.
cupola   dome supported either on a circular wall or on four arches making a square in plan

dado   lower few feet of room-wall, faced with wood or coloured differently from upper part
dagh   mountain
darwaza   (Persian) door, gate or portal, especially of monumental proportions
daulat khana   (Persian) 'abode of majesty' king's palace enclosure
dinar   from Latin denarius, gold coin, usually in a ten to one ratio with silver
dirham   from Greek *drakhme*, silver coin, weight 2.8 or 2.9 grams
diwan   (Persian) royal court or audience place; *diwan-i am* for public audience, *diwan-i khas* for private ones; also state administrative council
dhoti   piece of cloth wrapped around the loins

earthenware   a ceramic body made from clay maturing at *c.*850-1200°C

ghazi   a warrior for Islam, frontier soldier, hero or martyr
glaze (lead, tin)   vitreous (glassy) coating applied to the surface of a pot to make it impermeable or for decorative effect. Lead glaze: a glaze fluxed with lead oxide. Ting: a glaze, lead-or alkaline-fluxed, opacified with tin oxide
Gupta   period beginning with the reign of Chandragupta I (320)

haft aurang   tile with colour design, with a slight depression between the colours
haft qalam   filigree engraving technique
haram   (Arabic) forbidden; haram sara, exclusive compound for royal women (as *zenana q.v.*); also a ritual enclosure employed mainly for the great shrines of Mecca and Medina, and for the Dome of the Rock and the al-Aqsa Mosque in Jerusalem
harmika   part of the top of a *stupa*, small room or receptacle for the reliquary
hasht behesht   (Persian) literally 'eight paradises'; octagonal palace pavilion, usually with alternating *iwans* and chambers to its side with a central two storey chamber
hazira   an enclosure around an unroofed tomb, with the addition of a mosque
Hepthalites (*White Huns*)
    Turco-Mongol nomads who dominated Central Asia and Afghanistan from the mid-fifth century to the late sixth century AD
Hinayana (*Lesser Vehicle*)
    one of the two branches of Buddhism
hypogeum   underground tomb chamber or group of chambers
hypostyle   hall with ceiling supported by columns

Il-khan	Mongol rulers of Persia of the line of Hulagu
imam	leader of prayer, religious leader in a wider sense,
imamzade	Muslim shrine, usually *shi'ite*, mausoleum of a descendant of one of the twelve *imams*
iwan	see *aiwan*
jataka	story of the earlier lives of Buddha Sakyamuni
kasr (*qasr*)	a fortified dwelling, a palace
khaniga (*khanga, khanaqah*)	hermitage or retreat of sufis or dervishes; monastery
kibla (*qibla*)	axis of prayer, wall of mosque facing Mecca
khan	Turkish title of prince or lord
Kufic	script with angular letter forms and ligature
kuriltay (*qurultay*)	Mongol council of princes
Kushans	people of Iranian origin, founders of a vast empire (first to third century AD) which included Afghanistan, Turkestan and North Pakistan
li	Chinese measure, 1 mile = 5 *li*
lead glaze	see glaze
lustre	a metallic sheen on the surface of a glaze used for its decorative effect
madrasa	reading place, religious college, school of Islam
Mahayana	(Great Vehicle) one of the two main branches of Buddhism
maiolica	tin-glazed earthenware
Maitreia	in Mahayana Buddhism, great bodhisattva, future saviour of the world
maksura (*maqsara*)	a protective barrier surrounding the minbar and the minrab in a Friday mosque
mandala	magical diagram in Buddhist iconography
Massagetae	confederation of nomadic tribes east of the Caspian
masjid	mosque; *jami masjid* (*juma'a masjid*): Friday Mosque
mihrab	niche in the main wall of the mosque marking direction of Mecca
minaret	mosque tower for calling Muslims to prayer
minbar	pulpit
Mithras	Persian god of light and sun; one of the three judges of the souls of the dead
Mithraism	Iranian religion also practised by the Romans
mudra	hand gesture conveying state of mind or attitude; important in Buddhist iconography
mukarnas (*muqarnas*)	multiple miniature *squinch* forms making 'honeycomb' pattern
musalla	an enclosure, usually unroofed; a place of prayer outside a city wall
naskhi	a cursive form of Arabic calligraphy
nastalik (*nastaliq*)	script characterised by the elongation of certain letters, the smoothing out of the line and generally diagonal movement
Nataraja	King of Dance (attribute of Shiva)

nokers	(Mongol) company of guards
noyon	(Mongol) noble, lord
octagon	figure or architectural form with eight sides
pakhsa (pise)	sundried bricks of beaten clay mixed with gravel
Parthia	province of Iran south-east of the Caspian
pendentive	concave form which results when a horizontal quarter-circle is joined to two arches at right angles to each other; by building pendentives in the corners of four arches forming a square, a dome or drum can be placed upon them
pentagon	five-sided figure, usually plane rectilineal
peristyle	row of columns surrounding a building
pilaster	flattened out version of a column with base, fluting, capital etc., built against a wall or a pier; section of pillar
pillar	any free standing support
pishtak (pishtaq)	rectangular screen framing a portal or an iwan
plinth	low projecting course at the foot of a wall or colonnade
pol (pul)	bridge
portico	colonnade connected by a roof to the external wall of a building
Prakrit	the 'common language' of ancient India derived from Sanskrit, the 'perfect language'
propylaeon	monumental entrance to a sacred enclosure
qaleh (Kala)	castle
qalam	pen; could be made of reed or of animal hair
raja	king
rauza (rawza)	mortuary complex of tomb and funerary mosque
rhyton	a drinking vessel in the form of an animal or an animal's horn, with single or double spouts for drinking
ribat	a fortified enclosure used as a dwelling or place of prayer
Safavids	Shi'a dynasty in Persia, gained power in 1501
Saka, Scythians	nomads of Iranian origin, who migrated to Western Asia from South Russia and Chinese Turkestan
samsara	transmigration of souls
sangha	order of Buddhist monks; sangharama-monastery
saray (sarai)	palace
shah	(Persian) king
shari'a	holy law of Islam
sharif	noble
sheikh	(Arabic) elder, chief; also descendant of the companions of the Prophet
shi'a	partisans of Ali and his descendants as the proper imams of the Muslims
socle	plain, low rectangular block serving as support for pedestal vase, statue etc.
Soghd, Soghdiana	Persian province north of Bactria, centered on Samarkand

squinch	arch across corner to effect transition from polygon to circle; serves the same purpose as pendentive
stelae	upright stone slabs, usually inscribed, marking graves or victories
stoneware	a ceramic body made from clay, harder and heavier than earthenware, maturing at c.1200-1300°C
stucco	carved or moulded plaster, often painted, used as ornamental and protective covering for mud-brick walls; the finest stucco was made of powdered marble
stupa	tumulus, burial or reliquary mound
sufi	Muslim mystic or hermit
sultan	emperor, supreme ruler
sunni	the major, or Orthodox, sect of Islam
tal, tel, tepe	artificial mound made of debris of foundations and collapsed walls
thuluth	bold rounded script with some swash letters used for titles
Timurid	dynasty founded by Timur (Tamerlane) in 1370, extinguished by the Uzbeks in 1506
tin glaze	see glaze
turbe (turbat)	Turkish term for a domed tomb
tympanum	space between the lintel of a doorway and the semicircular arch above it
ulus	domain, tribal area
vazir (vizier)	minister
vaqf (waqf)	a pious foundation used to support mosques, madrasas etc.
vault	stone roof or ceiling; barrel vault: continuous roof, usually semi-circular in section, resting on the walls on either side; groin vault: roof produced by the intersection of two equal barrel vaults. The weight of such a vault rests only on the corners
vihara	residential quarters of a Buddhist monastery
vimana	storyed building with receding terraces, main element in South Indian sanctuary
yurt	tent, household
zenana	(Persian) enclosed accommodation for women, gynaeceum
ziggurat	Mesopotamian temple composed of multiple tiers and resembling an artificial mountain
Zoroaster (Zarathushtra)	prophet and founder of the Zoroastrian religion, a reformed version of Mazdeism. His teachings are known as the *Avesta*

Bibliography

Abbreviations

AA	*Arts Asiatiques*, Paris (before 1954 *Revue des Arts Asiatiques*, Paris)
Aas	*Artibus Asiae*, Ascona
Afg	*Afghanistan*, Kabul
AFJ	*Afghanistan Journal*, Graz
AJA	*American Journal of Archaeology*
BSOS/BSOAS	*Bulletin of the School of Oriental (and African) Studies*, London
CAJ	*Central Asiatic Journal* (The Hague –Wiesbaden)
CRAI	*Comptes-rendus des séances de l'Académie des Inscriptions et Belles-Lettres*, Paris
EW	*East and West*, Roma
JA	*Journal Asiatique*, Paris
JISOA	*Journal of the Indian Society of Oriental Art*, Calcutta
JRAS	*Journal of the Royal Asiatic Society*
JASB/ JRASB	*Journal of the (Royal) Asiatic Society of Bengal*, Calcutta
Mém. DAFA	*Memoires de la Délégation archéologique française en Afghanistan*, Paris
Mon. Piot	*Fondation E. Piot, Monuments et mémoires publiées par l'Académie des Inscriptions et Belles-Lettres*, Paris
OA	*Oriental Art*, London
RA	*Revue Archéologique*, Paris
SPACH	*Society for the Protection of Afghanistan Cultural Heritage*
ZDMG	*Zeitschrift der Deutschen Morgenländischen Gesellschaft*, Wiesbaden
ZS	*Zentralasiatische Studien*, Bonn Bibliography

General

Afganskii spravochnik, Moskva 1964
Afghan Studies, vol. 1, London 1978, vol. 2, London 1979
Area handbook for Afghanistan, Washington 1969
Ball, W., Gardin, J.-C., *Archaeological Gazeteer of Afghanistan*, 1982
Bennigsen, A., & Lemercier-Quelquejay, C., *Islam in the Soviet Union*, London 1967
Caroe, Sir O.K., *The Pathans*, London 1976
Clifford, M.L., *The Land and People of Afghanistan*, Philadelphia and New York 1973
Davies, R., *An Historical Atlas of the Indian Peninsula*, New Delhi, 1949
Dupree, L., *Afghanistan*, Princeton 1973

Dupree, N.H. *Status of Afghanistan Cultural Heritage*, SPACH Library Series No 1., Peshawar, 1998
Geiger, W., 'Die Sprache der Afghanen, das Pasto. Grundriss der Iran', *Philologie* I, part 2, Strasbourg 1898-1901
Gilles, R., Cambon, P., 'L'Afghanistan, cinquante ans d'archéologie, vingt ans de guerre', *Archéologia*, 3/2000
Fraser-Tytler, W.F., revised by M.C. Gillett, *Afghanistan*, London 1967
Hahn, H., Die Stadt *Kabul (Afghanistan) und ihr Umland. I:* Gestalt-wandel einer orientalischen Stadt, Bonn 1964
Humlum, J., *La géographie de l'Afghanistan*, Copenhagen 1959
Jentsch, C.H., *Das Nomadentum in Afghanistan*, Meisenheim 1973
Jettmar, K., *Die Religion des Hindukusch* (Religion der Menschheit, Ban 4), Stuttgart 1975
Kauffer, R., Le guépier afghan, *Historia* 1/2010
Klimburg, M., *Afghanistan. Das Land im historischen Spannungsfeld Mittelasiens*, Wien 1966
Knobloch, E., 'Survey of Archaeology and Architecture in Afghanistan' (Part I, The South), *AFG* I (8, 1981)
Knobloch, E., *Monuments of Central Asia*, London 2001
Knobloch, E., *Russia and Asia*, Hong Kong: 2007
Kraus, W., *Afghanistan* (Natur, Geschichte, Kultur, Staat, Gesellschaft, Wirtschaft), Tübingen 1972
Lesny, V., *Buddhismus*, Praha 1948
Le Strange, G., *The lands of the Eastern Caliphate*, Cambridge 1905
Lewis, B. ed., *The world of Islam*, London 1976
Lewis, J., 'Pillage d'une culture. Le patrimoine afghan en peril', *Archeologia* 3/2000
Lobanov-Rostovsky, A., *Russia and Asia*, Ann Arbor 1951
Neidermayer, O. von & Diez, E., *Afghanistan*, Leipzig 1924
Rashid, A., *Taliban*, London 2000, Jihad, *Yale* 2002, *Descent into Chaos*, London 2008
Robertson, G., *The Kafirs of the Hindu Kush*, London 1900
Schurmann, H., *The Mongols of Afghanistan*, The Hague 1942
Sidky, M.O., 'Buddhism in Afghanistan', *Afg* 3, 1976
Tate, G.P., *The frontiers of Baluchistan*, London 1909, reprint Lahore 1976
Thomas, D., *Between Rocks and a Hard Place*, Minerva, 7-9/2010
Wheeler, G., *The peoples of Soviet Central Asia*, London 1966
Wilber, D.N., 'Afghanistan, independent and encircled', *Foreign Affairs* 31, 3, 1953
Wilber, D.N., *Afghanistan, its people, its society, its culture*, New Haven 1962

History

Adamec, L.W., *Afghanistan 1900-1923: a diplomatic history*, Berkeley 1967
Akhmedzhanov, G., *Geratskii vopros v XIX veke*. Tashkent 1971
Babur, *Babur-nama*, tr. A.S. Bereridge, London 1921
Barthold, W., *Herat unter Husein Baiqara, dem Timuriden*, Leipzig 1938
Barthold, V.V., *Turkestan down to the Mongol invasion*, London 1928
Becker, S., *Russia's Protectorates in Central Asia*, Cambridge, Ma. 1968

Belenitsky, A., *The ancient civilisation of Central Asia*, Genève and London 1969
Bosworth, C.E., *The Ghaznevids: Their empire in Afghanistan and Eastern Iran 994-1040*, Edinburgh 1963
Bosworth, C.E., *Sistan under the Arabs*, Rome 1968
Bosworth, C.E., *The Medieval history of Iran, Afghanistan and Central Asia*, London 1977 (various reprints)
Bosworth, C.E., 'The early Islamic history of Ghur', *CAJ* VI, 1961, reprinted in 'The Medieval History of Iran', Afgh. and C. Asia, London 1977
Bosworth, C.E., 'The imperial policy of the early Ghaznavids', *Islamic Studies*, Karachi I, 3, 1962, reprinted in *The Medieval History of Iran, Afgh. and C. Asia*, London 1977
Bosworth, C.E., 'Notes on the pre-Ghaznavid history of Eastern Afghanistan', *The Islamic Quarterly* IX, Oxford 1965, reprinted in *The Medieval history of Iran, Afgh. and C. Asia*, London 1977
Bosworth, C.E., 'The development of Persian culture under the early Ghaznavids', Iran VI, London 1968, reprinted in *The Medieval history of Iran, Afgh. and C. Asia*, London 1977
Bosworth, C.E., 'Barbarian incursions: the coming of the Turks into the Islamic world', in Islamic civilisation 950–1150, ed. D.S. Richards, Oxford 1973, reprinted in *The Medieval history of Iran, Afgh. and C. Asia*, London 1977
Bosworth, C.E., 'The armies of the Saffarids', *BSOAS* XXXI, London 1968, reprinted in *The Medieval history of Iran, Afgh. and C. Asia*, London 1977
Bosworth, C.E., *The later Ghaznavids, 1040-1186*, Edinburgh 1978
Brockelmann, C., *Geschichte der islamische Völker und Staten*, 2nd ed. München und Berlin 1943
Concise History of Islam, Amsterdam 1957
Coulson, N., *A history of Islamic law*, Edinburgh 1964
Durand, Sir H.M., *The first Afghan War and its causes*, London 1879
Dyakonov, M.M., 'Drevnyaya Baktria', in *Po sledam drevnikh kultur*, Moskva 1954
Eyre, V., *The Military Operations at Cabul*, London 1843
Eyre, V., *The Kabul Insurrection of 1841-42*, London 1879
Elliot, H. & Dowson, J., ed., *History of Gazni*, 2 vols. (first published 1869), Calcutta 1953
Elphinstone, M., *An account of the kingdom of Caubul*, London 1815
Ferrier, J.P., *History of the Afghans*, London 1858
Foot, R., 'The changing pattern of Afghanistan's relations with its neighbours', *Asian Affairs*, XI, I, February 1980
Frumkin, G., 'Afghanistan, carrefour des civilisations', *Journal de Genève* no. 156, July 1957
Gibb, H.A.R., *Arab conquest in Central Asia*, London 1923
Grousset, R., *L'empire des steppes*, Paris 1939, 1960
Haenisch, E., (tr.), *Die geheime Geschichte der Mongolen*, Leipzig 1948
Heissig, W., *Die Mongolen: Ein Volk sucht seine Geschichte*, 2nd ed. München 1978
Hookham, H., *Tamburlane the Conqueror*, London 1962
Kohzad, A.A., 'Les Ratbils Shahs de Kaboul', *Afg* 2 1950
Kohzad, A.A., 'Two of the last Buddhist rulers of Ghazni and Bamiyan', *Afg* 4, 1950
Kohzad, A.A., 'Huit légendes concernant la fondation de la ville de Herat', *Afg* 4, 1951

Kruglikova, J.T. ed., *Drevnyaya Baktria*, Moskva 1976

Leyden, J., and Erskine, W., (tr.), *Memoirs of Zahir-ud-Din Muhammed Babur, Emperor of Hindustan, written by himself, in the Jaghatai Turki*, London 1826, Oxford 1912

Lockhart, L., *The fall of the Safavid dynasty and the Afghan occupation of Persia*, Cambridge 1958

Lukonin, V.G., 'Sasanian conquest in the East of Iran and the problem of Kushan chronology', in *Abstracts of Papers by Soviet Scholars, International Conference on the History, Archaeology and Culture of Central Asia in the Kushan Period*, Dushanbe 1968

Macrory, P., *Signal Catastrophe*, London 1966

Marvin, Ch., *The Russians at Merv and Herat, and their power of invading India*, London 1883

Masson, V.M., 'Problema drevnyey Baktrii i novyi arkheologicheskii material', *Sov. arkheologiya* 2, 1958

Masson, V.M., 'Drevnyeyshii Afghanistan', *Sov. Arkheologiya* 2, 1962

Masson, V.M. & Romodin, A.A., *Istoriya Afganistana* I, Moskva 1964

Masson, V.M., *Srednyaya Azia i drevniy vostok*, Moskva and Leningrad 1964

Masson, V., Sarianidi, V., *Central Asia, Turkmenia before the Achaemenids*, 1972

McChesney, R.D., *Waqf in Central Asia: Four hundred years in the History of a Shrine, 1480-1889*, (Mazar-i-Sharif) Princeton, 1991

Narain, A.K., *The Indo-Greeks*, Oxford 1957

Noorani, A.G., *Soviet ambitions in South Asia International Security*, 4.3, 1979-80

Rahmany, M., 'La reine Gawarchade', *Afg* 2 1949

Sale, Lady Florentia, *A Journal of the Disasters in Afghanistan 1841-2*, London 1843

Sanders, J.H. (tr.), *Tamerlane*, by Ibn Arabshah, London 1936

Schlumberger, D., 'Les traits originaux de l'historie de l'Afghanistan', *Afg* 4 1961

Sellman, R., *An Outline Atlas of Eastern History*, London 1954

Singh, G., *Ahmad Shah Durrani: Father of Modern Afghanistan*, New Delhi 1959

Spuler, B., *Iran in früh-islamischer Zeit*, Wiesbaden 1952

Stavisky, Bongard & Levin, 'Central Asia in the Kushan period', *Abstracts of Papers by Soviet Scholars, International Conference on the History, Archaeology and Culture of Central Asia in the Kushan Period*, Dushanbe 1968

Stein, A., 'Afghanistan in Avestic geography', *Indian Antiquary* XV, 1886

Sykes, P., *History of Persia*, 2 vols, London 1915, 1930

Sykes, Sir P., *History of Afghanistan*, London 1940

Talbot-Rice, T., *The Scythians*, London 1961

Tarn, W.W., *The Greeks in Bactria and India*, 2nd ed., Cambridge 1951

Tate, G.P., *Seistan, a memoir on the history, topography, ruins and people of the country*, 4 parts, Calcutta 1910-12

Tauer, F., *Dejiny a kultura islamu*, Praha 1940

Tolstov, S.P., *Po sledam drevnie – khorezmiiskoy tsivilisatsii*, Moscow 1948

Toynbee, A., 'Afghanistan as a meeting-place in history', *Afg* 2 1960

Victor, J.-C., *La cite des murmures*, Paris 1983

Vogel, R., *Die Persien – und Afghanistan Expedition Oskar Ritter von Niedermayers 1915-16 (Studien zur Militärgeschichte, Militärwissenschaft und Konfliktsforschung, Band 8)*, Osnabrück 1976

Watson, B., *Szu-Ma Chien, grand historian of China*, London 1958

Zeymal, E.V., '278 AD – The date of Kanishka', *Abstracts of Papers by Soviet Scholars, International Conference on the History, Archaeology and Culture of Central Asia in the Kushan period*, Dushanbe 1968

Travel

Dupree, N.H., *An historical guide to Afghanistan*, Kabul 1971
Dupree, N.H., *An historical guide to Kabul*, 2nd ed. Kabul 1972
Dupree, N.H., *Herat. A pictorial guide*, Kabul 1966
Dupree, N.H., *The road to Balkh*, Kabul 1967
Dupree, N.H., *The valley of Bamiyan*, 2nd ed. Kabul 1967
Barger, E., 'Exploration of ancient sites in Northern Afghanistan', *Geographical Journal* XCIII, 5, May 1939
Beal, S. (tr.), *Travels of Fa-Hsien (400) and Sung Yun (518)*, London 1869
Beazley, C.R., *Texts and versions of Carpini and Rubruck*, London 1903
Burnes, A., *Cabool, being a personal narrative of a journey*, London 1842
Burnes, A., *Voyages de l'embouchure de l'Indus à Lahor, Caboul, Balkh, et à Boukhara et retour par la Perse, pendant les annees 1831, 1832 et 1833*, 4 vols, Paris 1835
Burnes, A., *Travels into Bokhara*, 3 vols, 2nd ed., London 1835
Burnes, A. & Gerard, J.D., 'Continuation of the route of lieut. A. Burnes and dr. Gerard, from Peshawar to Bokhara', *JASB* II, 1833
Byron, R., *The road to Oxiana*, London 1937
Ferrier, J.P., *Voyages en Perse, dans l'Afghanistan, le Beloutchistan et le Turkestan*, 2 vols, Paris 1860
Gibb, H.A.R. (tr.), *The travels of Ibn Battuta*, London 1929
Gibb, H.A.R. (tr.), *The travels of Ibn Battuta AD 1325-1354*, 3 vols, Cambridge 1958-71
Giles, H.A. (ed.), *Fa-Sien, travels 399-414 AD or Record of Buddhist kingdoms*, Cambridge 1923
Honigberger, J.M., 'Journal of a route from Dera Ghazni Khan, through Vaziri country to Kabul', *JASB* III 1834
Julien, S. (tr.), *Hiun-Tsiang, Mémoires sure les contrées occidentales*, Paris 1857
Komroff, M., *Contemporaries of Marco Polo*, London 1928
Lal, M.M., *Journal of a tour through the Punjab, Afghanistan, Turkistan, Khorasan and part of Persia in company with Lieut. Burnes and Dr Gerard*, Calcutta 1834
Latham, R.E. (tr.), *The travels of Marco Polo*, Lonodn 1958
Le Strange, G. (tr.), *Clavijo, Ruy Gonzales de, Embassy to Tamerlane 1403-1406*, London 1928
Lunt, J., *Bokhara Burnes*, London 1969
Toynbee, A., *Between Oxus and Jumna*, London 1961
Wood, J., *A personal narrative of a journey to the source of the river Oxus by the route of the Indus, Kabul and Badakhshan 1836-38*, London 1841
Wood, J., *A journey to the source of the river Oxus*, London 1976
Yate, C.E., *Northern Afghanistan*, Edinburgh and London 1888
Yate, C.E., *Khurasan and Sistan*, Edinburgh and London 1900
Yule, H. (tr., ed.), *The book of Ser Marco Polo*, 2 vols, 3rd ed. New York 1929
Wolfe, N.H., see Duprée, N.H.

Architecture, archaeology and art

Afghanistan, une histoire millénaire, Catalogue, Musée Guimet, Paris 2002
Allchin, F.R. & Hammond, N. (eds), *Archaeology of Afghanistan*, London-New York, 1978
Ancient Art of Afghanistan (Catalogue of an exhibition), London 1967
Arberry, A.J., *Classical Persian Literature*, London 1958
Arts de l'Islam des origins à 1700 dans les collections publiques françaises, (catalogue d'une exposition), Paris 1971
Ashrafi, M.M., *Persian-Tajik poetry in XIV-XVII centuries, miniatures from USSR collections*, Dushanbe 1974
Auboyer, J., *Afghanistan et son art*, Paris 1968
Bachinsky, N.M., *Reznoye derevo v arkhitekture Srednei Azii*, Moskova 1947
Bahari, E., Bihzad, *Master of Persian Painting*, London 2000
Ball, W., *The monuments of Afghanistan*, London 2008/ incl. Gazetteer of several hundred names
Blanc, J.-C., *Afghan trucks*, London 1976
Borovka, G.I., *Scythian art*, London 1928
Bruno, A., 'The planned and executed restoration of some monuments of archaeological and artistic interest in Afghanistan' (Italian archeological mission in Afghanistan), *EW* XIII, 2-3, 1962
Centlivres-Demont, M., *Volkskunst in Afghanistan (Malereien an Lastwagen, Moscheen und Teehäusern)*, Graz 1976
Creswell, K.A.C., *Early Muslim architecture*, 2 vols, London and New York 1932, 1940
Critchlow, K., *Islamic patterns*, London 1976
Cohn-Wiener, E., *Turan*, Berlin 1930
Dagens, B., Le Berre, M. & Schlumberger, D., 'Monuments préislamiques d'Afghanistan', *Mém. DAFA* XIX, Paris 1964
Dani, A., *Gandhara art in Pakistan*, Peshawar 1968
Diez, E., *Churasanische Baudenkmäler*, Berlin 1918
Diez, E., *Persien. Islamische Baukunst in Churasan*, Hagen I.W.- Darmstadt-Gotha 1924
Diez, E., *Iranische Kunst*, Wien 1944
Diez, E., 'Die Siegestürme in Ghazna als Weltbilder', *Kunst des Orients* I, 1950
Dupree, N.H., Dupree, L. & Motamedi, A.A., *The National Museum of Afghanistan. An illustrated guide*, Kabul 1974
Fischer, K., *Schöpfungen indischer Kunst*, Koln 1959
Foucher, A., 'The decoration of the stuccoed stupas', in *Excavations at Taxila – The stupas and monasteries at Jaulian by Sir John Marshall*, Calcutta 1921
Foucher, A., 'De Kàpisi à Pushkarâvati', *BSOS* VI, 1930-1932
Foucher, A., *L'art Gréco-bouddhique du Gandhâra*, 2 vols in 4 parts, Paris 1905-51
Franz, G.H., 'Der buddhistische Stupa in Afghanistan', *AFJ* 4, 4, 1977 and 5, I, 1978
Frumkin, G., *Archaeology in Soviet Central Asia (Handbuch der Orientalistik. Siebente Abteilung: Kunst und Archäologie. Band III: Innerasien)*, Leiden 1970
Frye, R.N., 'Notes on the history of architecture in Afghanistan', *Ars Islamica* XI-XII, 1946

Frye, R.N., 'Observations on architecture in Afghanistan', *Gazette des Beaux-Arts*, March 1946
Ghirshman, R., *Études iraniennes II – un ossuaire en Pierre sculptée*, AAs XI, 4, 1948
Ghirshman, R., *Persian Art, 249 BC–AD 651*, New York 1962
Ghirshman, R., *The art of ancient Persia*, Paris and New York 1964
Ghirshman, R., *Perse – Proto-iraniens – Mèdes – Achéménides, Iran – Parthes et Sasanides*, Paris 1962
Ghirshman, R., *Iran*, Paris 1951, Engl. tr. London 1954
Grabar, O. & Hill, D., *Islamic architecture and its decoration AD 800-1500*, London 1964/7
Grabar, O., *Studies in medieval Islamic art*, London 1976
Grube, E.J., 'The decorative art of Central Asia in the Timurid period', *Afg* 2-3, 1971
Hackin, J., *L'art bouddhique de la Bactriane et les origins de l'art Gréco-bouddhique*, Kabul 1937
Hackin, J., *Buddhist art in Central Asia: Indian, Iranian and Chinese influences from Bâmiyân to Turfân. Studies in Chinese art and some Indian influences*, London 1938
Hackin, J., Carl, J. & Meunié, J., 'Diverses recherches archéologiques en Afghanistan 1933-1940', *Mém. DAFA* VIII, Paris 1959
Hoag, J.D., *Islamic Architecture*, London 1987
Hrbas, M. and Knobloch, E., *The art of Central Asia*, Praha and London 1965
Iran – *miniatures persanes, bibliothèque impériale* (Introduction by B. Gray & A. Godard), Coll. UNESCO de l'art mondial, 1956
Knobloch, E., *Beyond the Oxus*, London 1972
Kohzad, A.A., 'Recherches archéologiques en Afghanistan', *Afg* 2, 1953
Kühnel, E., *Islamische Schriftkunst*, Berlin und Leipzig 1942
Lefevre, J. *The Persian carpet*, London 1977
Marshall, Sir J., *Taxila*, 3 vols, Cambridge 1951
Masson, M.E., *Termezskaya arkheologicheskaya ekspeditsiya 1936-38*, 2 vols, Tashkent 1941-43
Matheson, S., *Persia: An Archaeological Guide*, London 1972
Matheson, S., *Time off to dig*, London 1961
Motamedi, H., 'Archaeological survey of Kyoto University in Afghanistan', *Afg* 3, 1976
Otto-Dorn, K., *Kunst des Islams*, Baden-Baden 1964
Paiman, Z., Kaboul, les Buddhas colorés des monastères, *Archéologia* 473/2010
    Kaboul, foyer de l'art bouddhique, *Archéologia* 461/008
    Découvertes à Kaboul, *Archéologia* 430/2006
    Région de Kaboul-nouveaux monuments bouddhiques, *Archéologia* 419/2006
Pinder-Wilson, R., *Islamic art*, London 1957
Pope, A.U., *A survey of Persian art*, 6 vols, London and New York 1938-39, 1964
Pope, A.U., *Persian Architecture*, London 1965
Pugachenkova, G.A., *Po drevnim pamyatnikam Samarkanda i Bukhary*, Moscow 1968
Pugachenkova, G.A., 'Mazar Arab-ata v Time', *Sov. Arkheologiya* 1961
Pugachenkova, G.A. & Rempell, L.I., *Vydayushchiye pamyatniki arkhitektury Uzbekistana*, Tashkent, 1958
Pugachenkova, G.A., 'Les monuments peu connus de l'architecture médiévale de l'Afganistan', *Afg* I, 1968
Pugachenkova, G.A., *Iskusstvo Afghanistana*, Moskva 1963
Pugachenkova, G.A., 'The architecture of Central Asia at the time of the Timurids', *Afg* 3-4, 1969-70

Rempel, L.I., *Arkhitekturnyi ornament Uzbekistana*, Tashkent 1961
Renz, A., *Geschichte und Stätten des Islam. Von Spanien bis Indien*, München 1977
Riter, C.F., 'Persian and Turkish architectural decoration', *OA* XV, 3, 1969
Rosenfield, J.M., *The dynastic arts of the Kushans*, Berkeley 1966
Rostovtzeff, M., *The excavations at Dura-Europos*, New Haven 1943-49
Rowland, B., *Ancient art of Afghanistan. Treasures of the Kabul Museum*, New York 1966
Rowland, B., *Art in Afghanistan; objects from the Kabul Museum*, London 1971
Rowland, B., *The art and architecture of India*, London 1953
Safadi, Y.H., *Islamic calligraphy*, London 1978
Shishkin, V.A., *Goroda Uzbekistana (Tashkent, Samarkand, Bukhara)*, Tashkent 1943
Sims-Williams, N. & J. Cribb, 'A new Bactrian Inscription of Kanishka', *The Great Silk Road Art and Archaeology*, 4, Kamakura, 1995-96
Sourdel, D. & J., *La civilisation de l'Islam classique*, Paris 1968
Sourdel-Thomine, J., 'Deux minarets d'époque seljoukide en Afghanistan', *Syria* XXX 1953
Sourdel-Thomine, J. and Spuler. B., *Die Kunst des Islam*, Berlin 1973
Stein, M.A., *Archaeological recconnaissances*, London 1937
Stierlin, H., *Architecture de l'Islam*, Fribourg 1979
Szabo, A & Barfield, T.J., *Afghanistan: An Atlas of Indigenous Domestic Architecture*, 1991
Tadgell, C., *The History of Architecture in India*, London 1990
Talbot-Rice, T., *Ancient art of Central Asia*, London 1965
Tolstov, S.P., *Po sledam drevnie-khorezmiiskoy tsivilisatsii*, Moscow 1948
Trever, K.V., *Pamyatniki Greko-baktriyskogo iskusstva*, Moskva and Leningrad 1940
Trousdale, W., 'Rock-engravings from Tang-i Tizao in Central Afghanistan', *EW* XV, 3-4, 1965
Veymarn, B.V., *Iskusstvo Srednei Azii*, Moskva 1940
Vogt-Göknil, U., *Grands courants de l'architecture islamique-Mosquées*, Paris 1975
Waldschmidt, E., *Gandara, Kutscha, Turfan*, Leipzig 1925
Welch, S.C., *A King's Book of Kings (The Shah-Nameh of Shah Tahmasp)*, New York 1972
Welch, S.C., *Persische Buchmalerei*, München 1976
Wheeler, R.E.M., *Charsada*, Oxford 1962
Wheeler, R.E.M., *The Indus civilisation*, 3rd ed., Cambridge 1968
Wheeler, R.E.M., *Flames over Persepolis*, London 1968
Wilber, D.N., *The architecture of Islamic Iran. The Il Khanid period*, Princeton 1955
Zasypkin, V.N., *Arkhitektura Srednei Azii*, Moskva 1948
Zasypkin, V.N., *Arkhitekturnyie pamyatniki Srednei Azii*, Moskva 1928
Zestovsky, P.I., 'Esquisses d'architecture afghane: Herat-Kabul-Herat', *Afg* 3, 1949.
Zodchestvo, *Uzbekistana*, Tashkent 1959

4 Sites and monuments – Pre-Islamic

Adriani, A., 'Le scoperte de Begram et l'arte alessandrina', *Archeologia classica* VII, 2, 1955
Auboyer, J., 'Ancient Indian ivories from Begram, Afghanistan', *JISOA* XVI, 1948
Barthoux, J.J., 'Les fouilles de Hadda'
    Paris-Bruxelles 1930: Figures et figurines, *Mém. DAFA* VI
    Paris-Bruxelles 1933: Stupas et sites, *Mém. DAFA* IV

Bernard, P., 'Les fouilles de Kuhn Masjid', *CRAI* 1964
Bernard, P., 'La premiere campagne de fouilles a Ai Khanoum', *CRAI* 1966
Bernard, P., 'Deuxième campagne de fouilles d'Ai Khanoum en Bactriane', *CRAI*, 1967
Bernard, P., 'Ai Khanoum – Troisième campagne de fouilles à Ai Khanoum', *CRAI*, 1968b
Bernard, P., 'Fouilles d'Ai Khanoum', *Afg* 2, 1973 and 4, 1976
Bernard P., Francfort, H.P., *Etudes de géographie historique sur la plaine d'Ai-Khanoum*, 1978
Buhot, J., 'Les antiquités bouddhiques de Bamiyan d'après A. Godard, Y. Godard et L. Hackin', *RAA* IV, 3, 1927
Burnes, A., 'On the colossal idols of Bamian', *JASB* II, 1833
Carl, J., 'Le monastère bouddhique de Tepe Marandjan', in Diverses recherches archéologiques en Afghanistan, Paris 1959, *Mém. DAFA* VIII
Casal, J.-M., 'Mundigak', *Afg* 4, 1952
Casal, J.-M., 'Mundigak: un site de l'age du Bronze en Afghanistan', *CRAI*, 1952
Casal, J.-M., 'Quatre campagnes de fouilles à Mundigak 1951-1954', *AA* I, 1954
Casal, J.-M., 'Fouilles de Mundigak', 2 vols, Paris 1961, *Mém DAFA* XVII
Casal, J.-M., 'Mundigak, ou l'Afghanistan à l'aurore des civilisations', *Archéologie* 1966
Caspani, P.E., 'Les murs de Kaboul', *Afg* 2, 1946
Castaldi, E., 'Preliminary report on the researches at Hazar Sum' (Samangan), part II (Italian archaeological mission in Afghanistan), *EW* XIV, 3-4, 1963
Curiel, R, & Fussman, G., 'Le trésor monétaire de Qunduz', Paris 1965, *Mém. DAFA* XX
Dagens, B., 'Monastères rupestres de la vallée de Foladi', Paris 1964, *Mém. DAFA* XX
Dagens, B., 'Fragments de sculptures inedits', Paris 1964, *Mém. DAFA* XX
Edelberg, L., 'An ancient Hindu temple in Kunar', *Afg* 3, 1960
Fischer, K., 'Pre-Islamic fortifications, habitation and religious monuments in the Kunar Valley', *Afg* 3, 1960
Fischer, K., *Kandahar in Arachosien*, Wiss. Zeitung der Martin-Luther-Univ. Halle-Wittenberg, VII, 6, 1958
Foucher, A., 'Note sur les antiquités bouddhiques de Haibak' (Turkestan Afghan), *JA* July-September 1924
Foucher, A., 'Notice archéologique sur la vallée de Bamiyan', *JA* April-June 1923
Franz, G.H., 'Das Chakri Minar als buddhistische Kultursäule', *AFJ* 5, 3, 1978
Ghirshman, R., 'Fouilles de Begram' (Afghanistan), *JA* 1943-1945
Ghirshman, R., avec la collaboration de Mme T. Ghirshman, 'Begram, Recherches archéologiques et historiques sur les Kouchans', Cairo 1946, *Mém. DAFA* XII
Ghirshman, R., 'Fouilles de Nad-i-Ali dans le Seistan Afghan', RAA XIII, I, 1939-1942
Godard, A., Godard, Y. & Hackin, J., 'Les antiquites bouddhiques de Bâmiyân', Paris-Bruxelles 1928, *Mém. DAFA* II
Hackin, J., 'Les fouilles de la Délégation archéologique française à Hadda (Afghanistan): la mission de Foucher, Godard, Barthoux (1923-1928)', *RAA* V, 2, 1928
Hackin, J., 'Sculptures gréco-bouddhiques du Kapiça', *Mon. Piot* XXVIII, 1925
Hackin, J., 'The colossal Buddhas at Bâmiyân, their influence on Buddhist sculpture', *Eastern Art* I, 2, 1928
Hackin, J., & Carl, J., 'Nouvelles recherches archéologiques à Bâmiyân', Paris 1933, Paris 1933, *Mém. DAFA* III

Hackin, J., & Carl, J., 'Recherches archéologiques au col de Khair-khaneh près de Kabul', Paris 1936, *Mém. DAFA* VII

Hackin, J., and Hackin, R., *Le site archéologique de Bamiyan. Guide du visiteur*, Paris 1934

Hackin, J., avec la collaboration de Mme J.R. Hackin, 'Recherches archéologiques à Begram, Chantier no. 2 (1937)', Paris 1939, *Mém. DAFA* IX

Hackin, J., 'The Buddhist monastery of Fondukistan', *Journal of the Greater Indian Society* VII, 1940

Helms, S.V., *Excavations at Old Kandahar in Afghanistan*, 1976-8, London 1997

Henning, W.B., 'Surkh Kotal und Kaniska', *ZDMG* 115, I, 1965

Jettmar, K., 'Zum Heiligtum von Surkh Kotal', *CAJ* V, 1960

Klimberg-Salter, *The Kingdom of Bamiyan: Buddhist Art and Culture in the Hindu Kush*, Rome, 1989

Kruglikova, I.T., *Dilberdzhin, khram Dioskurov*, 1986

Lezine, A., 'Trois stupa de la région de Caboul', *AAS* XXVII, 1-2, 1964

Masson, C., 'Notes on the antiquities of Bamian', *JASB* V, 1936

Meunié, J., 'Shotorak', *Mém. DAFA* X, Paris 1942

Meunié, J., 'Le couvent des otages chinois de Kaniska au Kâpisa', *JA* 1943-1945

Mizuno, S., *Haibak and Kashmir-Smast. Buddhist cave temples in Afghanistan and Pakistan surveyed in 1960*, Kyoto 1962

McNicoll, A., 'Excavations at Kandahar 1975', *Afghan Studies* I, 1978

Mostamandi, M. & S., 'Nouvelles fouilles à Hadda (1966-67) par l'Institute Afghan d'archéologie', *AA* XIX, 1969

Mustamandi, S., 'Recent excavation of Hadda', *Afg* 2, 1969

Motamedi, H., 'Buddhic monastery of Fundukistan', *Afg* I, 1971

Papin, C., 'Fouilles de'Ai-Khanoum', *Mém. DAFA*, vol. 8, Paris 1992

Puglisi, S.M., 'Preliminary report on the researches at Hazar Sum' (Samangan), 'part I: General survey' (Italian archeological mission in Afghanistan), *EW* XIV, 1-2, 1963

Rowland, B., 'The colossal Buddhas at Bamiyan', *JISOA* XV, 1947

Rowland, B., 'Studies in the Buddhist art of Bamiyan: the Bodhisattva of group E', in *Art and Thought*, ed. by K. Bh. Iyer, London 1947

Sarianidi, V., *The golden hoard of Bactria*, N. York 1985

Scarre, C. (ed.), *Seventy Wonders of the World*, London 2000

Scerrato, U., 'A short note on some recently discovered Buddhist grottoes near Bamiyan, Afghanistan', *EW* XI, 2-3, 1960

Schlumberger, D., 'Surkh Kotal, a late Hellenistic temple in Bactria', *Archaeology* VI, 4, 1953

Schlumberger, D., 'Surkh Kotal: un sanctuaire du feu d'époque kouchane en Bactriane', *AA* I, 1954

Schlumberger, D., 'Surkh Kotal in Bactria', *Archaeology* VIII, 2, 1955

Schlumberger, D., 'The excavations at Surkh Kotal and the problem of Hellenism in Bactria and India', *Proc. of the British Academy* XLVII, 1961

Schlumberger, D., 'La nécropole de Shakh Tépé, près de Qunduz', *CRAI* 1964

Schlumberger, D., 'Ai-Khanoum, une ville hellénistique en Afghanistan', *CRAI* 1965

Schlumberger, D. & Bernard, P., 'Ai-Khanoum', *Bulletin de Correspondance Hellénique* LXXXIX, 1965

Schlumberger, D., 'Les fouilles de Surkh Kotal en Bactriane' (I-IV), *CRAI* 1953, 1954, 1955, 1957, 1961, 1963

Schlumberger, D., 'Le temple de Surkh Kotal en Bactriane' (I-IV), *JA* 1952, 1954, 1955, 1964

Simpson, W., *Buddhist architecture: Jalalabad*. Trans. of the Royal Institute of British Architects, 1879-1880

Simpson, W., 'Buddhist remains in the Jalalabad valley', *Indian Antiquary* VIII, 1879

Simpson, W., 'The Buddhist caves of Afghanistan', *JRAS* XIV, 1882

Taddei, M., 'Tapa Sardar; First preliminary report', *EW* XVIII, 1968

Taizi Zemaryalai, *Architecture et décor rupestre des grottes de Bamiyan*, Paris 1977

Talbot, M.G., Maitland, P.J. & Simpson, W., 'The rock-cut caves and statues of Bamian', *JRAS* XVIII, 1886

Whitehouse, D., 'Excavations at Kandahar 1974', *Afghan Studies* I, 1978

Young, R.S., 'The South wall of Balkh-Bactra', *AJA* LIX, 1955

5 Early Islamic

Baker, P.H.B., Allchin, F.R., *Shahr-i Zohak and the History of the Bamiyan Valley*, 1991

Bivar, A.D.H., 'Seljukid ziyarats of Sar-i Pul', *BSOAS* XXIX, 1966

Bombaci, A., 'Ghazni', *EW* VIII, 3, 1957

Bombaci, A., 'Introduction to the excavations at Ghazni' (Summary report on the Italian archeological mission in Afghanistan, I), *EW* X, 1-2, 1959

Bruno, A., 'Le minaret de Djam', *Courrier de l'UNESCO*, octobre 1979

Bulliet, R.W., 'Naw Bahar and the survival of Iranian Buddhism', *Iran* XIV, 1976

Caspani, P.E., 'Nau-Bahar of Balkh', *Afg* I, 1947

Davary, D., 'Die Ruinenstadt Bost am Helmand', *Afg* 4, 1976

Dorn'ich, C., *Minar-i-Chakari*, SPACH Library Series No.3, Peshawar, 1999

Flury, S., 'Le décor épigraphique des monuments de Ghazna', *Syria* VI, 1925

Gardin, J.-C., 'Lashkari Bazar, une résidence royale ghaznévide II', Paris 1963 (*Mém. DAFA* XVIII)

Glatzer, B., 'The madrasah of Shah-i Mashad in Badgis', *Afg* 4, 1973

Godard, A., 'Ghazni', *Syria* VI, 1925

Golombek, L., 'Abbasid mosque at Balkh', *OA* XV, 3, 1969

Guya I'Témadi, 'The general mosque of Herat', *Afg* 2, 1953

Herberg, W. & Davary, D., 'Topographische Feldarbeiten in Ghor. Bericht über Forschungsarbeiten zum Problem Jam – Ferozkoh', *AfJ* 3, 2, 1976

Kieffer, C.M., 'Le minaret de Ghiyath al-Din à Firouzkoh' (Minaret de Djam), *Afg* 4, 1960

Kohzad, A.A., 'Lashkargah', *Afg* I, 1949

LeBerre, M., *Lashkar-i Bazar*, Paris 1978

Leshnik, L., 'Ghor, Firuzkoh and the Minar-i-Jam', *CAJ* XII, I, 1968

Malleson, G.B., *Herat, the granary and garden of Central Asia*, London 1880

Maricq, A. & Wiet, G., 'Le minaret de Djam. La découverte de la capitale des sultans Ghorides, XIIe-XIIIe siècles', Paris 1959 (*Mém. DAFA* XVI)

Melikian-Chirvani, A.S., 'Remarques préliminaires sur un mausolee ghaznévide', *AA* XVII, 1968

Melikian-Chirvani, A.S., 'Eastern Iranian architecture: apropos of the Ghurid parts of the Great Mosque of Herat', *BSOAS* XXXIII, 1970

Melikian-Chirvani, A.S., 'La plus ancienne mosquée de Balkh', *AA* XX, 1969

Mukhtarov, A.M., *Balkh in the Late Middle Ages*, Bloomington 1993

Naimi, A.A., 'Boste', *Afg* 4, 1948

Naimi, A.A., 'Les monuments historiques et les mausolées de Ghazni', *Afg* 2, 1952

Najimi, A.W., *Herat: The Islamic City*, London, 1988

Pope, A.U., 'The mosque at Qal'a-i Bist', *Bull. Am. Inst. Persian Art and Archaeology* IV, 1935

Pugachenkova, G.A., 'Mechet No Gumbat v Balkhe' (Afghanistan), *Sov. Arkheologiya*, 3, 1970

Saljooki, F., 'The complete copy of the ancient inscription of the Ghiassuddin Grand Mosque in Herat', *Afg* 3, 1967

Scerrato, U., 'The first two excavation campaigns at Ghazni, 1957-1958', Summary report on the Italian archaeological mission in Afghanistan, II, *EW* X, 1-2, 1959

Schlumberger, D., 'Les fouilles de Lashkari Bazar', *CRAI* 1948, 1949, 1950, 1951, 1952

Schlumberger, D., 'Les fouilles de Lashkari Bazar: recherches archéologiques de l'époche ghaznévide', *Afg* 2, 1949

Schlumberger, D., 'Les fouilles de Lashkari Bazar', *Afg* 4, 1950

Schlumberger, D., 'La grande mosquee de Lashkari Bazar', *Afg* I, 1952

Schlumberger, D., 'Le palais ghaznévide de Lashkari Bazar', *Syria* XXIX, 1952

Trousdale, W., 'The minaret of Jam: a Ghorid monument in Afghanistan', *Archaeology* XVIII, 2, 1965

Whitehouse, D., 'The barrow cemetery at Kandahar'. *Annali, Ist. Orient. di Napoli*, vol. 36, 4, 1976

6 Timurid and late Islamic

Adamec, L.W., *Herat and Northwestern Afghanistan*, Graz 1975

Brown, P., *Indian architecture (The Islamic Period)*, Bombay 1942

Byron, R., 'The shrine of Khwaja Abu Nasr Parsa at Balkh', *Bull. Am. Inst. Persian Art and Archaeology* IV, I, 1935

Byron, R., 'Timurid monuments in Afghanistan', *IIIe Congrès International d'art et d'archéologie Iraniens*, Leningrad 1935

Centlivres, P., *Un bazar d'Asie Centrale. Forme et organisation du bazar de Tashqurghan, Afghanistan*, 1972

Davary, D. & Erdmann, H., 'Die Moschee von Takhta Pol in Nordafghanistan', *AFJ* 4, 3, 1977

Frye, R.N., 'Two Timurid monuments in Herat', *Aas* XI, 3, 1948

Golombek, L., *The Timurid shrine at Gazur Gah*, Toronto 1969

Guya I'Temadi, 'Le Dome Vert ou le mausolée des princes timurides', *Afg* I, 1946

Mustamandy, S., 'A building by the name of Gowarshad in Kohsan of Herat', *Afg* 4, 1968

Parpagliolo, M.T.S., 'The Bagh-i Babur', *Afg* 3, 1975 and 4, 1976

Pugachenkova, G.A., 'A l'étude des monuments timourides d'Afghanistan', Afg 3, 1970

Saljuqi, F., *Khiyaban*, Kabul 1964

Vogel, J. Ph., *Tile mosaics of the Lahore Fort*, Karachi 1977 (1st ed. 1920)

Index

Entries in **bold** refer to figures. *Italics* indicate the page containing the main discussion of an entry

Abbas Safavid shah of Persia 145, 146
Abdali, tribe, see Durrani 35, 36, 37
Abdul Razzak, sultan, see Sultan Abdul Razzak
Abdurrahman, amir 39, 40, 46, 72, 134, 161, 162
Ab-i Panj, river 16
Ab-i Wakhan, river 16
Abul Al'a Maududi, preacher 45
Abu al-Valid, mausoleum, Herat *148*
Abu'l-Fath Muhammad, Ghorid sultan 124
Abu'l Kasim Mahmud, see Mahmud of Ghazna 109
Abu'l Kasim, mausoleum, Herat *132*
Abu Nasr Parsa, Balkh, see also Khoja Abu Nasr Parsa **colour plate 9**, *149*, 71-5
Abu Said, Timurid sultan 34
Achaemenian, dynasty 25, 47, 54, 58, 73, 76, 78, 85, 96
Afghan Institute of Archaeology 88
Afrasiab, site, Samarkand 55, 58, **62**
Agra 37, 50, 63, 71, 103, 109, 110, 160
Ahmad, desc. of Shahrukh 137
Ahmad Khan Abdali, see Ahmad Shah Durrani 36
Ahmad Shah Durrani, amir 36, 37 mausoleum 160, 162
Ahmad Shah Masud, resistance leader 45
Ahmad Yassevi, mausoleum, Turkestan 158
Aibak, site 52, **76**, **30**, **31**, **32**
Aimak, tribe 19, 20, 22
Ajanta, caves, India 89, 94, 95
Akbar, Moghul emperor 68
Akcha, town 98, 99, 101, 107
Ala-ad-daula, son of Baisanghur 137
Ala-ud-Din Jahan Suz, Ghorid sultan 108, 116
Alexander 25, 26, 50, 53, 78, 96, 118
Alexandria 81
  Ariana 25, 118, 120
  Eschate 26
  of the Arachosians 78

Alexandrias 72
Algeria 45
Ali, caliph 147, 156
Ali Shir Nevai, vazir and poet 121, 137, 139
Alptigin, Turkish commander 31, 107, 108
Altai, mountains 29, 101
Amanullah, king 41, 42, 90
America, American, see also United States 24, 45, 46, 97, 162
Amu Darya, river, see also Oxus 14, 16, 19, 32, 35, 37, 38, 40, 41, 43, 73, 79
Anatolia 32, 57, 58
Anbir, see Sar-i Pul
Ansari, Khoja Abdullah, see Khoja Abdullah Ansari 127, 138, 139, 144, 146, 148
Aphrodite 53
Apollo 53
Apsidenhalle 51
Arabs, Arabic 19, 21, 29, 30, 45, 63, 76, 96, 100, 103, 105, 107, 119, 149, 162
Arab-Ata, mausoleum, Tim 64, 107
Arachosia, Persian satrapy 25, 26, 27, 47
Aral Sea 16, 29, 30, 34
Aramaic, language 79, 80
Arghandab, river 17, 43, 116
Ariana, Persian satrapy 25
Arsacids, dynasty 53
Aryans 96, 114
Armenia 32, 57, 58
Ashoka, Mauryan emperor 27, 50, 78, 79, 80
Ashraf, Ghilzai amir 35, 36
Asia Minor 32
Assyria 49, 50, 54
Austria 13
Avesta 118
Ay Khanum, site 12, 23, 72, *73*, 79, 97
Ayub Khan 40
Azadan, village 148

Azerbaidjan 32

Baba Hatim, mausoleum, Balkh *106*, 107
Babrak Karmal, politician 44
Babur, Moghul emperor 34, 35, 68, 71, 108, 109, 132, 133, 149, 158
  tomb of 161
  gardens 68, 71, 160, **colour plate 6**
Babylon 26, 49, 50, 57
Bacha Sakkao, Tajik usurper 42
Bactria, Bactriana, Persian satrapy 25, 26, 27, 28, 29, 51, 53, 55, 74, 76, 79, 86, 96, 98, 101, 103
Badakhshan 14, 24, 79, 81, 136
Badghiz, province 119, 126
Bad-i-sad-o-bist-ruz, wind 19, 119
Bagh, India 95
Bagh-Gai, Hadda 85
Bagh-i Bala, palace, Kabul 162
Bagh-i Bihzad, Herat 134
Bagh-i Firuzi, Ghazni 109
Bagh-i Murad, Herat 139
Bagh-i Jahan Aray, Herat 139
Baghlan, village 75
Bagolango 75
Bahramshah, tower of, Ghazni **23**, **45**, **46**, **47**, 106, *112*, *114*, 122, **colour plate 19**
Baihaqi/Bayhaki, Persian historian 116
Baisanghur, son of Shahrukh 137
Bajaur 26
Bala Hissar, Balkh 96, 98
  Herat 119, **49**, *131*
  Kabul *103*, 161
Balalyk-Tepe, Turkestan 55
Balkh/Bactra 29, 32, 33, 34, 35, 37, 39, 43, 54, 61, 81, 88, 90, *96*, 99, *104*, 106, 107, 119, 154, 156, 161
  citadel **21**, **41**
  Timurid monuments 68, 69, *149*, **colour plate 23**
Baluch 19, 20, 22
Bamiyan **1**, 12, 14, 16, 23, 26, 30, **37**, 38, **38**, **40**, 45, 52, 53, 55,

88, 96, 101, 108, 128, 130, **colour plate 1**
Bamiyan Rud, river 16
Band-i Amir, lakes **6**, **colour plate 2**
Battuta, see Ibn Battuta
Begram, see Kapiça
Benelux 13
Bessus, satrap 96
Bibi Khanum, mosque, Samarkand 68
Bihzad, painter 70, 71
Bishapur, site, Iran 54, 55, 56
Bivar, A.D.H., author 106
Bost, site, Sistan 17, 31, 60, 106, 107, *116*, 117, 118
Bostan Serai, Kabul 162
Bosworth, C.E., author 108
Brahma, Brahmin, see also Hindu 30, 82, 107
Brahui, tribe 19, 20, 21
Britain, British 13, 35, 37, 38, 39, 40, 41, 46, 90, 109, 134, 161
British-Afghan Treaty 42
British India, see India 42
British Institute of Afghan Studies 78
British Museum 72
Buddha, Buddhism 11, 23, 28, 29, 30, 52ff, 75, 79, 80, 82, 84, 85, 86, 88, 96, 98, 102
Buddhist architecture 50, 51, 55ff, 63, 81, 118, 160
sites 76, 78, 79, 89ff, 100
Bukhara, town and khanate 30, 32, 34, 36, 37, 38, 42, 49, 60, 61, 64, 66, 68, 106
Burnes, Sir Alexander, traveller 90
Byron, R., author 110, 115, 122, 126, 134, 136, 139, 146, 151, 153, 158
Byzantine Empire 29, 32

Cairo 57
Caspian Sea 32, 38
Caucasus 20
Central Asia 12, 28, 38, 39, 40, 42, 43, 45, 49, 58, 60, 63, 67, 68, 79, 81, 95, 96, 103, 127
Chaghatay, son of Chingiz-Khan 33
Chahar Bagh, gardens 68, 161
Chahar Su, bazaar, Herat 68, 147
Chahar Suq 162
Chahr Chatta, bazaar, Kabul 161
Chakhil-i Ghundi, Hadda 85
Chandragupta, Mauryan emperor 27
Chapriar, river 85
Charikar, town 82, 96
Charsada, site, Pakistan 28
Chechnya 45
Chehel Sina, site, Kandahar 79

Chehel Sotun, pavilion, Isfahan 68
Chehel Sotun, Masjid, Ziyarat Gah 148
Chilsotoon, palace, Kabul 162
China, Chinese 23, 28, 29, 41, 66, 69, 70, 80, 81, 85, 94, 96, 98, 103, 125, 144, 146
Chinese Turkestan, see Turkestan
Chingiz-Khan 20, 32, 116, 127, 130, 156
Chingizid, dynasty, Herat 139, 143
Chisht, Herat 126, 127
Chitral 21, 88
Clavijo, Spanish envoy 68, 149
Connolly, traveller 133
Corinthian 74, 85, 86, 96
Crimean War 38
Ctesiphon, palace 58
Cyrus the Great, Persian king 118

DAFA 42, 90
Damghan, town 60
Daoud Khan, Muhammad, President 43, 44
Dari, language 20
Darius I, Persian king 49, 50
Dasht-i Margo, desert 15
Dawlatabad, minaret, Balkh 61, *106*, 122
Deh Ghundi, Hadda 85
Deh Morasi Ghundai, site, Kandahar 73
Delbarjin, site, Akcha *101*
Delhi 32, 35, 36, 37, 45, 50, 66, 67, 103, 127, 134, 160
Deobandism, radical doctrine 45
Diez, E., author 114
Dokhtar-i Nushirwan, site, Pul-i Khumri 55, *101*
Dost Muhammad, Amir 37, 38, 39, 145, 157
Drangiana, Persian satrapy 25, 26, 27, 47
Dravidian 20, 21
Duprée, L., author 13
Dura Europos, site, Syria 54, 74
Durand, Sir Mortimer 41, 42
Durrani, tribe 20, 37, 42, 44

Ecbatana, site 50
Egypt 37, 47, 49, 50, 57, 81
Elam 50
Ellenborough, Lord 109
Ellora, caves, India 89
Elphinstone, Sir Mountstuart 89
Erg Kala, Merv 54
Ethiopia 44
Eyre, Vincent, Lt, author 90

Farah Rud, river 18
Farsi, language 20, 21
Fa Sien/Hsien, Chinese pilgrim 88
Ferdausi/Ferdawsi, poet 115
Ferghana, province 30, 34, 35, 160
Ferrier, J.P., traveller 132, 133, 145
Firuz, see Peroz
Firuzabad, palace, Iran 54, 55
Firuzkuh, site, Ghor 127
Fischer, K., author 51
Flury, S., author 109, 111, 112, 115
Foladi, Valley 14, 52, *95*, 130
Foucher, A., author 77, 90
France, French 13, 42, 73, 74, 85, 88, 90, 97, 117, 127
Franz, G.H., author 51, 85
Frumkin, G., author 55
Frye, R.N., author 124, 125
Fundukistan, site, Charikar *95*, 96

Gandamak, treaty of, 1879 39
Gandhara, province 25, 27, 29, 80
art 52ff, 75, 76, 82, 85, 86, 94, 95
Ganges, river 34
Gar Nao, Hadda 85
Gardez, town 82, 85
Gawhar Shad, queen 131, 132, 133, 158
mausoleum, Herat 67, 121, **61**, *135*, **62**, **63**, 137, 147, **colour plate 10**
mausoleum, Kohsan *148*
Gazurgah/Gazur Gah, Herat 69, 72, 121, 127, *138*, **64**, 139, **65**, 140, **66**, **67**, **68**, **69**, **70**, 146, 148, 153, 160, **colour plates 21 & 21**
Gedrosia, Persian satrapy 27
Gerard, Dr, traveller 90
Germany, German 13, 41, 42
Ghalwar 148
Ghaznavid dynasty 17, 30, 103, 108, 116, 119, 128
empire 31, 32
architecture 64ff, 110
monuments 106, 107, 109
Ghazni/Ghazna, town 14, 25, 29, 31, 37, 38, 57, 59, 60, 61, **63**, 64, *107*, 109, 110, 114, *158*
Ghilzai, tribe 20, 35, 36, 37, 38, 44
Ghirshman, R., author 50, 55, 80
Ghiyat-ad-dunya Wa-d-din Muhammad, Kart sultan 125
Ghiyat-ud-Din, Muhammad ben Sam, Ghorid sultan 120, 123, 124, 127
Ghor 15, 31, 127, 128

Index

Ghorid dynasty 31, 32, 66, 118, 119, 128, 139, 146
  architecture, monuments 64ff, 120, 124, 125, 126, 127
Ghorband, river 16, 26, 80
Giraldi, painter 145
Gobi, desert 32
Godard, A., author 90, 109, 110, 115
Golden Horde 34
Goldsmid, General 41
Golombek, L., author 71, 105, 127, 137, 138, 143, 144, 146, 154
Grabar, O., author 57, 58, 60, 61
Greek 16, 26, 28, 50, 51, 52, 74, 78, 85, 88, 92
Greco-Bactrian 52, 53, 72, 73, 96, 98, 101
  Buddhist 29, 53, 75, 80
  Iranian 53, 54
  Indo-Greek 75
  Roman 63, 81, 86, 101
Green Mosque, Balkh, see also Khoja Abu Nasr Parsa 69
Guimet, Musée 12, 88
Gujerat 28, 109
Gul Ahmad 102
Guldara stupa, Kabul 82, **33**, **34**, 85, 102
Gulistan Serai, Kabul 162
Gupta, Indian dynasty 28, 29, 51, 53, 82, 92, 94, 96
Gurganj/Urgench/Jurjaniya, site, Turkestan 32

Habibullah, king 41, 162
Hackin, J., author 81, 90, 91, 94
Hadda, site, Jalalabad 52, 64, *85*, 86, 87
Hadji Piyade, mosque, Balkh 106
Hafiz-i Abru, Persian historian 131
Hafizullah Amin, politician 44
Haft qalam, tombstone, style 143, 146
Haft Tepe, site, Iran 50
Hairava/Herat 118
Hakim Mirza, grandson of Babur 161
Hamun-i Helmand, lake 17
Hanafi, sunnite sect 21
Harakuwatis 78
Harappa, site, Pakistan 25, 74
Hari Rud, river 14, 15, 17, 22, 40, 41, 118, 119, 126, 127, 128, 138
Harun ar-Rashid, caliph 32
Harut Rud, river 18
Hawkal, see Ibn Hawkal

Hazara, tribe 19, 20, 21, 22, 95, **colour plate 4**
Hazaratjat 14
Hazret Ali, mausoleum, Mazar-i Sharif 71, *156*, **80**, **81**, **colour plate 16**
Hebron 146
Heliocles, Bactrian king 27
Hellenistic, see also Greek 50, 51, 55, 74, 76, 79, 81, 82, 92, 101
Helmand, river 17, 19, 22, 26, 41, 43, 116, 117
Hepthalo-Buddhist 72, 102
Hephthalites, White Huns 23, 28, 29, 52, 55, 80, 88, 96, 99, 101, 102, 103, 107, 119, 128, 149
Herat, city 13, 15, 17, 19, 20, 21, 24, 25, 29, 32, 33, 34, 35, 36, 37, 38, 40, 61, 64, 70, 71, 96, 107, 128, 131, 133, 134, 145, 146, 147, 148, 149, 153, 157, 160
  medieval monuments 65, 67, *118*
  Timurid monuments 67, 68, 69, **50**, **51**, **52**, **53**, **54**, **55**, *131*, **colour plates 12, 24 & 25**
Herberg, W. & Davary, D., authors 127
Hilo, country of Hadda 85
Hinayana 98
Hindu, Hinduistic 19, 21, 30, 52, 66, 68, 82, 100, 109, 114, 116
Hindukush, mountains 14, 17, 22, 25, 26, 27, 28, 29, 37, 89, 96, 98, **colour plate 22**
Hindushahi, dynasty 30, 31, 82, 103, 107
Hindustan 108
Hittite 49
Hoag, J., author 66, 117, 137
Honigberger, J.M., traveller 90
Hulagu, Il-Khan, grandson of Chingiz-Khan 33, 34
Humayun, Moghul emperor 103, 160
Humlum, J., author 13, 15
Husayin, Amir of Balkh 33, 34
Husayin Baykara, Timurid sultan 34, 66, 70, 121, 132, 133, 134, 137, 138, 139, 143, 145, 147, 148, 156
Hyde, T., author 98
Hydreuma, Syrian fort 52

Ibn Battuta, Arab traveller 103, 104, 108, 109, 119
Ibn Hawkal, Arab geographer 119, 120
Ibn Tulun, mosque, Cairo 57

Ibrahim, Ghaznavid sultan 64, 109, 111, 115
Ibrahim, Timurid sultan 137
Ili, river 29
Il-Khans, dynasty 33
Imam-i Kalan, mausoleum, Sar-i Pol 107
Imam-i Khurd, mausoleum, Sar-i Pol 106
India, Indian 12, 13, 21, 22, 23, 26, 28, 29, 30, 31, 34, 35, 36, 37, 39, 41, 42, 45, 50, 71, 81, 88, 89, 92, 94, 96, 107, 108, 109, 127, 134, 156, 158, 160
  architecture 53, 61, 65, 66, 68, 70, 72, 79, 86
Indian Ocean 16
Indo-Afghan 53
  European 27
  Greek 26, 27, 80
  Muslim 109
  Parthian 80
Indus, river 16, 23, 25, 26, 27, 37, 47, 74
Irak/Iraq 63, 116
Iran, see also Persia 12, 13, 17, 20, 21, 26, 28, 32, 33, 41, 44, 45, 47, 49, 50, 53, 54, 55, 67, 74, 75, 79, 82, 102, 105, 106, 108, 143, 147
Iranian architecture 51, 57, 58, 60, 61, 63, 66, 94, 105, 115, 146, 158
Irtysh, river 32
Isfahan 35, 36, 68
Ishrat Khana, Samarkand 68
Isfizari, Persian historian 120
Iskander, see Alexander
Islam 30, 33, 40, 42, 44, 45, 55, 58, 63, 71, 103, 114, 115
Islamic architecture 58, 63ff, 68, 95, 127, 136, 138, 146, 156
  early 67, 78, 79, 99, *103*
  Timurid 131ff
Islam Kala, town 24
Ismail, Safavid Shah of Persia 34
Ismail Samanid, mausoleum, Bukhara 64
Ismaili, tribe 21
Istakhri, Arab geographer 108
Istanbul 50
Italy, Italian 42, 53, 100, 116, 145, 158

Jahangir, Moghul emperor 161
Jalalabad 14, 16, 19, 26, 38, 41, 46, 85, 88
Jalal ad-Din Muhammad, poet 160

Jam, minaret, Ghor 57, 65, 115, 126, *127*
Jami, poet 147
Japan 42
Jaulian, monastery, Pakistan 53, 82
Jawand 126
Jaxartes, river, see Syr Darya 26
Jayhun, river, see Amu Darya
Jebe Noyon, Mongol commander 32
Jews 19
Jirga, Afghan tribal assembly 42
Jhelum, river 26
Jochi, son of Chingiz-Khan 34
Jurjaniya, see Gurganj
Juzjan, province 106

Kabul city 13, 14, 19, 23, 26, 28, 29, 30, 31, 34, 35, 37, 38, 39, 40, 41, 42, 43, 46, 52, 71, 80, 96, 100, 102, 107, 109, 115, 128
    Gorge **3**
    monuments, medieval 68, 82, *103*
    late 72, *160*
    museum 12, 45, 73, 74, 75, 81, 82, 95, 118
    river 16, 26
    valley 19
Kabulshah, dynasty, see Ratbil Shahs
Kafirs, see also Nuristanis 21, 40
Kairouan 57
Kaital/Qaitul Range, mountains 78
Kajar, Persian dynasty see Qajar
Kakrak, Valley 14, **88**, 95, 130
Kala-i Bost, see Bost
Kala-i Dokhtaran, Bamiyan **59**, 130
Kala-i Hinduwan, Balkh 97
Kala-i Zal, site, Kunduz 79
Kandahar 13, 14, 19, 25, 26, 29, 35, 36, 37, 38, 40, 46, 73, 100, 134
    Old city/Shahr-i Kuhna 78, 79
    monuments *160*
Kanishka, Kushan king 28, 74, 75, 76, 81, 82
Kapisa/Kapiça, see also Begram 26, 28, 29, 45, 52, *80*, 81, 82, 88, 103
Kara Kum, desert 14, 17
Karakhanid, dynasty, Turkestan 108
Kara Tepe, site 55
Kart, dynasty/Kart Maliks, Herat 33, 119, 120, 121, 124
Kashan, town, Iran 60
Kashmir 37
Kasr-i Naranj, site, Kandahar 78

Kazakhstan 158
Kazwini, Persian geographer 103, 119
Kerulen, river 32
Khair Khane, site, Kabul *82*, 102
Khalchayan, site 55
Khalk, journal, political party 43, 44
Khanikov, traveller 137
Khawak Pass 26
Khisht Tepe, site, Kunduz 79
Khiva, town, khanate 36, 38, 42, 72
Khoja Abdullah Ansari 138
Khoja Abu Nasr Parsa 69, *149*, **71, 72, 73, 74, 75, colour plate 9**
Khoja Parda, see Hadji Piyade
Khojend, town 26
Khondamir/Khwandamir, Persian historian 132
Khorasan 29, 30, 31, 32, 34, 36, 37, 53, 104, 107, 108, 119, 120, 138
Khorezm/Khwarizm 31, 32, 34, 54, 55, 108
Khorezmshahs, dynasty 32, 119
Khosroes Anushirwan, Sasanian king 29
Khulm, see Tashkurgan 76, 162
Khulm, river 101
Khwaja Muhammad, Range 14
Khwaja Safa 102
Khyber Pass 17, 38
Kidara Kushans, tribe 53
Kirghiz 19, 21, 22
Kirman, town 35
Kizil, site, Xinjiang 92
Kizil Kala, port 24, 43
Kizilbashi, tribe 21
Koh-i Mori, stupa, Kabul 82
Koh-i Nur, diamond 36
Kohsan, village 148
Kokand, khanate 38
Kokcha, river 16, 73
Konya 60
Kopet Dagh, mountains 38
Koy Krylgan Kala, site, Uzbekistan 54
Kucha, site, Xinjiang 92
Kufa, Irak 64
Kuhandiz, castle 103, 162
Kuh-i Baba, Range 14, 17, 23, 130, **colour plate 14**
Kuhna Masjid, site, Pul-i Khumri *75*
Kumtura, site, Xinjiang 92
Kunar, river 17, 26, 88

Kundjakai 102
Kunduz, town 26, 43, 73, 79, *162*
Kunduz Ab, river 16
Kunya Urgench, see Gurganj
Kushans 28, 29, 75
Kushan architecture 51, 52, 53, 55ff, 81, 82, 95, 99
    sites 72, 74, 78, 80, 84, 85, 102
    dynasty 53, 76, 79, 96, 98, 100, 101, 103, 118, 128
Kushka, town 24
Kushribat, caravanserai, Herat 148
Kutub Minar, Delhi 127

Labi Hauz, Bukhara 68
Laghman 80
Lahore 31, 37, 50, 68, 71, 103, 108, 160
Lashkar-i Bazar, site, Sistan 17, 63, 64, 115, *116*
Lashkargah, see Laskar-i Bazar
League of Nations 42
Le Berre, M., author 99
Levant 23
Libya 45
Liyavandak, see Bukhara 55
Logar, river 17, 82
Long-men, site, Xinjiang 89

Madinah 141, 146
Mahayana, Buddhist doctrine 52, 80, 88
Mahmud ben Sam, Ghorid sultan 124
Mahmud of Ghazna, sultan 31, 32, 102, 104, 107, 108, 109, 110, 111, 115, 117, 119, 158
Mahrattas 37
Maiwand, village 40
Makdisi, Arab geographer, see Mukaddasi
Malwa, India 28
Marco Polo 104
Mashad, town 36, 37, 69
Masjid-i Chehel Sotun, Ziyarat Gah *148*
Masjid Hadji Piyade, see Noh Gumbad
Masjid-i Baland, Bukhara 56
Masjid-i Hauz-i Karboz, Herat 148
Masjid-i Kalan, Bukhara 61
Masjid-i Shah, Mashad 69
Masjid-i Shah Do Shamshira, Kabul 162
Masjid-i Sabz/Green Mosque, Balkh, see Khoja Abu Nasr Parsa

Masjid-i Suleiman, Iran 50
Masud I, Ghaznavid sultan 31, 64, 108, 109, 116, 117
Masud III, Ghaznavid sultan 115
  palace of 115, 116, 160
  tower of **22**, **44**, 111, *112*, **48**, **colour plate 18**
Masudi, Arab historian, geographer 98
Masson, Ch., traveller 90, 102
Mathura, India 53
Maurya, Indian dynasty 27, 50, 51, 85
Maydan-i Shah, Isfahan 68
Mazar-i Sharif 23, 71, 74, 90, 98, 99, 149, 154, **79**, 162
Mazdeism, religion 98
McMahon, boundary commission 41
Mecca 98, 132, 141, 146
Megasthenes, Greek traveller 50
Melikian-Chirvani, A.S., author 69, 105, 107, 121, 122, 124, 127
Merv 29, 32, 33, 39, 40, 54, 107, 119, 134
Mes-i Aynak 102
Mesopotamia 47, 54, 79, 106
Meunié, J., author 82
Minar-i Chakri, Kabul *85*
Ming, Chinese dynasty 69, 125
Mir Mahmud, Ghilzai Amir 35, 36
Mir Wais, Ghilzai Amir 35
  mausoleum of 160
Mir Zakah 79
Miran, site, Xinjiang 89, 95
Mirza Hindal, son of Babur 161
Mithra, Iranian deity 82
Mizuno, S., author 77
Moghul, Indian dynasty 33, 35, 36, 37, 71, 103, 149, 160
  architecture 50, 68, 160
Moghulistan 34
Mohenjo Daro, site, Pakistan 25
Mohi, village 101
Mohra Moradu, monastery, Pakistan 53, 82
Mohun Lal, Munshi, traveller 124, 133
Mongols 19, 20, 21, 23, 29, 30, 32, 33, 34, 60, 63, 65, 66, 67, 96, 104, 116, 118, 119, 120, 130, 149
Moorcroft, W., traveller 90
Moscow 34, 42, 44
Muhammad ibn Abd al-Wahhab, preacher 45
Muhammad Akbar Khan, son of Dost Muhammad 38

Muhammad Daoud Khan, see Daoud Khan 43
Muhammad Nadir Shah, see Nadir Shah, king 42
Muhammad Sheybani, Uzbek khan 34
Muhammad Zahir Shah, see Zahir Shah, king 42
Mukaddasi, see also Makdisi 76, 104, 108, 119, 126
Mulla Kalan, khaniga, Herat *147*
Multan 31
Mundigak, site, Kandahar 25, *73*, 78
Murghab, river 17, 126
Musalla, site, Herat *132*, **60**, 134, 143, 158
Mustawfi, Arab geographer 76, 108, 119

Nadir Khan, Shah of Persia 36, 37, 71, 92
Nadir Shah, king 23, 42, 82
Nagarahara, see Hadda 85
Najibullah, president 44
Naksh-i Rustam, site, Iran 101
Namakdan, pavilion, Herat 139, *146*
Namazgah/Namaz Gah, mosque, Turkestan 132
Napoleon 37
Nasr ben Ali, mausoleum, Uzkend 58
Nasser Khosrow, library 11
Naw Bahar, Balkh 97, 99
Nayin, town 58
Nevai, Ali Shir, see Ali Shir Nevai
Niedermeyer, O. von, traveller 124, 133
Nisa, site, Turkmenistan 54
Nishapur 32, 37, 107, 119
Noh Gumbad, mosque, Balkh 58, 65, **24**, *104*, **43**, 107, **colour plate 13**
North-West Frontier, Pakistan 39, 42
Now Ruz/New Year 156
Nur Muhammad Taraki, see Taraki 43
Nuristan, province 14, 19, 21, 40
Nuristanis, tribe 19, 20

Oghuz, Turks 104
Onon, river 32
Otrar, town 32
Ottoman, empire 32
Oxiana, see Transoxania
Oxus, river, see also Amu Darya, Jayhun, Panj 16, 22, 23, 25, 26, 29, 31, 53, 55, 101, 104, 108

Paitava, stupa, Kabul 81, 82
Pakistan 14, 17, 18, 19, 20, 22, 42, 43, 44, 45, 46, 53, 82, 88
Paktia, province 18, 19, 102
Pamir 15, 16, 19, 41
Panipat, battle of 35
Panj, see Ab-i Panj, river
Panjdeh, oasis 40, 41, 134
Panjshir/Panjsher river 16, 17, 26, 80, 81
Parni, Parthian tribe 53
Paropamisus, mountains, Safid Kuh Range 15, 22, 118
Parsiwan/Persians 21
Parthia 28, 53, 58, 101, 118
Parthian architecture 50, 53ff, 58, 60
Pasargadae, Iran 50
Pashto, language 20
Pataliputra, site, India 50
Pathan, see Pushtun
Peacock throne 36
Pendzhikent, Tajikistan 55
Pentagon 45
Peroz, the last Sasanian 29
Persepolis 50, 85, 101, 118
Persia, see also Iran 22, 23, 25, 26, 29, 30, 34, 36, 37, 38, 41, 52, 70, 71, 74, 75, 79, 96, 101, 108, 115, 160
Persian architecture 50, 53, 57, 64, 65, 68, 85, 94, 127
  language, see Farsi
  Gulf 45
Persians 19, 20, 35, 103
Peshawar 17, 24, 28, 37, 46, 81
Pol-i Malan, bridge, Herat 126, **55**, **colour plate 5**
Pollock, General 38, 161
Pope, A.U., author 58
Porus, Indian king 26
Prakrit, language 79, 80
Prates, Hadda 85
Pugachenkova, G.A., author 105, 106, 137, 148
Pul-i Khishti, mosque, Kabul 162
Pul-i Khumri, town 74, 76
Punjab 25, 26, 28, 29, 31, 37, 38, 41, 52, 53, 85, 88, 98
Pushkalavati, see also Charsada 28
Pushtun 19, 20, 22, 35, 37, 43, 44
Pushtunistan 42, 43

Qaitul Range, see Kaital
Qajar/Kajar, Persian dynasty 37
Quetta, town 25, 38

Rabi'a Balkhi, poetess 154
Ratbil Shahs, dynasty, see

Turkshahis 103, 162
Rashid, A. 46
Rauza, village 108, 158
Rawlinson, J.A., soldier, scholar 111
Red Army 42
Registan, desert 14
Registan, Samarkand 68
Renz, A., author 114, 158
Robatak, site, Samangan 76
Romanus Diogenes, Byzantine emperor 32
Rome, Roman 52, 53, 55, 63, 81, 86, 88
Rostovtzeff, M., author 74
Roui, village 101
Roxana, wife of Alexander 96
Rum, sultanate of 32
Russia, Russians, see also Soviet Union, USSR 13, 22, 24, 34, 37, 38, 39, 40, 41, 42, 45, 81, 102, 134, 147

Sabuktagin, founder of Ghaznavid dynasty 31, 32, 107, 108, 111, 115
Safavid, Persian dynasty 30, 33, 34, 35, 36, 68, 71, 121, 125, 139, 146, 149
Saffarid, Sistan dynasty 30, 32, 100
Safid Kuh Range, see Paropamisus
Saka/Scythians 27, 28, 101
Salang, tunnel 23
Sale, Lady, authoress 90
Saljuqi, F., author 122, 137
Samangan, town 76
Samanid, dynasty 30, 31, 107, 108, 154
  architecture 69ff
Samarkand 32, 33, 34, 36, 38, 40, 58, 61, *62*, 66, 67, 68, 69, 131, 146
Samarra 58, 105, 106
Sanjar, Seljuk sultan 32
Sarianidi, V., author 101
Sarmatians 81, 101
Sar-i Pol, village *106*
Sasanian, Persian dynasty 28, 29, 75, 80, 88, 98, 100, 101, 115, 118, 128
  architecture 53ff, 57, 58, 63, 82, 94, 96, 99, 105
Sattagydia, Persian satrapy 25
Saudi Arabia 45
Sayid Subhan Kuli Khan, madrasa, Balkh *154*
Schlumberger, D., author 53, 63, 99, 118, 128
Scythians, see Saka
Seh Oghor, mausoleum, Kabul 161

Seleucid, dynasty 52, 53, 118
Seleucus, succ. of Alexander 26
Seleucus Nicator, ruler of Persia 27
Seljuks, Turkish tribe 30, 31, 32, 57, 108, 119, 149
  architecture 57, 65ff, 67, 68, 106, 126
Semirechiye 32
Shah Foladi, mountain 14
Shah Jahan, Moghul emperor 161
Shah Mahmud, amir 37
Shah-i Mashad, madrasa, Herat 126
Shah-Shahid, mausoleum, Ghazni *160*
Shah Shuja, amir 37, 38, 161
Shah-i Zinda, Samarkand 68, 146
Shahab ud-Din, Ghorid sultan 120
Shahname, epos by Ferdawsi 115, 128
Shahr-i Gholghola, site, Bamiyan *128*, 58, *130*, **colour plates 3 & 15**
Shahr-i Kuhna, site, Kandahar *78*, 79
Shahr-i Kuhna, site, Tashkurgan 162
Shahr-i Zohak, site, Bamiyan **56**, *128*, **57**
Shahrak, village 127
Shahrisabz, palace, Uzbekistan 66
Shahrukh, son of Timur 34, 66, 69, 70, 120, 121, 131, 132, 139, 146, 147, 148, 149
Shahrukh ibn Sultan Abu Said, Timurid prince 137
Shahzade Abu'l Kasim, mausoleum, Herat *147*
Shahzade-i Chin, Shotorak 81
Shapur, Sasanian king 54, 80
Sheikh Abdullah, see Khoja Abdullah Ansari
Sheikh Amu, philosopher 138
Sheikh Sadr-ud-Din Armani, khaniga, Herat *148*
Sheikhzade Abdullah, mausoleum, Herat *147*
Sher Khan Bandar, port 24
Shewaki, stupa, Kabul *85*
Shibergan, village 101
Shi'ite, religion 21, 106, 156
Shibar Pass 16, 23, 26
Shiraz 67
Shir Ali, amir 39
Shortugai, site 74
Shotorak, site 53, *81*, 82
Shul Tepe 162
Sialkot, town, Pakistan 29
Siberia 29, 38, 101
Sigiriya, site, Ceylon 95

Sikhs 19, 21, 37, 38
Silk Route 81
Sind, province 31, 37
Sircali madrasa, Konya 60
Sirkap, Taxila 51
Sistan, province 17, 18, 25, 27, 29, 30, 31, 32, 33, 37, 41, 107, 108, 116, 119, 120
Siyahgerd, village 96
Soghdiana, Persian satrapy 26, 29, 55, 105
Somnath, temple, India 63, 109
Sourdel-Thomine, J., author 106, 114
Soviet Union, see also Russia 42, 44, 45
Soviet-Afghan Treaty, 1921 42
  1978 44
SPACH 12, 135
Srinagar 68, 71, 161
St Petersburg 134
Stein, Sir Aurel, explorer, author 161
Sufi, sufism, doctrine 57, 138, 147
Suen Tsang/Hsüen Tsang, Chinese pilgrim 80, 81, 88, 98, 99, 103, 162
Sultan Abdul Razzak, mausoleum, Ghazni *158*, **82**, **83**
Sultan Muhammad, painter 70
Sunnite, doctrine 21, 45, 66
Surkh Kotal, site 55, *74*, 76, **29**, 79, **colour plate 11**
Surkhan Darya, river 101
Surya, deity 82
Susa 49, 50, 118
Swat 26, 53
Syr Darya, river, see also Jaxartes 26, 29, 32, 34, 38
Syria 52, 74

Tabriz 70, 71
Tadgell, Ch. author 50
Tahmasp I, Safavid shah of Persia 36, 70
Tahmasp II, last Safavid 140
Tajik, Tajikistan 16, 19, 20, 22, 42, 44
Takht, Gazurgah 145
Takht-i Babur, Kandahar, see also Chehel Sina *160*
Takht-i Bhai, monastery, Pakistan 82
Takht-i Pol, mosque, Mazar-i Sharif 72, **76**, *154*, **77**, **78**
Takht-i Rustam, site Aibak 76
Takht-i Rustam, site, Balkh 98, *99*
Takht-i Sanghin, site, Tajikistan 101
Takht-i Shah, mountain 85

191

Index

Talas, river 29
Talbot, M.G., traveller 90
Taliban, Islamic fundamentalists 11, 24, 44, 45, 46, 95, 162
Tali Barzu 55
Tamerlane, see Timur 33
Taq-i Bostan, site, Iran 101
Taraki, Nur Muhammad, politician 43, 44
Tareb Khana, Herat 149
Tartars, White and Black Sheep, tribes 34, 104
Tashkent 38
Tashkurgan 76, *162*, **colour plates 7 & 17**
Taxila, site, Pakistan 51, 53, 55, 77, 80, 81, 85
Tedzhen, river 17
Temuchin, see Chingiz-Khan 32
Tepe Darra, site, Kabul *82*
Tepe Fullol, site, Badakhshan 79
Tepe-i Kafariha, site, Hadda 85
Tepe Kalan, site, Hadda 85
Tepe Khazana, site *82*, 102
Tepe Maranjan, site, Kabul *82*, 102
Tepe Naranj 102
Tepe Rustam, site, Balkh 98, *99*
Tepe Sardar, site, Ghazni 55, *100*, **42**
Tepe-i Shotor, site, Hadda *88*
Termez, town 24, 107
Tibet 41, 92
Tilla Tepe, site 45, 72, *100,101*
Tim, town, Uzbekistan 64, 107
Timur/Tamerlane 33, 34, 67, 97, 116, 119, 120, 121, 131, 149
Timurid dynasty 34, 35, 70, 123, 137, 146
 architecture 49, 58, 65, 66ff, 69, 71, 121, 122, 125, 145, 147, 148, 149, 158
 monuments *131*
Timur Shah Durrani, amir 37, 103
 mausoleum 161
Tirpul, town 148
Tokharistan 28
Tokhtamish, khan of the Golden Horde 34
Top Kapi Saray, Istanbul 50
Toprak Kala, site, Uzbekistan 55
Trans-Caspia 39
Transoxania 26, 27, 28, 29, 30, 32, 33, 34, 35, 36, 55, 57, 67, 68, 88, 96, 110
Trebeck, G., traveller 90

Tribal territory 46
Tripartite Treaty, 1838 38
Tulun, see Ibn Tulun
Tumchuk, site, Xinjiang 96
Tung Shih-hu, Yabghu 92
Tungus, tribe 32
Turkestan 105
 Afghan 38, 154
 Eastern/Chinese 15, 32, 81, 89, 92, 95, 118
 plain 14
 Western/Russian 29, 39, 106
Turkestan city 158
Turkey 32, 41, 42
Turkic languages 21
 peoples 29, 88
Turkmenistan 17, 54, 147, 148
Turkomans, see also Tartars 19, 21, 34, 39, 40, 70
Turks 21, 29, 31, 32, 70, 96, 107, 108, 119, 128, 154
Turk-Shahi, dynasty 29, 30, 103, 107
Tus, town 32

Udny's boundary commission 41
Ulughbeg, son of Shahrukh 34, 131
 uncle of Babur 161
Ulugh Beg Miranshah 158
Umayyad, caliphs 58
UNESCO 128
United States of America 42
USSR, see also Soviet Union, Russia 42, 43, 44, 158
Uzbeks, Uzbekistan 16, 19, 21, 22, 34, 35, 44, 64, 66, 68, 70, 149
Uzkend/Uzgand, site, Kirghizstan 58, 60, 106, 114, 127

Vabkent, minaret, Uzbekistan 60, 61, 66, 106
Vajrapani 102
Varakhsha, site, Uzbekistan 55, 58
Victoria, Queen 134
Vietnam 44
Vigne, G., traveller 109, 110, 114
Vogt-Göknil, U., author 56
Volga, river 34

Wahhabism, radical doctrine 45
Wakhan, corridor 15, 41
Wakhsh, river 98
Warwaliz, town 162
White Huns, see Hephthalites
Wilber, D.N., author 122, 124

Wilford, F., traveller 89
Wolfe, N.H., author 137
World War, First 41
World War, Second 41, 42
World Trade Center, New York 45
Xerxes, Achaemenian king, Persia 50
Xinjiang, see Chinese Turkestan 15, 32, 53, 81, 89, 92, 95

Yakub Khan, son of Shir Ali, Amir 39
Yakublais Khan 102
Yakubi, Arab geographer 104
Yakut, Arab geographer 76, 104, 116, 119
Yate, C.E., traveller 97, 98, 99, 132, 133, 137
Yemshi Tepe, village 101
Yue-che /Yüe-czi, tribe 27, 28, 79
Yun-kang, site, Xinjiang 89

Zabulistan 29, 30
Zahir Shah, king 24, 42, 44, 162
Zamzam, cistern, Herat 146
Zanghir Gah, mountain 138, 139
Zaranj, site, Sistan 29, 33, 116
Zarathustra 96
Zarnigar Khana, pavilion, Herat 69, 139, *145*, 146, 148
Zestovsky, P.I., author 124
Ziyarat-i Ashukan-o-Arefan, shrine, Kabul 162
Ziyarat Gah, village 147, 148
Ziyarat-i Ghiyat ud-Din, shrine, Herat 123
Ziyarat-i Hazret-i Tamin, shrine, Kabul 162
Ziyarat-da-Kherka-i Sharif, shrine, Kandahar *160*
Ziyarat-i Mir Sahib, shrine, Kandahar 78
Ziyarat-i Mir Shahid, shrine, Herat 147
Ziyarat-i Mui Mubarak, shrine, Ghazni 115
Ziyarat-i Sher Sukh, shrine, Kabul 161
Zohak 128
Zoroastrism, religion, see Zarathustra 12, 54